*With appreciation for your support
as a Contributing Member of the
Smithsonian National Associate Program*

ENGINES OF CHANGE

The American Industrial Revolution, 1790–1860

BROOKE HINDLE and STEVEN LUBAR

Smithsonian Institution Press   *Washington, D.C., and London*

Library of Congress Cataloging-in-Publication Data

Hindle, Brooke.
Engines of change.

Bibliography: p. 285
Includes index.
1. United States—Economic conditions—To 1865.
2. United States—Industries—History.   3. Technological
innovations—Economic aspects—United States—History.
I. Lubar, Steven D.   II. Title.
HC105.H66   1986   338′.06   86-6709
ISBN 0-87474-540-3
ISBN 0-87474-539-X (pbk.)

Contents

Preface

THE MATERIAL ASPECTS OF AMERICAN LIFE UNDERWENT GREAT CHANGE in the period from 1790 to 1860, a pattern of development often referred to as the American Industrial Revolution. At the center of this transformation was a series of technological developments that were directly associated with labor, management, and organizational change.

This book's discussion begins with physical survivals of technologies of that era, most of them preserved in the Smithsonian Institution. The book, like the exhibition from which it is derived (also entitled *Engines of Change*), endeavors to look through these artifacts to gain an understanding of the Industrial Revolution that differs significantly from popular perceptions. Specific insights can be gained from three-dimensional survivals and from two-dimensional views that are neither available in written accounts nor communicable through words alone. The photographs, drawings, and maps included here are, consequently, more than mere illustrations, more than a pleasant way to underline the written text. Indeed, in some ways they constitute the book's primary message.

At the same time, the most obvious message conveyed by artifacts and pictures is limited by its unavoidable specificity. It must always be placed in a larger and broader context. Occasionally, observers bring enough context with them to interpret the artifacts they see, but usually extended verbal explanation is required to make objects and pictures truly meaningful. That is the purpose of the text of this book—to provide the context, to look through the physical survivals to an enriched comprehension of the technology and related aspects of the American Industrial Revolution.

The bulk of the artifacts and drawings pictured here are displayed in the Smithsonian Institution, most of them in the related exhibit. Gaps have been filled by pictures or loans from friends at several institutions. Particularly helpful have been the Hagley Museum and Library, the Museum of American Textile History, the New-York Historical Society, the New York State Historical Association, Rensselaer Polytechnic Institute, Slater Mill Historic Site, and Sleepy Hollow Restorations. Maps to fill specific needs have been prepared by James Wiedel of the University of Maryland.

Portions of the text have been read and improved by Carolyn Cooper, Pete Daniel, Judith A. McGaw, G. Terry Sharrer, and Merritt Roe Smith. Roger G. Kennedy's support and suggestions have been helpful. Many curators and specialists at the National Museum of American History have helped in research, in locating and identifying artifacts, and in obtaining photographs. They include Richard E. Ahlborn, Silvio A. Bedini, Edward Ezell, Francis Gadson, Craddock Goins, Anne C. Golovin, Elizabeth M. Harris, Harry Hunter, William A. Jacobs, Barbara S. Janssen, Claudia B. Kidwell, James A. Knowles, Arthur P. Molella, Robert P. Multhauf, Susan H. Myers, Rodris Roth, John T. Schlebecker, Anne M. Serio, Ann M. Seeger, David Shayt, Carlene Stephens, John Stine, Robert M. Vogel, Robert A. Walther, Deborah Warner, John H. White, Jr., Roger B. White, William W. Withuhn, William E. Worthington, Jr., and Helena P. Wright. Our thanks also to the Smithsonian Office of Photographic Services, and to Claire Beerman, Marjorie Berry, and Juanita Morris for typing the manuscript.

I

The Industrial Revolution and Technological Change

THE INDUSTRIAL REVOLUTION WAS ONE OF THE GREAT TURNING POINTS of modern history. It signals the most clear-cut beginning of the mechanization and industrialized production on which our present world rests. Before that period of change, craft technology was dominant, depending on hand tools, simple machines, individual skills, and small shop or home production. After its impact, powered special-purpose machines, high-skill technicians but limited-skill wage operatives, and factories increasingly became part of the economy. The volume and diversity of products increased, while costs dropped, and the income of some groups, especially the middle and well-to-do, accelerated. Most consumers benefited, but some workers lost their vocations and factory operatives often suffered from constricting, boring, and insecure jobs. The United States experienced the onset of these critical changes between the American Revolution and the Civil War.

Even before the War for Independence, Americans had begun to bring in desired advances of the Industrial Revolution. Mechanization and powered machinery were the most visible aspects of the changes that were transferred by the mid-nineteenth century, although methods of organizing and putting them to use were imported at the same time. From transfer and adaptation, Americans moved quickly in some areas to creative innovation and widening economic and social change. The significance of the many new ways of production was not immediately perceived at home and even less abroad. In 1851, Great Britain was suddenly shocked by the American achievements displayed at the first world fair, held in London at the Crystal Palace. Americans were also surprised but pleased to observe the positive reactions to their work. One book and associated chromolithograph, entitled *American Superiority at the World's Great Fair*, publicized prevailing reactions by celebrating primarily the process of mechanization (fig. 1–1).

Fig. 1–1. *"American Superiority at the World's Great Fair." Shown are some of the American products that won prizes at the 1851 Crystal Palace Exhibition.*

EARLY FOUNDATIONS

Behind the changes and achievements of the United States lay not only the British advances that were borrowed directly, but a long European history of mechanical development. The phrase "industrial revolution" was first applied to changes made in Britain in the late eighteenth and early nineteenth centuries, when that country assumed leadership in several lines of technological and organizational development. Mechanization, however, had begun long before, and even factories were centuries old. The Greeks had used gear trains, pumps, and waterpower.

During the sixteenth and seventeenth centuries, a sequence of elaborate books called "theaters of machines" appeared in Italy, France, and

Germany—but not in England. In retrospect, these volumes seem to forecast the Industrial Revolution. Through beautiful engravings, they depicted newly designed military, agricultural, and production machines; water-raising mechanisms were among the most prominent. Nearly all of the components were well-known devices on which the mechanization of the Industrial Revolution was based. Some of the machines were actually built, while others remained merely dreams.

One of the most elegant of these books was Agostino Ramelli's *Le diverse et artificiose machine*, published with parallel French and Italian texts in Paris in 1588. Ramelli was an Italian military engineer, brought to Paris by Henry III because of his recognized skill in constructing fortifications. His book enhanced the king's stature by celebrating machines, at the same time providing a resource for mechanics and designers that would last two centuries.

The machines themselves were important, but even more widely useful were the carefully drawn components, which were the foundation of all expansion in mechanization. Among these devices, gear trains are prominent. Spur gears seem today the most familiar type of gearing; they were made then by cutting, rounding, and filing each gear tooth so that it meshed as well as possible with the adjoining gear (fig. 1–2). Wooden lantern and candle gears were already much used in water mills and windmills, and they continued to be (fig. 1–3). Cams are rotating devices with a specifically designed shape to the edge that produced repeating but noncontinuous actions (fig. 1–4). Pistons and cylinders were already used successfully for pumping water (fig. 1–5).

England gave no early indication it could take the lead in fulfilling the dreams promised by these books. The country's economic and technological development had long lagged behind the Continent in most respects. Besides, even by the sixteenth century, the English were far behind in printing and bookmaking. By the seventeenth century, publica-

Fig. 1–2. Spur gears

Fig. 1–3. Lantern and candle gears

Fig. 1–4. Cam

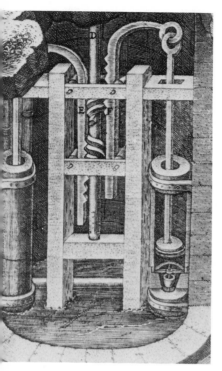

Fig. 1–5. Piston and cylinder pump

tion output had improved, but the best machine publications produced were how-to-do-it books. Instead of celebrating current achievements in a grand style and looking toward the future as the theaters of machines did, these works were intended to help artisans improve their work. They encouraged those who made and worked with such machines to do their own work and to move forward on their own.

For the most part, they described in detail basic production machines. A good example is Joseph Moxon's series of publications entitled *Mechanick Exercises*. His initial volume, *The Doctrine of Handy-Works*, was begun in 1678 but took two years to complete because it was published serially in the form of pamphlets at six pence each. Moxon pictured and described several lathes, one of the most important machines in use for both wood and metal work (fig. 1–6). The blacksmith's forge was even more fundamental for iron work (fig. 1–7).

A major disadvantage England continued to suffer was her shortage of wood, the primary industrial fuel. This problem, however, became an advantage, because it led to the use of an alternative and, for many uses, a better fuel: coal, and its derivative coke. There was nothing new about the use of coal; indeed, England was able to import skilled miners with the required techniques from Germany to develop her own deep coal mines. What was new was her success in converting to coal nearly all industries requiring the use of heat, including ceramics, glass, and

Fig. 1–6. Lathe

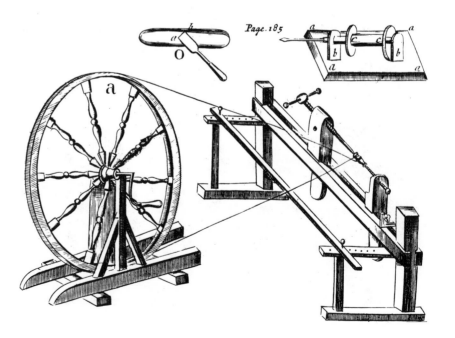

metal casting. The means for converting iron production, the final great wood-based industry, to coal was not found until 1709, when coke reduction of iron ore succeeded.

England's conversion of her heat-using industries to coal from the previous dependence on wood was a fundamental change with major implications. Some have even called it "the first industrial revolution." Coal could be substituted for wood only after technological adaptation; in some cases, significant invention and development were required. Space heating with coal was relatively easy, but the impurities in coal made it impossible to use in the same way as wood in such processes as glassmaking. That problem was solved by the use of fine clay crucibles and the development of the reverberatory furnace, which very simply shielded the coal fire from the materials being heated, preventing the infiltration of impurities.

The use of coal instead of charcoal for iron reduction was more difficult. The direct use of coal did not work, nor did initial efforts to convert the coal to coke as a replacement for charcoal in a blast furnace. The first major success was attained by the Quaker Abraham Darby at Coalbrookdale in 1709 (fig. 1–8). Darby used a standard blast furnace, the iron ore most accessible to him, and the sort of lime normally used. Not all iron ores could be reduced as successfully with coke, however. As a result, the use of coke did not spread rapidly. However, toward the end

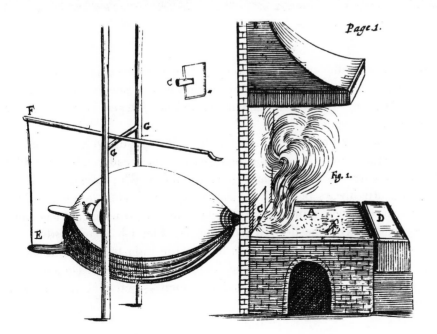

Fig. 1–7. Blacksmith's forge

Fig. 1–8. Upper works, Coalbrookdale

of the eighteenth century, coke became England's primary means for reducing iron. This not only solved the problem of wood/charcoal shortage, but gave that country unanticipated advantages in accelerating industrial development.

Over a long time span, England slowly caught up with the leading continental nations in most technologies and got ahead in a few, notably clockmaking, instrument making, and gunnery. The catching-up process nearly always began in the same way the English had learned to conduct deep coal mining, by bringing in foreign artisans and mechanics familiar with the desired technologies. Flemish weavers were attracted to provide the foundation of a textile industry that flourished. French glassworkers and clockmakers brought their crafts. On her own, England took a lead in some products, such as scientific instruments and iron cannon.

MAJOR AREAS OF
TECHNOLOGICAL REVOLUTION

The classical Industrial Revolution did not involve all production. Many crafts did not change at all, and those that were mechanized and industrialized changed at very different rates. The four most dramatic changes occurred in (1) iron production, (2) the rise of the steam engine, (3) the mechanization of textile production, and (4) precision machine work.

The iron revolution of this period involved coke ore reduction and new methods for making malleable iron (or iron that was not brittle but could bend and be machined). These methods, called puddling and rolling, replaced more expensive and more labor-intensive processes toward the end of the eighteenth century. Puddling involved heating pig iron, or iron that had been reduced from the ore, in a reverberatory furnace and having a man stir or move about the molten iron in order to remove impurities and some of the carbon. Rolling was the next step, which ran the iron through a set of rollers that could produce different shapes but usually turned out bars of malleable iron similar to those previously hand-produced by heating and hammering the molten pig iron.

Coke iron was not as generally useful as charcoal iron, but because it was so much cheaper, it became very successful. In many ways, iron was the key material of the Industrial Revolution. Because England had good supplies of iron ore and coal, its solutions to the economical production of iron gave the country a growing advantage.

The second change of the Industrial Revolution, the steam engine, represented a great new power source. Like other technological changes, it, too, had ancient roots, running back to the Greek Hero. Giovanni Branca's 1629 theater of machines book pictured a useful application of a steam wheel powered by a jet of steam (fig. 1–9). Later in that century, the French-born Denis Papin gave a new turn to ideas about steam when he applied it to piston and cylinder experiments that he carried out in England.

Shortly afterward, in 1689, Thomas Savery patented the first working steam engine (fig. 1–10). This device is best thought of as a steam pump, because it had no moving parts and was not applicable to the operation of mechanisms. It was used to pump water out of deep mines by admitting steam to a chamber, then condensing it by admitting a spray of water, which created a partial vacuum into which atmospheric pressure pushed the water below through a tube. Steam was then admitted below the water in the chamber to push it further up through another tube. This pump worked but was unreliable and subject to explosions and steam leaks.

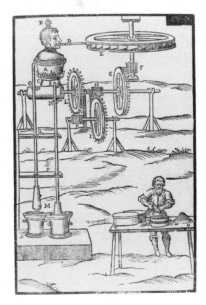

Fig. 1–9. Branca's steam wheel

Fig. 1–10. Savery's steam engine

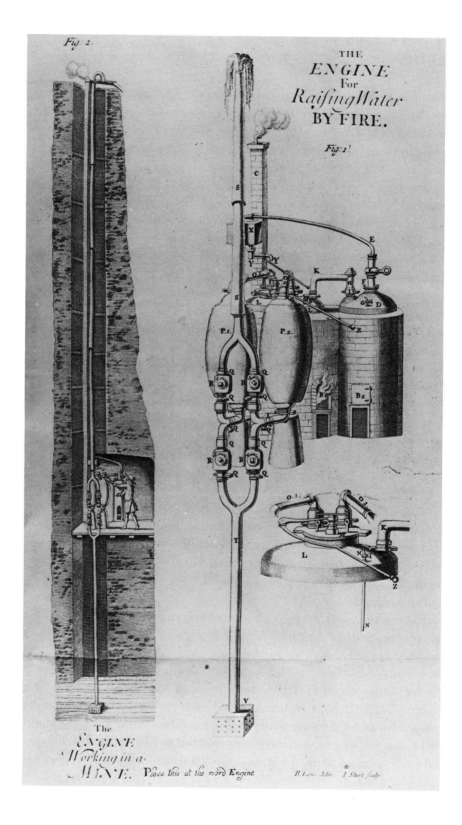

ENGINES OF CHANGE

The biggest step was taken by Thomas Newcomen, whose engine was in use by 1712 (figs. 1–11, 1–12). Using a piston and cylinder, he applied Savery's condensation of steam to create a vacuum and atmospheric pressure to push the piston into the cylinder. This produced mechanical motion, which was applied to moving a mechanical water pump. The Newcomen engine, too, was used to pump water out of deep mines. It was, however, inefficient, hard to keep running, and consumed a great deal of fuel. On the positive side, it was susceptible to extended improvement and development, as are most significant inventions.

James Watt, the man most associated with the steam engine, produced his first commercial engine in 1776. Beginning with the Newcomen engine, he soon moved the steam engine to new levels of performance (figs. 1–13, 1–14). He used the pressure of steam to move the piston, first in only one direction and ultimately both up and down. He also incorporated a separate condenser into which the used steam was diverted for condensation—at a great saving in efficiency and cost, because

Fig. 1–11. Newcomen engine

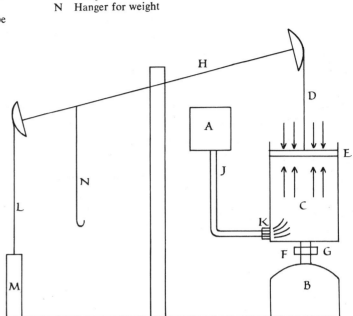

A	Water reservoir	J	Water pipe
B	Boiler	K	Water valve
C	Cylinder	L	Pump rod
D	Piston rod	M	Pump
E	Piston	N	Hanger for weight
F	Steam pipe		
G	Valve		
H	Beam		

Fig. 1–12. Schematic of Newcomen engine

the cylinder no longer had to be subjected to great changes in temperature and resultant heat loss.

The steam engine proved an important technological change, with remarkable social and economic results. Using wood or coal as fuel, it could power manufacturing plants in almost any location, including the center of cities. Other power sources were not that adaptable; waterpowered mills had to be located at a "waterpower site," usually near the falls of a river, and windmills were also restricted in possible locations. In an even more striking manner, the steam engine offered new flexibility in transportation. It proved capable of use for both land and water transportation in circumstances where waterpower was never usable and wind power often was not.

Mechanized textile production in a factory, the third great change, is often seen as the essence of the Industrial Revolution. If food, shelter, and clothing are humanity's most basic needs, clothing—made mostly from textiles—is the need most susceptible to industrialized production. Indeed, the process of mechanizing textile production had begun centuries earlier with the fulling mill (fig. 1–15). This was a machine, usually powered by a waterwheel, that pounded woolen cloth immersed in water in order to make it clean, compact, and strong. The hand loom also emerged early. This device was based on a frame to hold the warp yarn in parallel lines while the woof yarn was woven through the warp by hand (fig. 1–16).

The spinning wheel emerged in the sixteenth century to mechanize, in some degree, the process of spinning yarn, an operation previously accomplished by the use of distaff and drop spindle. Early spinners, usually women, held the roving to be spun in one hand on a rod or distaff while pulling and twisting the raw fibers into yarn that was tied to the drop spindle (fig. 1–17). The spinning wheel was usually operated by a treadle that rotated the wheel and pulled and twisted the yarn onto a bobbin while the operator held and fed the raw fibers into the device (fig. 1–18). Most spinning and weaving were done in the home.

The technological changes in textile production that were associated with the Industrial Revolution went much further than these early efforts. Primarily, they related to spinning and weaving. John Kay's flying shuttle of 1733 shot the woof yarn through the separated yarns of the warp, reducing human effort in weaving on a loom. James Hargreaves's spinning jenny of 1770 permitted a single operator to spin several yarns

Fig. 1–13. Watt engine replica

Fig. 1–14. Schematic of Watt engine

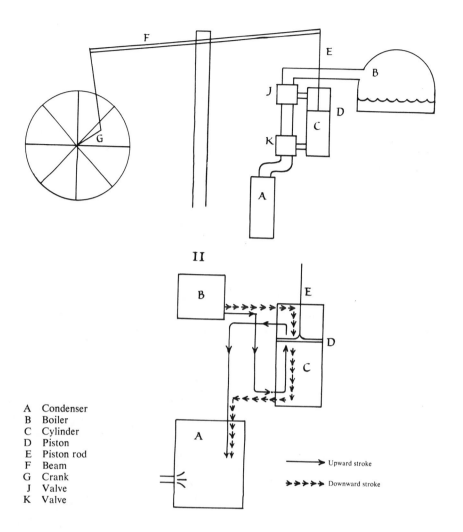

A	Condenser
B	Boiler
C	Cylinder
D	Piston
E	Piston rod
F	Beam
G	Crank
J	Valve
K	Valve

simultaneously (fig. 1–19). Spinning frames with multiple spindles and powered by water came next. Power looms appeared a little later, succeeding first with cotton and then with wool. Both spinning and weaving increasingly came to be done in factories, and before long the factory incorporated an extensive division of labor (fig. 1–20). Factory production had been used in Italy as early as the thirteenth century, but the mechanized, steam- or water-powered textile factories of the early nineteenth century represented something new in the world.

Less dramatic but more fundamental and more widely influential was the fourth change, the improved machining of both metal and wood, which was a requirement and a stimulus for increased mechanization of all sorts. The lathe was an ancient machine, but it was improved in many ways, especially by the slide rest that held the cutting tool in a fixed position and permitted more complicated and more reproducible work. Grinding machines and drill presses similarly became more accurate and precise, and the power planer emerged as an important device. Perhaps the most striking development was in the growth of special-purpose machines, each designed to perform one very specific and increasingly complex function. Increased precision in machine work speeded the development of steam engines and textile mills; it also opened new opportunities in many other fields.

RELATED SOCIOECONOMIC CHANGES

All these technological changes were accompanied by related social and economic changes, some facilitating development of the new technology and others resulting from it. New patterns of organization, management, and labor were an integral part of the Industrial Revolution. A new attitude toward economics and business permeated these developments.

Fig. 1–15. Early fulling mill

Fig. 1–16. Hand loom

Fig. 1–17. Drop spindle   *Fig. 1–19. Spinning jenny*

Fig. 1–18. Flax spinning wheel

Fig. 1–20. Textile mill workers

The most influential statement on this subject was Adam Smith's *Wealth of Nations*, published in 1776; it became the foundation of classical economics. Smith wrote little that was specific about mechanization but did assert that the marketplace would best determine when and where machines ought to be used. He offered more detail in urging increased division of labor, but there, too, as in all economic activity, he favored free enterprise. His position, one that came to be generally accepted, was that the individual who worked successfully within the marketplace for the purpose of profiting himself would at the same time benefit society. The "invisible hand," as Adam Smith identified destiny, would work to that end.

The factory system and the substitution of wage labor for craft independence made labor dependent on owners and managers. Capital became more self-directed. Urban concentration grew, and English manufacturing cities became crowded, smoky, and unpleasant. Critics began to talk of the "dark satanic mills."

At the same time, human benefits grew increasingly evident. Manufactured goods became cheaper as their production was mechanized and carried out in a water- or steam-powered factory. When cotton goods dropped in price, they were more widely used. Clothing and bed clothes were changed and washed more frequently, and personal cleanliness and health rose. Housewives and domestics were burdened with new chores, but the most visible effect was a rising quality of life.

THE ROLE OF GREAT BRITAIN

Britain's trade flourished, because it gained an important edge over competitors in producing desired products. This advantage was immediately recognized by other countries, which responded by seeking to import the new ways of making and doing things. The British tried to counter such moves by legislation prohibiting the export of steam engines, textile machinery, and other new machines. They recognized, too, from their own past experience that the best way to transfer technology from one country to another was to bring in mechanics who knew how to build and use the machines that were needed. Now, to prevent their own mechanics from leaving with technological secrets they did not want to lose, they prohibited such emigration. They made substantial efforts to enforce both of these restrictions, but with limited success.

These measures impeded the spread or diffusion of the Industrial Revolution, and Britain's advantage was maintained, primarily because of what has been called technological momentum. Continental nations continued to industrialize, but they could not quickly accelerate to Britain's pace.

The United States was the most fortunate nation in obtaining the benefits of British advances, having had long experience during the colonial era in importing tools and machines as well as the people who made and used them. These individuals came mostly from England but also from Germany, Scotland, Ireland, and other countries, bringing varied and sometimes conflicting techniques. They introduced tools and technology almost automatically. More planning and specific effort, however, were required to bring in certain crafts that were needed.

Some specialties that were not well developed in England were imported from the Continent, just as England had done to improve her own economy. For example, Italian silk reelers, Dutch and Polish glassworkers, and German sawyers were sent to Jamestown by the Virginia Company in the early seventeenth century. Silk culture was not a part of the English scene, her shortage of wood made sawyers scarce, and foreign glassworkers were more ready than Englishmen to go to America. Many technologies were purposely transferred to America, nearly always by bringing in people familiar with them.

Most of this transfer was from the British Isles, so the Americans were well positioned at the end of the colonial period to import the Industrial Revolution from their former mother country—despite her restrictive laws. When the United States was established, Americans became foreigners to the British and were subject to the same restrictions imposed on other nations. However, their long experience within the British system, their command of the same language, and their friends and relatives in England, especially, gave them access to her mechanics and technology. After the War, British migration to America resumed, and British mechanics found a special welcome here. Mills and shops using the new technology often had at least one English mechanic. In time, these men came to resent, correctly, the fact that they were valued only for the knowledge they brought with them.

The real beginning of the American Industrial Revolution coincided remarkably with the American Revolution. As the Americans attained independence, they came to recognize the colonial nature of their economy. They became more sensitive to the beginnings of the Industrial Revolution in England and realized that the new technologies offered economic advantages that were needed as they had not been during the colonial era. They made more serious efforts to promote manufactures than before the War, and gradually met some success. The new nation began its life encouraged by the enthusiasm of a minority that hoped to promote economic development by importing the new and growing technologies.

Today, the term Industrial Revolution is under challenge—on the accurate charge that the changes took place over too long a period and in too many places to be regarded as a revolution. The term arose out of English developments, and for a time England led the developments, but the changes that emerged were never exclusive to England. Also, the changes were too diverse and diffuse to be placed within a specific number of years.

But what happened *was* revolutionary. It changed the world. It is the most important change that separates our present world from the course of history prior to the Industrial Revolution. For the United States, it was especially important, beginning as it did, coincidentally, with its own independence. The material success and prosperity of this country rested on its great natural resources, but the rapidity of exploitation of this wealth and the directions in which it was deployed were functions of industrialization. More than that, much of American culture and character derived from the continuing influences of technology and from an early sense of its positive potential.

The New United States:
Land of Opportunities

WHAT WAS IT ABOUT THE UNITED STATES THAT ENCOURAGED EFFECTIVE response to the appeal of the Industrial Revolution and permitted the fulfillment of so many of its promises? Much of the reason for such successes rested upon its natural resources, but perhaps even more upon its people—their attitudes, reduced institutional constrictions, and personal drives for material improvement. These largely unplanned circumstances produced a country with great opportunities that could have moved in a variety of directions. One resultant move was accepting and integrating technological innovation into its social life.

MATERIAL IMPROVEMENT

The drive for material wealth, which became an attribute of many Americans, had a long history. From the earliest Spanish discoveries, dreams of great and instant wealth had arisen. Gold loomed as free riches. It captured many, including Sir Walter Raleigh, who founded the lost colony of 1585 at Roanoke Island, North Carolina, with the anticipation of great profit. He went into ecstasy over the gold purported to be held by the "emperor" of Guiana, of whom he wrote, "All the vessels of his home, table and kitchen were of gold and silver and the meanest of silver and copper. . . . He had in his wardrobe hollow statues of golde. . . . He had also roles, budgets, chests and troughs of golde and silver, heaps of billets of golde. . . ."[1] Raleigh failed to find that promised realm but did discover that no wealth was free, a truth experienced by all who followed him. Long and complex input was required before the real wealth of America could be found and turned into usable riches.

In fact, lives, sweat, tears, and money were poured into America before much was accomplished. For the earliest settlers, mere survival in the "strange new world" became the most pressing objective. The odds against the promised gain were great. Problems included new diseases and old ones that flourished anew in the new setting, the resistance of native Americans that sometimes became lethal, and the attacks of rival powers on precarious footholds. The mother country was at war nearly half the time, and the colonies were always involved in greater or lesser degree. Even when peace prevailed, war was understood to be in the offing.

Making ends meet required confronting an alien scene and engaging in activities that were wholly or partially new. Those who agreed to emigrate to America to escape an English jail usually brought inadequate health and skills with them; their survival rate was low. Slaves, who were imported in considerable numbers from the later seventeenth century, arrived to fulfill opportunities for those who bought them, not for themselves. Still, they adapted, learned new skills, and survived at a higher rate than might have been expected. By the eighteenth century, the rank and file of European immigrants and of Americans of European descent had come to feel themselves favored by fate.

REDUCED CONSTRICTIONS

Many European rigidities had been left behind, but so had many institutional supports. The British government was far away, and its representatives here found themselves with limited power. Even the provincial governments were relatively remote from most people. Only the local governments, towns, townships, and counties were in continuing touch with individuals. In most colonies the lack of a strong established church permitted competing denominations; churches had less strength and less effectiveness than in Europe. Most of those who grew up here, or who immigrated, were more on their own than they could have been in Europe. That condition had two sides to it, however. It conferred a responsibility for doing things for which no one had prepared, but it also conveyed a new freedom. The limitation on political and religious control and the undeveloped economic environment offered an unfamiliar freedom of choice—especially a freedom to enter new occupations with little restriction beyond that of the marketplace.

Many of those who came to America came to escape constrictions, and their descendants counted on remaining free of them. The stories are well known of those who sought to escape persecution by an established church, escaping from England, Germany, France, and elsewhere. Residents of Ireland, predominantly Scotch-Irish, came to escape high rents and such economic restrictions as the Woolen Act. Scottish losers in the political rebellions moved to America to escape attitudes that had become antagonistic. Such immigrants usually attained some of the specific freedoms they sought and sometimes expanded their hopes to reach toward a more just, more free society.

Individuals, families, and communities were on their own in a new way. They had the freedom to succeed or fail, with both positive and negative effects. For example, it was easier to run away here than in longer established countries, to escape from commitments as well as from external restraints. Indentured servants and apprentices, of whom Benjamin Franklin is the most famous, often left their homes and started new lives in other colonies where no one knew of their past. Franklin's experience was not unusual except for his own unusual capabilities. At the standard age of twelve, he was apprenticed to his brother James, a printer and newspaper publisher. In a few years, Benjamin wrote some of the most influential articles in the paper and, during two periods while his brother was jailed for political reasons, managed the newspaper. When he reached the age of seventeen, Benjamin decided that he could no longer endure his brother's domination, but he was still four years from completing his apprenticeship and therefore barred from employment as a printer anywhere in the Boston area. He then ran away, carrying a sense of guilt, first to New York City where he was unable to get a job and then to Philadelphia. There he found employment as a journeyman printer and launched one of the most spectacular careers in American history.

Europeans were accustomed to living among those with varying degrees of freedom, but in America only slaves and prisoners had a total lack of freedom. Among others with degrees of unfreedom, wives were conspicuous. Slaves, whose bondage grew tighter after 1690, escaped to occasional small, hidden communities of runaway slaves in the South. More often, they ran away to the North where, if they escaped capture, they might find protection among the growing number of free blacks. Wives, and sometimes husbands, deserted to another colony to escape the bonds and responsibilities of matrimony. Newspapers carried continuing advertisements by husbands to free themselves legally from financial claims against wives who had run away from their "bed and board."

The eighteenth-century Age of Enlightenment emphasized the dignity of the individual, the environmental approach to improving life, and confidence in the laws of nature and the progress of mankind. Thomas Paine was looking backward when he concluded, "This new world hath been the asylum for the persecuted lovers of civil and religious liberty from every part of Europe."[2] Thomas Jefferson, too, was thinking of past attainments when, in the Declaration of Independence, he defined freedom as "Life, Liberty, and the pursuit of Happiness."[3]

ENGINES OF CHANGE

The new Constitution of the United States codified freedom. The most explicit statement set out the freedoms of the First Amendment, the beginning of the Bill of Rights: "Congress shall make no law respecting an establishment of religion, or prohibiting the free exercise thereof; or abridging the freedom of speech, or of the press; or the right of the people peaceably to assemble, and to petition the government for a redress of grievances."[4]

The assertion of freedom as an ideal immediately called into question some of the most fundamental aspects of American life. Slavery, for example, was the absolute opposite of human freedom. How could a nation that celebrated freedom tolerate slavery? This shattering question had to be answered during the American Revolution, because it challenged all the proclaimed objectives. Every northern state replied by abolishing slavery within its borders, either immediately or through laws requiring gradual emancipation. The southern states also were torn but could not bring themselves to give up slavery, because too much of their life rested upon it. That left this ultimate challenge to freedom alive and well, and the South, the land of slavery, was the only part of the country that responded with only occasional enthusiasm to the Industrial Revolution (fig. 2–1).

In most other areas, freedom could and did advance; advocates of material improvement were especially anxious to base their efforts on American freedom. Historians have given political and religious freedom much more attention, but economic freedom deserves at least equal notice as a determinant of American material prosperity. Contemporaries praised freedom for its aid to the growth of agriculture, commerce, and especially manufactures. Tench Coxe, an early promoter of manufacturing, spelled out the connection. "The blessings of civil and religious liberty in America, and the oppressions of most foreign governments, the want of employment at home and expectations of profit here, curiosity, domestic unhappiness, civil wars and various other circumstances will bring manufactures to this asylum for mankind."[5] The importance accorded freedom in economic development grew out of American aspirations, but it also rested on European attitudes and writings, including Adam Smith's *Wealth of Nations*.

The thinking of the Enlightenment included the belief that science and technology underlay material advance and were moved forward by freedom. Joseph Priestley, the discoverer of oxygen, who migrated to this country in 1794, associated the spirit he found here with freedom. He asserted, "It will soon appear that Republican governments, in which every obstruction is removed to the exertion of all kinds of talent, will be far more favorable to science, and the arts [that is to technology], than any monarchical government has ever been."[6]

Fig. 2–1. Liberty Displaying the Arts and Sciences. *This 1792 painting by Samuel Jennings expresses the hopes of the directors of the Library Company of Philadelphia for the effects of freedom upon the new nation. The central figure of Liberty, holding her cap, is surrounded by many symbols, including painting, music, poetry, and sculpture, but also astronomy, geometry, commerce, architecture, and mechanics. At her feet is a broken chain, which expresses the abolitionist anticipation of happy, free blacks, as shown in the background. They, too, celebrate freedom by holding up a liberty pole with a laurel wreath.*

Freedom to pursue one's own business or economic goals was understood as the opportunity to operate within marketplace restrictions, with limited institutional and government restraints. An eager market was expected to encourage machines and technological change wherever they were truly of economic benefit. Workers as well as entrepreneurs, and of course consumers, would be benefited by this sort of freedom. Because freedom flourished here, technological change and economic improvement were expected to flourish. The Industrial Revolution could only be welcomed.

NATURAL RESOURCES

Freedom has been emphasized and reasonably well understood by Americans. Less acknowledged are the vast material advantages to which they fell heir. They have not been forgotten, but Americans tend to allot most of the credit for their accomplishments to the movers and shakers in each effort—and to a kind of spiritual superiority. Yet, the enormous, undeveloped wealth of the country was so fundamental a dependence that it must be given more attention. Material advance depended directly upon it. More than that, some of the qualities believed to be most deeply American grew out of material plenty.

American material growth rested upon the vast natural resources of the thinly settled continent. Immigrants, the investors who provided the required funding, and the governments that cleared the way—all anticipated economic profit. The land, forests, and mineral deposits offered new opportunities in almost all dimensions of life and living. The individual who profited financially would improve his social position and perhaps gain political roles from which he had previously been barred. Investors saw so many new sources of income that the New World loomed as a gigantic money tree. Governments saw means for strengthening themselves and their people: they would acquire sources of needed raw materials under their own flag rather than that of a foreign power, gain strategic positions, expand their trade and influence, and provide opportunities for the growth and success of their citizens. Groups seeking religious or social patterns at variance with those of the mother country could find in this new setting material support for their other objectives.

Land

The greatest and most recognized magnet was land. Land in the Old World was the foundation of economic, social, and political power. Nations were defined by their territories, which determined much about their wealth and power. The feudal system had been based upon land holding and the English aristocracy was still based upon land holding. The gentry were landowners from whom justices of the peace were chosen—key figures in the English legal system. In the colonial period, England's new sources of wealth did not come from its own land but from commerce, manufacturing, and the development of colonies. Yet, the newly rich, wherever they got their money, always felt the need to acquire landed estates in order to establish their social position.

These patterns underlay American development. Despite the openness of society and the absence of rigidity, the spirit of the English system permeated the development of America. Land in the colonies continued to be the great source and the great index of wealth. The possibilities of financial gain from holding land were greater than in the mother country, because the greatest unrealized wealth of the country still lay in undeveloped land, and landowners understood correctly that population and material growth would inevitably increase land value. It became the great speculation, a source of riches for the fortunate but of disaster for the unlucky. The well-to-do Robert Morris, "financier of the Revolution," finally went bankrupt from his land speculations.

Those with political power frequently used it to obtain land grants from the individual colonies, and this opportunity was critical to many leaders. Even William Byrd of Virginia, one of the wealthiest of planters, made a practice of cashing in on his land grants to bail himself out of recurring debts, debts that were almost necessarily a part of the tobacco-planting scene and not a result of individual incompetence.

To the small farmer and the would-be farmer, land was the first requirement, a need that had become next to impossible to fulfill in England for those without large means. Those without means had to work as rural laborers or cotters—or seek jobs in the city. A poor man could only accept the reality that land was not for him.

The development of the American colonies opened a new option that increasing numbers in Britain and on the Continent accepted—migration to America in the hope of owning their own farm. Virtually all immigrants, whatever their primary motivation, were conscious of this opportunity. They might have to accept passage from their church or sell their labor for a few years as indentured laborers—but in time they hoped to work as free men and acquire their own land. Those with some money came, especially from Germany, as "redemptioners." They paid the captain of the ship whatever they could for transporting themselves and their family and signed an indenture to work off however many years or months were required to pay the balance. At the beginning, many did not even outlive their indenture, but, over time, most immigrants became free men and won their own land. This hope was used as a carrot when many of the colonies offered headrights to each newcomer—usually fifty acres of land. The value of the vast acreage of undeveloped land was thus recognized and used.

Land, however, was more than a farmstead, more than the greatest economic incentive. It was also fundamental in the political process. In England, the freeholder or yeoman who cultivated his own land was entitled to vote, and this "county franchise" became the generally copied model in the colonies. Here the most usual voting requirement was the ownership of fifty acres of land or £50 of personal property. Few colonials had so much as £50 and most of those who did lived in the cities. A large proportion of families came to own fifty acres of land, however. The suffrage automatically became broader in the colonies than it was in the mother country, because a larger proportion of the population owned land. Only men, of course, could vote (except in a few, almost accidental, cases when women were permitted to vote in small localities). The son of a voting farmer might not own land and thus not be able to vote at the age of twenty-one, but by the time he became thirty or thirty-five, he often acquired land and became a voter.

Economic security and the right to vote rested for many on land. So did their social status. More even than in the Old World, the independent farmer was honored and celebrated. Many who had not attained that level sought it as their goal. Large landowners had correspondingly greater political power and social position. Everyone understood the meaning of land, and nearly all but those not permanently barred from owning land (as were the slaves) looked forward to the ownership of land or the ownership of more land.

When the United States became a nation, land was still of pervasive importance. The shape of its society and the nature of its culture owed much to land-related patterns. The economy, still largely colonial in its dependence upon the export of raw materials and farm produce, rested on land and land usage. In future development, nothing appeared to be more important than land. The ability to produce more food, fibers, leather, and other farm products was a necessary foundation for all material improvement. Land and the manner in which it was already being used gave the nation advantages that could not be matched anywhere in the world.

Wood

The importance of land in American development was enormous; the lesser but parallel importance of wood was more directly related to the Industrial Revolution. The American advantage over the mother country in wood paralleled her advantage in land. In both cases, the colonies enjoyed a vast plenty, while Britain's scarcity limited her options. In the case of land, scarcity increased prices, reduced the number of owners, and severely limited agricultural production. In the case of wood, the scarcity was so extreme that much of the wood used had to be imported, while wood substitutes were pursued where possible.

The technologies and the economy imported to the colonies from England and the Continent were based mostly on wood. Wood served three functions. It was, first, a material used in structures from houses to ships and for making wagons, tools, scientific instruments, and many household and work devices. Its second use was as a fuel for cooking, space heating, and industrial heating, including the smelting of iron. The third use of wood was for the chemicals derived from it; these included potash (an industrial alkali), naval stores such as turpentine, tannin for tanning leather, and maple sugar. Because wood was so nearly a universal necessity, America's vast supply can hardly be overrated.

Wood was the primary building material used through the colonial and early national period. Because it was so plentiful, it was used more extensively than in Britain or even in France, Spain, or Italy, where brick or stone public and domestic buildings were usual. New settlements in America were almost always constructed of wood. The log cabin was introduced by Scandinavian and German settlers, but it became standard in most initial frontier construction. In time the log cabin came to be cherished as a symbol by Americans, nearly all of whom quickly moved beyond it.

Wood frame buildings dominated New England even after extended development because of the lack of good building stone and brick clay. Elsewhere, wooden housing continued to be much used, although in towns and cities brick predominated and was often required in cities to reduce the fire hazard. Stone housing and public buildings usually marked an area where building stone was plentiful, as in eastern Pennsylvania. Different regions of the country soon developed their own distinctive styles of wood frame building (fig. 2–2).

The cheapness of wood favored ship construction to the extent that, by the Revolution, one-third of the ships flying the British flag were American built. At an early stage England reserved tall, straight American trees for use as masts; they were located, marked with an arrow, and shipped out for use by the Royal Navy. Timber and planking also were exported in large quantities, both to the Caribbean and to the mother country. Buying American-made ships was cheaper, however, than importing the wood and building them in England. The flourishing of American shipbuilding benefited the country in two ways: ship sales to Americans and to Europeans were profitable, and purchase by Americans contributed to the increase of oceanic commerce (fig. 2–3). The

Fig. 2–2. The Hart House, a seventeenth-century wood frame building from Ipswich, Massachusetts

construction of small boats fed internal commerce as well. Although the traditional technology of shipbuilding prevailed, American builders did begin to introduce innovations and distinctive designs.

The heavy use of wood permeated and affected the entire population, not merely carpenters and professional builders. Wood could be worked with less skill and less special equipment than iron or stone—and it was less expensive. For those living in wooded areas, it was almost free. As a result, farmers, who were isolated and had so little money they bought nothing they could make themselves, used wood for many unexpected purposes. They made hooks, hinges, and such devices as trammels, used to suspend pots over a fire, out of wood instead of metal as was usual in the mother country (figs. 2–4, 2–5).

Wood provided the most important early industrial chemical made in America—potash, or potassium carbonate, an alkali used in the manufacture of glass and soap. Glass was produced by heating a mixture of

alkali and sand; soap, by heating alkali and vegetable oil. Britain had a growing need for potash and, because of her own wood shortage, had to import it either from northern Europe or from her colonies. As a result the British encouraged American production of potash.

Potash was easy to make. Ashes collected from the burning of logs were leached, that is, water was poured over them, and the resulting solution was boiled down to the consistency of syrup. This then was further heated until it became a fused mass called potash, usually contain-

Fig. 2–3. Smith and Dimon Shipyard in New York City, 1833

Fig. 2–4. Wooden hinge

Fig. 2–5. Wooden trammel

Fig. 2–6. German-American fireback, 1748

ing less than 25 percent potassium carbonate. Much wood was available from the continuing clearance of the land; converting it into potash had the additional advantage of reducing the cost of the clearing effort.

The cold American winters, combined with the plentiful supply of wood, raised space heating to a level of necessity and significant development. Fireplaces and chimneys were essential in nearly all buildings, domestic and commercial, and improving them became important. Firebacks, a major product made of American cast iron, were placed at the back of fireplaces to radiate heat and increase efficiency (fig. 2–6). Cast iron heating stoves also came into use because of their improved heat efficiency.

The most famous attempt to improve space heating was Benjamin Franklin's Pennsylvania Fireplace, usually called the Franklin stove (fig. 2–7). This was an iron stove placed in a fireplace; it contained an air box designed to warm air before circulation by passing it through a succession of heated baffles. Despite its widespread publicity, the stove never worked well. Neither did Franklin's efforts to solve the endemic

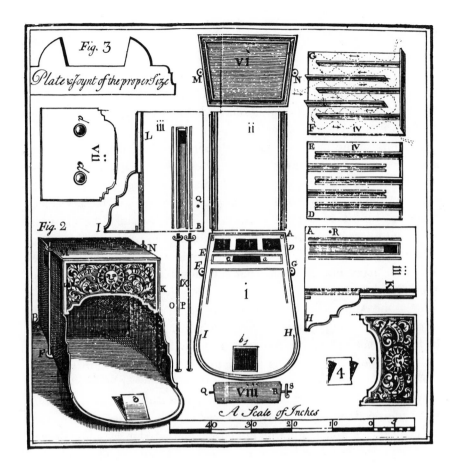

Fig. 2–7. Franklin's Pennsylvania Fireplace. The Pennsylvania Fireplace was really a cast iron stove placed within a standard fireplace. The air box (items iv) was a two-inch-wide box of baffles, placed toward the rear of the stove. Air was admitted to it from beneath the bottom plate (item i) through the Q-R vent. It then passed around the baffles, being heated as it moved; it flowed into the room through each side of the stove. The wood fire was placed on the bottom plate immediately in front of the air box, the smoke passing over the box, down beneath the back of the bottom plate, and into the chimney. Initially, the stove sold well and, when in full operation, worked as planned. Getting the fire burning and the smoke flowing through to the chimney proved to be too difficult, however, and the air box was soon abandoned.

problem of smoky chimneys, which continued until 1797 when Count Rumford, an emigré American, invented the smoke shelf. This has become the standard way to construct fireplaces—the fireplace back being placed a few inches forward of the chimney back, creating a shelf to deflect the smoke.

Wood also had more subtle effects on American material culture. Because of its availability, low cost, and ease in working, large numbers of people worked with wood and did not restrain themselves by trying to avoid waste. After all, much of the wood that was cleared for farming was simply destroyed, and Americans felt a sense of progress in converting woodland into farmland. Americans with a fingertip acquaintance with wood technology were encouraged to experiment and innovate in the use of wood without feeling they were wasting it. Its abundance made them prodigal.

Iron

Iron is often regarded as the prime material of industrialization, and America's richness in iron ore had been recognized early. Combined with a plentiful supply of wood, which was required for making the charcoal used in reducing iron ore, this richness gave the new country a great advantage. As a result colonial pig and bar iron production grew to exceed that of the mother country. Britain encouraged her colonies to produce raw iron by eliminating all duties upon it but, in 1750, prohibited the erection of further finished ironworks in America. Her policy was to exchange her own manufactured goods for such colonial raw materials as iron. That did not work as intended, because the colonials continued to erect rolling and slitting mills and to produce a variety of finished iron products. Connecticut, indeed, was conspicuous in producing so many iron products that raw iron had to be imported from other colonies.

Along the Appalachians, many ironworks, or iron plantations as they were generally called, had been established before the Revolution. Each was close to iron ore deposits; initially bog ore was easily available, but soon shallow mining was required. Each at the start was surrounded by forests, so the wood that had to be burned in a hump covered by earth to produce charcoal was equally accessible. Limestone from which the needed lime was obtained was usually relatively close, too. The central operation of the iron plantation consisted in reducing the ore in a blast furnace into which air was pumped by bellows, often powered by water. Ruins of many of these furnaces still survive; one of the best restorations is at Hopewell Village, Pennsylvania (fig. 2–8).

Independence brought the United States both advantages and disadvantages. The country was no longer within the British tariff and economic system but had become a foreign power. Americans still possessed the same resources in ore and wood and continued to produce good iron, but the market for it declined rapidly. This was caused both by the loss of special advantages in trading with Britain and by Britain's success in circumventing her wood shortage by using coke for iron reduction. Coke iron was not as superior in most characteristics as charcoal iron, but it was cheaper and satisfactory for many uses. The American iron production potential remained, but for a time after the attainment of independence its development languished.

HUMAN RESOURCES

The most important resource of all was people—but unlike other resources, the supply of people was seriously short. The lack of a popu-

lation density similar to that of European countries had increasing disadvantages. Cities were fewer and smaller; while Americans congratulated themselves on escaping the misery and crime they associated with cities, they also were denied an equivalent concentration of talent, money, trade, and manufacturing. Farming, commerce, and manufactures were all interdependent. The vast American distances, served by poorer transportation than other civilized countries, contributed further disabilities. The material development of the country required increasing numbers of inhabitants.

This deficiency, of course, had been present from the first settlements. The need for human resources brought in thousands of immigrants each year and was responsible for the device of indentured servitude. It also produced and fastened on the country the monumental evil of slavery. Slavery did supply workers essential for many needs, principally for hand labor in agriculture. The need for more hands also produced an unusually high birthrate. Americans liked to attribute their high natural increase in population to healthy living conditions and the lack of restraints, but those advantages were only part of the story.

The population was so widely separated and isolated that the great cultural and attitudinal differences brought in by immigrants could not be suppressed. Social and political accommodation of European immigrants proved difficult, uneven, and partial. Yet, it was far less unsatisfactory than the accommodation and integration of slaves and American Indians. Even the best motivated efforts to educate and integrate freed slaves and young native Americans were woefully unsuccessful. England alone, and Great Britain even more, embraced many different cultural and social groups, tightly differentiated from one another. This diversity was inconsiderable, however, compared with that in the United States. The need here for more people was so great that continuing development could only produce still more diversity and more unaccommodated differences among the population.

The scarcity of people put a higher value on each individual and on the skill and capabilities each possessed. The need for hands and for human enterprise of all sorts was so great that, in this lightly restricted society, divergent ways of doing things were more acceptable.

LAND OF OPPORTUNITIES

America, from the earliest discoveries, had been seen as a wonderful cornucopia of wealth and material prosperity. Reality produced many defeats but did not dim the dream. Settlements continued to be launched with such names as the "Land of Eden" and the "New Found Eden." Fulfillment was sufficient to keep the prophets vocal, and they were never more enthusiastic than at the time of establishing the United States.

The material foundation of the dream remained the vast, sparsely settled continent: the land, the plenty of wood, and "inexhaustible" minerals such as iron. Nothing, of course, could be done in the way of fulfillment except by and through people—but the population in residence or to be brought in was not so much reckoned as an asset as it was seen as a great unrealized need. Native Americans were occasionally exalted, mostly by Europeans, as "noble red men," but they were generally perceived as an obstacle to be pushed out of the way or overcome. Slaves were praised for their strength and loyalty when they were being sold, but most of those who owned them were absorbed by the need to keep them under control and in working health, at as low a cost as feasible. Those who lived far enough away did not think about slavery, except for the minority who came to recognize the enormity of the injustice and to work toward freeing the slaves. As for residents of European origin, their diversity was accepted because it had to be, but the objective was to establish economic and governmental patterns based upon those of Europe, primarily on the English system.

This was the state of the new nation in 1790. It celebrated its advantages, some of them based on deviations from European standards. Most advantages related to material welfare, however, were derived from American resources. Most American deviations involved greater freedom for the individual. They had arisen out of the undeveloped condition of the country, the lack of institutional constrictions, and the ideals of the Enlightenment. Fulfilling even portions of the dreams of material prosperity and individual happiness seemed heavily demanding and dubious, but some Americans were beginning to work on applying advances of the Industrial Revolution, especially the new technologies.

The Promise of Technology

EVEN THOUGH THE UNDEVELOPED WEALTH OF THE NEW NATION WAS regarded as inexhaustible, the key word was "undeveloped." America lacked the hands to do the needed work and the capital to finance the required development. These deficiencies were reduced but by no means removed by rising immigration and by the establishment of banks. Another aid to development that rose rapidly was technology. This suddenly seemed to offer a magic solution to the needs.

More and more enthusiasts saw the technology of the Industrial Revolution, organized and applied as it was in England, as a double opportunity. First, it offered means for speeding the development of the country by processes requiring fewer hands and limited capital. Second, the anticipation of riches by entrepreneurs and inventors made the application of technology actionable. Americans brought to this effort a broad acquaintance with traditional technology as well as specific skills in many crafts.

Traditional technology was well developed throughout the country in most major areas of enterprise. Surprisingly, Americans were better acquainted with everyday technology than they would have been had the country been more urbanized. Nine out of ten of them lived on farms or in farming communities, where, because of their isolation, they had to be familiar with a variety of tools and machines that they sometimes made themselves and in nearly all cases maintained in operation. Shop crafts were well represented in the cities and towns, where European mechanics, knowledgeable about overseas advances, tended to settle.

ANONYMOUS TECHNOLOGICAL IMPROVEMENTS

Americans had long practice in introducing, adapting, and improving the technologies imported from Europe. Significant inventions and innovations were few, however, and most of those were slow evolutionary developments that remain largely anonymous. The names of nearly all the individuals are lost, as are the dates of their specific alterations. What is best known about the process is the actual device that finally emerged. Examples are the Conestoga wagon, the Durham boat, and the Pennsylvania rifle. The Conestoga wagon was developed in Pennsylvania from imported German horse-drawn wagons for moving grain and bulk products. In America, rough, steep, and often muddy roads and weather extremes led to a covered wagon with large-diameter wheels, six-inch treads, and an upward flare at the front and back of the wagon that gave it almost the shape of a boat. The Durham boat was a similar product of change that produced a large flatboat used primarily for carrying wheat. (The Pennsylvania rifle is examined on pages 51–52.)

The best example of anonymous technology may be the elegant American felling axe. Many different sorts of axes were imported from Europe, but the most critical change occurred in the felling axe, a crucial tool because of the vast effort required to clear woodlands. The American axe was unique in that the bit, or cutting edge of the axe, was just about the same weight as the poll or flat edge—giving the axe remarkable balance. In contrast, the European axe had a longer and narrower bit and hardly any poll at all. This difference permitted the American axe to be swung straight and clean, without the slightest wavering. In addition, the wooden handle was given a length and curve precisely fitted to the height and swing of the axman. The result was remarkable. A practiced American axman could fell three times as many trees in the same time as a man using a European axe (figs. 3–1, 3–2).

The American axe was fully developed before the Revolution, and it remains much the same today. Despite its advantages, it had strikingly little acceptance in Europe. When Samuel F. B. Morse visited Italy in 1830, he was amazed to encounter the inefficiency of the standard European axe that was still being used there. He remarked that if the Americans had been limited to the use of that axe, they would never have been able to clear their continent.

Fig. 3–1. European axe

Fig. 3–2. American axe

Gristmills were ubiquitous throughout the civilized world, but sawmills were not. From the seventeenth century there were a great many in America, while almost none appeared in England. The lack of sawmills in England was not wholly caused by the country's shortage of forests and wood. Wood remained an important construction material there, even though most of it had to be imported. In whatever form the imports were received, sawing was called for, and several efforts were made to introduce sawmills. They always aroused a negative reaction, and some were destroyed by disgruntled sawyers who feared the loss of their jobs. In fact, handsawing worked reasonably well in England and even throughout Britain, but it was not satisfactory in America where the sheer volume of sawing demanded the use of sawmills. Besides, sawyers did not constitute an organized force in this country. The largest concentration of sawmills in the early seventeenth century was in the Maine region, where the operatives brought in to man the mills were not sawyers being deprived of higher skilled jobs. This continued to be true of the rest of the country, with the result that sawmills were a particularly American form of mechanization, especially compared with the mother country.

Most sawmills depended upon waterpower, which placed them at waterpower sites on rivers and often near the fall line. Most of them used lantern and candle gearing, just like that pictured in many theaters of machines, and transmission shafts similar to those used in gristmills. The up-and-down sawmill, first developed on the Continent in the fifteenth century, became standard. Now the saw not only moved up and down, but the log being cut was advanced automatically after each stroke (fig. 3–3).

Because of the spread of sawmills through the country and because many farmers were part-time lumberers, the technology of sawmills was widely known. Even those who had only heard of sawmills were likely to be familiar with waterwheels and the gearing they saw in gristmills.

Another widespread use of gearing was in clocks and watches. Watches were relatively rare, and tall clocks in the home were also limited to the relatively well-to-do. Tower clocks, however, were present in almost every town, and several might be found in churches or public buildings in a city. They used spur gears similar to those publicized in the theaters of machines (fig. 3–4). In addition, clock escapements introduced those who viewed them to precision mechanization. Of course, only a few made or worked with the technology of mills or clocks, but none of those who had watched them operate could feel alien to the new machinery of the Industrial Revolution.

FARMER — ARTISANS

All farmers apply technology to specific ends. It is a mistake to think of farmers as less acquainted with technology than city dwellers, especially in the new American nation but even on farms today. The maximum division of labor was attained in the cities, where clerks, writers, artists, actors, businessmen, government employees, and many other individuals needed almost no direct facility in the use of technology. It was not so with farmers and farm families, all of whom were engaged in "making and doing things." The production of food and fiber and processing them involved the use of technology at every stage. Most of it

Fig. 3–3. Mid-nineteenth-century sawmill from Chester County, Pennsylvania

Fig. 3–4. Tower clockworks

was traditional technology or hand work, but tools and man-made devices were required at almost every turn. Because the farmer's isolation was greater here than in Europe, most Americans made their own tools and repaired them. This required a process of visual thinking and a cultivation of imagination different from what a clerk or a writer needs. It was very important training. Machines were familiar, from gristmills and sawmills to clocks and spinning wheels. More Americans were close to technology in 1790 than were most English people; in addition, they were more ready to work with the new mechanized technology that was emerging.

The variety of pursuits that might be demanded of a single American continued to amaze European visitors. Johann David Schöpf, a German physician who remained after the War for Independence, reported a conversation with a farmer-tavern keeper in New Jersey. The American told him, "I am a mover, a shoemaker, furrier, wheelwright, farmer, gardener, and when it can't be helped, a soldier. I make my bread, brew my beer, kill my pigs; I grind my axes and knives; I built those stalls and that shed there; I am barber, leech, and doctor." [1]

The variety of products made in this manner was large. Many country gristmills were run by farmers—but operated only when a customer brought in grain to be ground, a seasonal need that followed the harvest season. Farmers had better control over other seasonal activities, such as cutting timber. A large number of farmers engaged in seasonal lumbering, which they undertook when their farming duties were relatively slow. Some operated sawmills on a seasonal basis.

Some farmers were, in addition, engaged in a pattern of production that has only recently become clear. This may best be described as the output of the farmer-artisan, that is, the farmer who also made specific craft products for sale or exchange. Many farm families, of course, made their own tools, furniture, fabrics, clothing, and processed foods. Beyond this, some farmers functioned as part-time artisans, producing trade goods or services for the market.

The extent of craft production by farmers has only recently come to attention. Hervey Brooks, a Connecticut farmer-potter, is not atypical. Some of his ceramic pieces have survived and he was first known for them alone. It is now clear that he was first of all a farmer and that he made the ceramic pieces to bring in additional income (fig. 3–5).

Other farmers specialized in making hats, shoes, or clothing. It was an easy transition from a farm life in which so many different tools had to be managed and used. Gristmills and sawmills, of course, were mechanized operations, but a smaller measure of mechanization was even more widely practiced. A hammer and chisel or a saw or plane represented simple tools, but the potter's wheel (ancient as it was), the spinning wheel, the hand loom, and the fulling machine all represented degrees of mechanization that should not be underestimated.

Fig. 3–5.
Hervey Brooks ceramic milkpan

The highest levels of skill were possessed by shop artisans in towns and cities. The basis of this form of technological production had been imported from Europe and continued to be refreshed by artisans, especially from England, who brought their skills and knowledge of new techniques to America in the hope of vocational and social advancement.

The American scene for craft artisans became very different, however, from what it had been in the Old World, and the great political and economic power of the guilds was not imported. The apprenticeship pattern was transferred but in weakened form. The master was under a legal obligation, as in Europe, to carry out the terms of the indenture and associated liabilities. He had to provide food, lodging, clothing, and education appropriate to the apprentice's station. He, of course, had to train the apprentice in the craft and often provide him with tools of the trade upon completing the apprenticeship. The terms were enforceable by the courts.

American deviations from European patterns were primarily a result of the looseness of American society. Runaway apprentices were one index of the limited control exercised over labor, but more continuously significant was the manner in which artisans might set themselves up in crafts for which they had never been trained. The strange career of John Fitch rested on such opportunities. In 1762 he began an unusual apprenticeship to a clockmaker in Windsor, Connecticut, at the late age of eighteen; he completed it at the usual age of twenty-one. However, he felt incompetent to seek employment as a journeyman, complaining that he was never taught the craft of clockmaking, a charge made by many American apprentices against their masters. So he set up shop as a brass founder, the work upon which he had spent most of his apprenticeship. In 1769 Fitch moved to Trenton, New Jersey, where he succeeded very well in silversmithing, for which he had never trained. With the approach of the War for Independence, Fitch served as a militia officer and then undertook gunsmithing as a temporarily profitable business. After 1780 he undertook various other enterprises, turning in 1785 to mapmaking, another field alien to his apprenticeship. By that time, however, he had demonstrated an ability to master a variety of technologies sufficiently to work in them reasonably well.

Fitch certainly had more capacity than most artisans, but many others moved from trade to trade and colony to colony with a similar lack of restraint. The most effective restraint was the marketplace, which corrected against incompetent craftsmen. The lack of enforcement of standards of regulation that were effective in Europe, and especially in Britain, loosened craftsmanship generally. Americans were less likely to spend their entire lives in pursuit of a single craft skill. Consequently, skills were developed to lower levels here. With their eye on the marketplace, Americans made products as cheaply and quickly as possible. They moved easily from job to job within a trade and even to different trades as well.

Most of the components of Industrial Revolution machines were well known to these artisans. Just as gear trains were used in mills and clocks, pistons and cylinders were known primarily in the water pumps used especially for raising water from mines and for pumping out ships. Less familiar but particularly forward looking were the air pumps, which were often imported.

The air pump was based on well-known components that soon came to play a major part in machine development. It was not familiar to most people, because it was used for demonstration and experiment, chiefly in colleges and schools. It was basically a piston and cylinder pump, often used to pump air out of an enclosed space in order to produce a partial vacuum, permitting experiments that demonstrated the effect of lack of air on fire and animal life. This experience, in making a vacuum and in using the piston and cylinder with gases rather than for pumping water, pointed toward the application of piston and cylinder to the steam engine (fig. 3–6).

Precision machining was another requirement the Industrial Revolution brought with it, and the Americans had some experience in that area. Specialized tools were an old story, and special-purpose and precision machines were a part of the early scene. Cabinetmakers were accustomed to using a great variety of very specifically designed planes, saws, and files. Spinning wheels seem like general-purpose machines, but they had to be built differently for flax, wool, or cotton. Even precision machines such as lathes and drill presses were sometimes set up to perform specific jobs in a way that limited their general applicability.

The lathe was one of the oldest of machine tools, used since antiquity. Until the eighteenth century, however, it was overwhelmingly a woodworking tool. It rotated the piece being worked on in a manner permitting it to be cut by a single pointed tool held against it. Henry Maudslay, in England, introduced the slide rest, which permitted the cutting tool to be held by the machine itself and moved as needed with increased precision. From 1800 on, the lathe emerged as the most basic tool for much iron and steel work (fig. 3–7). Improving versions were imported to America as they developed, and they rapidly became a fundamental reliance.

A more American development in precision work was the Pennsylvania rifle (fig. 3–8). Close tolerances, far beyond what was required in clockmaking, were needed in gunmaking. This was especially true of

Fig. 3–6. Air pump

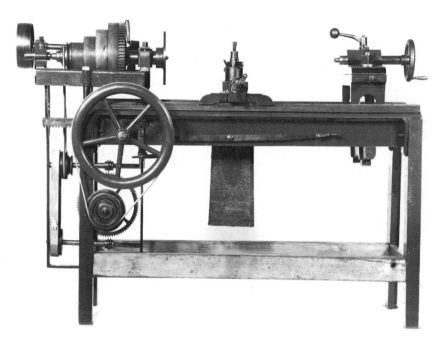

Fig. 3-7. American lathe, 1830

Fig. 3-8. Pennsylvania rifle

the anonymous riflemakers who had produced the Pennsylvania rifle years before the American Revolution. The German Jaeger or hunting rifle was a short-barreled, large-caliber gun brought to the colonies when the Germans first immigrated. Here, the riflemakers gradually converted it into a long-range, remarkably accurate piece by lengthening the barrel and reducing the bore. They also introduced a grease patch in which the bullet was placed before ramming it down the barrel. Despite the great precision required in fitting each component of the rifle, especially of the gun lock, every piece was cast, cut, and filed individually. It was traditional, craft technology.

The Pennsylvania rifle was sometimes called the secret weapon of the War for Independence, because it was so superior to the guns in general use. Muskets, including military muskets, had so little accuracy that they did not even have sights. They were fired by squads of soldiers creating a scatter pattern that could be effective. In contrast, the Pennsylvania rifle could pick off an individual at distances to 300 feet. It was less helpful in the Revolution than had been hoped, but it spread over the colonial and early national frontier. It was not designed as a military weapon but for hunting game, mostly small game, at which it proved much more effective. As the rifle moved west, it was sometimes called the Kentucky rifle—although its origin was clearly in German Pennsylvania.

THE NEW TECHNOLOGY: ENTHUSIASM VERSUS RESISTANCE

Technology was an integral part of American life, but for the most part, American craftsmen did not produce as elaborate or as high-quality products as the Europeans. They did not develop equivalent skill, and their market did not encourage uniqueness of design and fineness of finish. David Rittenhouse was one of the few craftsmen who reached the highest levels of skill and creativity.

Rittenhouse was the most celebrated craftsman of the Revolutionary era. Coming out of a farm background, he began his career as a clockmaker, moved on to making scientific instruments such as compasses, surveyor's levels, and telescopes, and finally into science where he was productive in mathematics, aspects of physics, and astronomy. After the founding of the new nation, Rittenhouse was seen as justification for the hope that the country could move forward in technology and industrial development. As a technologist-scientist, he was often viewed as Franklin's successor and, indeed, was elected to succeed him as president of the American Philosophical Society, the nation's first scientific society.

Rittenhouse's highest technological achievement was the two almost identical orreries, or mechanical planetariums, that he made a little before the Revolution (fig. 3–9). They were probably the most precise representations of the solar system produced to that time. All the planets then known revolved by clockwork about the sun and their satellites about some of them. With good accuracy, they could be cranked forward or backward 5,000 years. With his typical lack of restraint, Thomas Jefferson gave this work its greatest compliment, "We have supposed Mr. Rittenhouse second to no astronomer living; that in genius he must be the first, because he is self-taught. As an artist he had exhibited as great a proof of mechanical genius as the world has ever produced. He has not indeed made a world; but he has by imitation approached nearer its Maker than any man who has lived from the creation to this day."[2]

Incorporating the best astronomical understanding of the time, the orreries were a spectacular demonstration of precision technology—albeit of traditional, craft technology. More surprising, they had a peculiarly American air to them. Unlike the ornate European clockwork automata, they were sparely and simply designed with no excess ornamentation. The gear trains were complex, as they had to be to do their job, but the design was dominated by the effort to attain the objectives as easily and simply as possible (fig. 3–10).

"American improvement," or the material development of the country, became an objective as soon as cultural nationalism rose in the 1760s and 1770s. There was so much to be done that Americans reached for any help the new technology offered. New techniques could be applied to initial efforts of many entrepreneurs and individuals—without having to displace old methods, as was usually necessary in introducing new

Fig. 3–9. Rittenhouse orrery, 1767-71

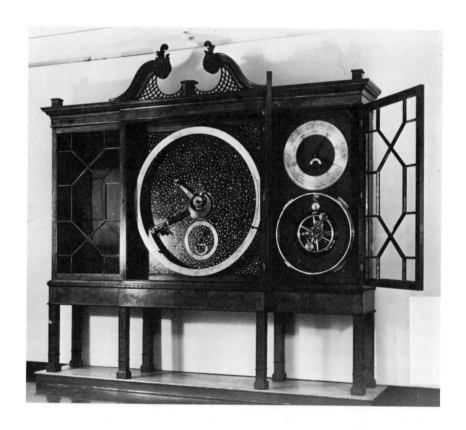

Fig. 3–10. The Saturn arm of the orrery

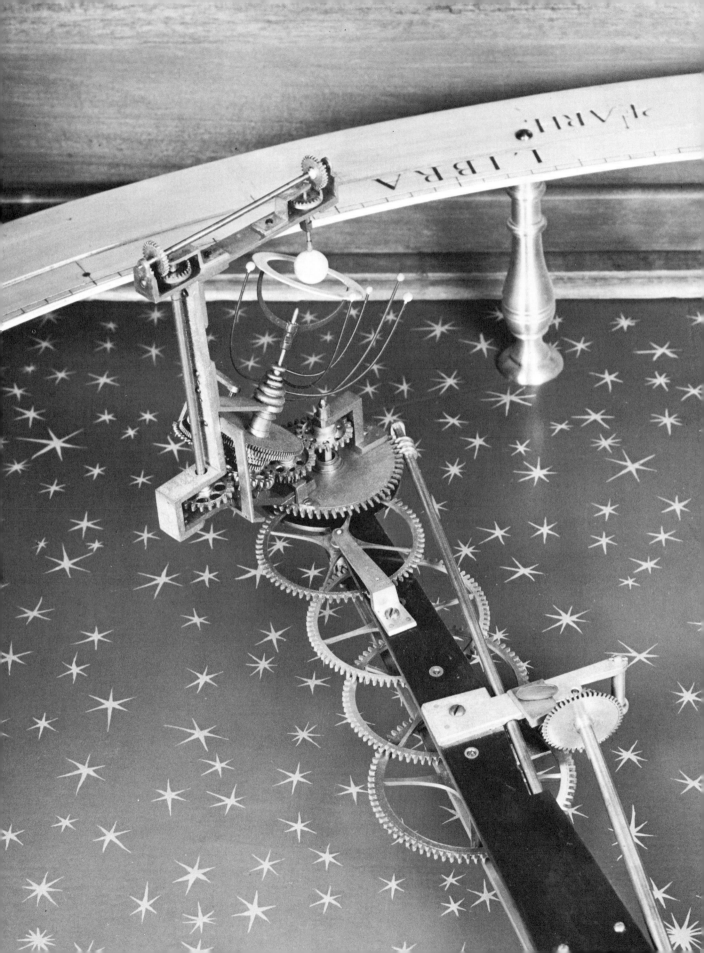

technology in established nations. A primary American advantage was a state of mind—a readiness on the part of many to apply mechanization wherever possible in order to reduce cost and human input. Often, the first step was to transfer, mostly from England, the more successful techniques and ways of managing them.

Some American leaders were captured early by this hope of applying new techniques to manufacturing. Benjamin Rush, a physician and signer of the Declaration of Independence, worked both before and after the war with manufacturing societies to encourage the importation of British technology—especially textile machinery. Very little of value was accomplished prior to independence, but by 1790 increasing numbers of political leaders had become attracted to the idea.

In fact, the new United States had the same advantage in applying new technologies that it had in applying the political aspirations of the Enlightenment. In writing the constitutions of new states and of the new nation, an opportunity was presented to introduce new concepts without having to demolish old ones. New manufacturing technologies could be introduced in a similar manner. Some political leaders supported the new approaches in both government and technology.

Among them, Alexander Hamilton has long been celebrated because of his *Report on Manufactures* of 1791. He said, "The Employment of Machinery forms an item of great importance in the general mass of national industry. It is an artificial force brought in aid of the natural force of man; and to all the purpose of labor, is an increase of hands, an accession of strength, unencumbered too by the expense of maintaining the laborer."[3]

Tench Coxe, who drafted much of Hamilton's report, was more specific. He reflected, "As long as we remained in our colonial situation, our progress was very slow, and indeed the necessity of attention to manufacture was not so urgent, as it has become since our assuming an independent station." In the new nation, he predicted, "Machines ingeniously constructed, will give us immense assistance."[4]

John Adams also was caught up in the enthusiasm for technology. He regarded changes of this sort as an integral part of the whole process of launching the new nation and included them in his *Defense of the Constitutions* [of the states]. He wrote, "The Inventions in Mechanic Arts, the discoveries in natural Philosophy, navigation, and commerce, and the Advancement of civilization and humanity, have occasioned Changes in the condition of the World and the human Character, which would have astonished the most refined Nations of Antiquity."[5]

Of the most celebrated leaders, Benjamin Franklin was as supportive as might be expected, and George Washington also sought to encourage technology as a means of American improvement. Toward this end, he urged specific patent legislation in his first address to Congress. He advised, "I cannot forbear intimating to you the expediency of giving effectual encouragement as well to the introduction of new and useful inventions from abroad as to the exertions of skill and genius in producing them at home."[6]

Yet such support was far from universal. Many were influenced by the long-standing conviction that American virtue was opposed by British vice, especially in London. This view had been enthusiastically publicized during the Revolution, which also sensitized Americans to other British evils. Conspicuous among them were the negative aspects of the Industrial Revolution, not only bad living and working conditions, but also the deadly dullness of the work of machine operators. Manchester was understood to be a gruesome, industrialized city that no one would want to emulate.

These attitudes produced an antagonism to mechanization, manufacturing, industrialism, and urbanization, which combined readily with the philosophical position that farming was the most virtuous occupation. Some worked vigorously to promote agriculture and to discourage manufacturing. George Logan and John Morgan worked hard to promote new agricultural practices in the United States. Logan saw a conspiracy: "The declared intention of establishing national manufactories, is to carry off the surplus produce of our agriculture."[7] Morgan declared, "Agriculture will more abundantly supply our wants, than the manufacturing of any kinds of goods can do."[8]

The most important negative was that of Thomas Jefferson, who believed that virtuous, representative government had to rest on self-sustaining, independent farmers. Despite his real, almost bubbling, enthusiasm for technological creativity, Jefferson long remained dubious that further mechanization and development of manufacturing could be carried through without seriously, perhaps fatally, damaging republican government in the United States. He was convinced that manufacturing cities produced evils incompatible with good government. Twenty years later he would reluctantly withdraw his opposition, but in 1785 and again in 1788 he castigated manufacturing and its technology without restraint. He pleaded, "Let us never wish to see our citizens occupied at a work-bench, or twirling a distaff. Carpenters, masons, smiths are wanting in husbandry; but for the general operations of manufacture, let our workshops remain in Europe."[9] He concluded that manufacturing was not merely undesirable but unsupportable in this country: "In general it is impossible that manufactures should succeed in America from the high price of labour."[10]

THE OPPORTUNITY

The new United States was fortunate in being launched at a time when the philosophy of the Enlightenment extolled the values of the individual, the environmental approach to social improvement, and a broadly based, elective government. The riches of the country were still being uncovered, but most of them required the application of some technology. The process of development could be speeded by adding more hands or more capital—but in many cases the most accessible aid was the new technology. The enthusiasts for technology could speed up the process, and opponents could slow it down. In the free, unstructured society of this country, however, the new technology offered so much and those who sought it were numerous enough that no conscious decision had to be made. Even against active opponents, the Industrial Revolution was transferred. The most critical transfer, however, was not machines but enthusiasm, enthusiasm for technology. This, coupled with American facility in technology, permitted the United States to seize the opportunity and make the most of it.

IV *The Transfer of Technology*

THE LONG AMERICAN EXPERIENCE IN TRANSFERRING TECHNOLOGY TOOK a critical turn with the American Revolution and the establishment of the new nation. The colonial period was marked by the immigration of many peoples from many European countries who brought with them differing cultural sets and sometimes competing technologies. For example, English and German ironmaking did not follow the same procedures and resulted in divergent processes being instituted within the colonies. The differences between Indian, African slave, and European technologies, of course, were even greater, and while the European patterns largely overwhelmed those inherited from other continents, they never did become uniform. Influences from Germany, Scotland, Scandinavia, France, and the Netherlands continued, as did technological transfer from those countries and England. In fact, every new immigrant brought with him or her a specific technological heritage—in some cases very limited, but always influential on attitudes.

Such diversity by no means ended with the American Revolution, but the remarkable coincidence of that series of events with critical developments of the Industrial Revolution altered the overall picture. Independence required that a more balanced economy be developed to replace the colonial economy, and those who pursued this need and opportunity recognized that some of the advances of the English Industrial Revolution offered a distinct opportunity. Efforts to encourage manufacturing brought attention immediately to English advances in production technologies and in related organizational patterns. However, internal and external commerce also had advantages to gain from some of the new technologies. Indeed, to some, even the efforts to mechanize certain agricultural processes seemed worth bringing in. The Industrial Revolution caused a heavy emphasis on the transfer of English and Scottish technologies.

Relationships with the former mother country were strained after the War, and former tariff and credit advantages were lost, but other means of help were still there. As former colonials, the Americans exploited their language, family, business, and friendship ties to give them better access to British innovations than any other country. Perhaps their unending experience in the transfer of technologies from many places was even more important. In any event, all their experiences were now concentrated more heavily than before on Great Britain and especially on England.

Americans were better positioned in other respects, too, than might have been anticipated. Their experience with technology permitted the easy reception, adaptation, and use of new machines. It even permitted the reproduction of machines developed in Britain with little more information about them than the basic concept. Most striking, the Americans were almost immediately able to improvise and invent new ways of doing some of the things accomplished by the new machinery.

Their improvisations and modifications of British machinery reflected the differing American context. Everything had to be adapted to American society and economy. Skill levels here were usually lower, capital was more scarce, labor more dear, distances enormously greater, and government weak and impoverished. These differences affected both the machines themselves and the manner in which they were put to use.

TRANSFER BY IMMIGRANTS: THE NEW TEXTILE TECHNOLOGY

The best example of successful technology transfer is found in the introduction of the new English system of mechanized textile production. The most pressing motivation to acquire this capability was the English success in supplying cloth more cheaply than it could be made in the United States. American efforts to gain this advantage for themselves had begun even before independence was attained. Colonial business and political leaders brought in English mechanics to set up mechanized textile production. After independence a still more compelling need arose to break free from the tyranny of English imports.

By then the English, afflicted by continental as well as American efforts to take over the advantages they had gained in making cheap textiles, had passed laws prohibiting the export of the new machines and the emigration of mechanics who knew about them. If successful, these laws would have cut off the two primary means for effecting technology transfer. They did not succeed. The United States was especially successful in gaining the needed knowledge, despite the laws. A few machines were imported by disassembling them into their component parts and packing them in disguised boxes. Because Americans were in a position to build machines themselves, however, once individuals here knew a little about them, they did not much rely on the importation of machines. The important transfer was the unbroken immigration of knowledgeable mechanics.

Samuel Slater was the most celebrated of these (fig. 4–1). He provided the key transfer of knowledge for building America's first successful textile mill, based on the Arkwright system of factory production. Other mechanics had come to America before him, but none had succeeded. Neither had Americans who sought to duplicate English machinery on the basis of inadequate information.

Fig. 4–1. Samuel Slater

Slater brought with him unusual advantages and found in this country a very favorable opportunity. Of a well-to-do family, he was apprenticed to Jedediah Strutt, who had been an associate of Richard Arkwright and who had become one of the largest textile manufacturers in England. As mill overseer for Strutt, Slater learned both technical and managerial skills.

When he completed his apprenticeship at the age of twenty-one, Slater learned that American states were giving bounties for the introduction of cotton textile machinery. Following a deception practiced by many English emigrants, he passed himself off as a farmer in order to board a ship for the United States. Landing at New York in 1789, he found the machinery and organization of the New York Manufacturing Society so inadequate that he gave up his effort to improve it. Instead he accepted the invitation of Moses Brown to visit him in Pawtucket, Rhode Island.

Moses Brown was a fiercely independent merchant and businessman who had come into conflict with his well-to-do family when he became a Quaker and again when, at an early stage, he opposed the slave trade. He had worked for two years at efforts to launch the machine manufacture of textiles. He assembled workmen and had a number of machines built, but when Slater saw them he pronounced the machines beneath any possibility of rescue for effective operation. He would have to build everything new. Promising to build an effective mill, he went to work in 1790 for William Almy, Brown's son-in-law, and Smith Brown, his cousin. In due time Almy and Brown became Almy, Brown, and Slater.

Slater's success would have been absolutely impossible without workmen competent to execute his designs—designs that were unfamiliar in the United States. Slater specified that, above all, he must have a man to work in wood who was bonded not to steal any of the designs. Sylvanus Brown (unrelated to Moses) filled this post with great success. Oziel Wilkinson not only took care of the parallel need for iron work but soon married Slater's daughter. Each of them engaged skilled and imaginative mechanics (millwrights, blacksmiths, brassworkers, carpenters, and leather workers) who had learned their trades in the United States. A country less developed technologically could not have carried through Slater's designs as they did.

The most important two machines upon which the production of cotton yarn depended were the carding machine and the spinning frame. The carding machine replaced the hand cards that sorters had previously used to make roving, which is a compacted and aligned roll of cotton fibers. The carding machine had a large cylinder, surfaced with protruding teeth or wires that were slightly bent—as they were on hand cards (fig. 4–2). As the cylinder rotated, its teeth passed by parallel but oppositely bent teeth on the "flats" that surrounded the top of the cylinder. This action aligned and compacted the roving. Mechanization thus eliminated the handwork and speeded the process of carding.

The spinning frame was a more complicated piece of machinery, but Slater actually took less time to get that in satisfactory working condition than he did with the carding machine. Just as a spinning wheel did, the spinning frame had to stretch and twist the roving until it became tight and uniform yarn (fig. 4–3). But Slater's spinning frame made forty-eight lengths of yarn simultaneously and did so without any human skill having to be applied. The operator's job was to keep the machine running, keep it supplied with roving, and fix it whenever a length of yarn

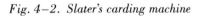

Fig. 4–2. Slater's carding machine

broke or any other breakdown occurred. The spinning head was the key element of the machine.

Both carding machines and spinning frames were powered by waterwheels in Slater's early mills. He first set them in motion in 1790 in an adapted building that was not a satisfactory mill; by 1793 he had built a large part of the mill that survives today (fig. 4–4). Waterpower was used also in England, although steam was beginning to take over. Moses Brown had, in fact, investigated the possibility of using steam power but concluded that it was impracticable. Of course, the United States had more usable waterpower sites than England, and most manufacturing operations, especially in New England, continued to depend on water.

Slater transferred not only the machinery and the general arrangement of the mill but the labor pattern as well. In the United States it was not usual for children to work formally until the age of fourteen, when they could be engaged as apprentices. In England younger boys and girls were introduced into textile mills as operatives, and Slater initially applied that pattern. His first mill used eight children between the ages of seven and twelve to operate both carding and spinning machines. These boys and girls were not apprentices but worked for wages—low wages.

Fig. 4–3. Slater's spinning frame

Fig. 4–4. Slater's 1793 mill,
Pawtucket, Rhode Island

When Slater expanded his operations, as he did into other towns, he ran into resistance. It was hard to find the children needed. Some families opposed the spinning mill in general, seeing it as an importation of the evils of the English factory system and as a threat to American liberties. Others objected to the low wages, believing their children more valuable on the farm or better served by waiting until they could learn a trade as an apprentice. Only the poorest farmers and the landless urban poor let their children work in a mill. That situation made it necessary to try approaches more in conformity with the American scene, such as the employment of young women and recent immigrants. Child labor never became as widespread in the United States as in England, but it was not eliminated.

Samuel Slater's transfer is the most dramatic example of successful transfer through the personal immigration of an individual familiar with a new technology. This was the means by which most textile technology was transferred. Between 1773 and 1775, more than 500 British immigrants had told customs officers that they worked in textile trades. Between 1824 and 1831, 5,000 immigrants reported these trades, including 153 textile machine makers. Most of the transfer effected was hard to discern and unrecorded, but it was real.

Next to Slater, Arthur and John Scholfield effected the most important transfer. They came to Massachusetts in 1793 and succeeded in building working woolen textile machinery. The mechanization of wool textile production was harder than cotton because of the nature of the fibers. The Scholfields put together a hand-operated spinning jenny and a hand loom very quickly, John Scholfield producing most of the design. They worked so well that support materialized for setting up a water-powered wool mill. For this purpose, they put together three carding machines in a Newburyport factory, all water powered as was the fulling machine (fig. 4–5). However, they continued to use the hand-operated jenny and loom. Their business soon failed, but knowledge of the carding machine was diffused through the state and into Connecticut. Although other English immigrants also reproduced individual carding machines in this country, the Scholfields were responsible for its successful diffusion here. It continued to be improved, and wool spinning and weaving were similarly mechanized.

Fig. 4–5. Scholfield wool carding machine

The most important remaining need was for a power loom, but that came by a different route. The most publicized transfer was that by Francis Cabot Lowell, who visited England in 1812 and carefully studied power looms there. He discovered how they worked and brought the information back to Massachusetts. Here he might never have been able to translate his knowledge into practice without the aid of an ingenious American mechanic, Paul Moody, who was able to adapt and improvise sufficiently to build a working loom. This transfer became important in the Lowell textile mills and was diffused from there.

The power-loom adaptation represented a different and higher level transfer from those of Slater and the Scholfields, because it skipped over the need for an immigrant mechanic. It depended on both the good understanding of Lowell and the well-developed technological skills of Americans, especially Moody. Of course, immigrants also built power looms, in the same manner that Slater had introduced cotton spinning, but, in this case, the more sophisticated transfer succeeded better. Still later, the transfer of calico printing was similarly effected by mechanics who visited Britain.

There was, in fact, a third and still more independent power-loom transfer that was hardly a transfer at all. This was the design and building of the machine by American mechanics without any significant information on English looms beyond the idea itself. The first American patent for a power loom was granted in 1810, but the American design that worked best was an earlier crank or "Scotch" loom, in the development of which David Wilkinson, son of Oziel, played a major role. This Rhode Island loom was able to compete with Lowell's, but the Lowell loom became more widely diffused. The power loom emerged quickly as an essential component of mechanized textile production (fig. 4–6).

TRANSFER BY IMPORTING MACHINES

British efforts to curb the transfer of Industrial Revolution technologies to other countries had limited success. Prohibition of the emigration of mechanics never much restrained those who wished to move to the United States. The prohibition against exporting specified new machines was more effective but not very injurious to Americans, who relied much more on immigrant mechanics, visits to England, drawings and descriptions, and the ingenuity of their own mechanics.

The surreptitious importation of restricted British machines did rise after the Revolution, textile machinery being more sought after than steam engines and other devices. Phineas Bond, Jr., the American-born British consul for the middle states, was particularly active in checking

Fig. 4–6. Power loom, c. 1868

incoming cargoes and reporting on violators. At an early stage, he identified two Englishmen who shipped from Liverpool to Philadelphia one carding and three spinning machines, "packed in Queen's ware crates and casks, to elude discovery."[1]

Throughout, the United States imported much less British machinery than did the continental nations. Clandestine imports cannot be enumerated, but legal American imports in 1840, the year before the restrictions were repealed, amounted to only £13,500, compared with £72,600 for France and £593,064 in total. British restrictions were intended primarily to prevent the export of machinery in order to reduce competing manufactures.

In fact, the export of some machines was not only permitted but encouraged, steam locomotives among them. From 1830 on the export of locomotives became an important trade item for Britain. As the United States sought to introduce railroading, the importation of a very few prototype locomotives proved the most important of all machine imports. The great story here is the importation and adaptation of the *John Bull* in 1831; this episode is examined in detail in chapter 8.

TRANSFER FAILURE: THE NEWCOMEN ENGINE

Constant selectivity was exercised in the transfer of new technology from abroad. It was usually exercised without conscious large-scale decision in a social process resembling the role of natural selection in biological evolution. Nearly all important technological changes associated with the English Industrial Revolution came to the attention of Americans, who usually attempted to transfer them. Which succeeded, which found a minor place, and which failed completely depended upon complex factors, most central of which was a clear and present need to apply the device in question to a profitable enterprise.

One of the earliest transfers related to the Industrial Revolution was the Newcomen engine. Its failure is instructive in view of its initial success in fulfilling the specific need for which it was brought here. Thomas Newcomen got his atmospheric steam engine working reasonably well by 1712, but it always remained a cranky engine, hard to adjust and to keep running well. It was voracious of fuel and inefficient, qualities that were acceptable at the British coal mines where it was used most for pumping water out of deep mines.

In 1753 Phillip Schuyler, who owned a deep copper mine in what is now North Arlington, New Jersey, arranged to import a Newcomen engine to pump the water out of his mine (fig. 4–7). In this case, before American mechanical skills had been widely developed, Schuyler had to import not only the engine but spare parts and mechanics to put it together, adapt it to the purpose intended, and keep it running. The immigrant in charge of this operation was Josiah Hornblower, of the Hornblower family, one of the leading manufacturers of engines in England.

The engine did succeed and, through several rebuildings based on imported components, was used to pump the water out until the mining operation became unprofitable. However, there was no other immediate need for such an engine. America did not have deep coal mines, and the one or two other copper mines did not require such an engine. The device could not become a part of the American economy because it was not needed. No modification or development compatible with the "state of the art" could have made it useful.

Fig. 4–7. Newcomen steam engine cylinder from the Schuyler mine

The steam engine did not become a part of American life until much later, when mechanical skills had risen to higher levels. When John Fitch, in 1785, first planned a steamboat, he began with a Newcomen engine of his own design. Although Fitch never built the Newcomen engine, his design is interesting (fig. 4–8). As early as 1736 Jonathan Hulls had obtained a British patent for a Newcomen-driven steamboat, and the Marquis de Jouffroy's boats of 1776 and 1783 also used Newcomen engines. When Fitch sought help in America, he talked to three men, including Josiah Hornblower, none of whom knew anything about engines other than Newcomen's. The Newcomen engine, therefore, was a reasonable beginning, but the massive, heavy engine with long working beams that was used at mines would not have worked on a boat. Fitch, therefore, modified the design by using springs to lower the piston in each of two cylinders—instead of weights as applied in stationary Newcomen engines. He also used ratchets to convert the reciprocal motion of the pistons to the required rotary motion. Before he put his 1787 and 1789 boats in operation, he learned of Watt's improvements and redesigned the engines.

Throughout this entire period transfer remained a part of life, but it differed greatly from one technology to another. Whether a transfer succeeded continued to depend wholly upon whether it sufficiently fitted specific American needs and capabilities.

DELAYED TRANSFER: THE ENGLISH IRON REVOLUTION

Technology transfer has to be understood not only for its outstanding successes, such as mechanized textile production and railroading, but also for such clear-cut failures as the Newcomen engine and for delayed transfers. One major aspect of the Industrial Revolution was transferred to the United States only after a remarkably long delay. This was the iron revolution, sometimes called the first iron revolution. It began with Abraham Darby's successful reduction of iron ore using coke rather than charcoal as the fuel, at what is now Ironbridge, England, in 1709. That achievement followed from England's depletion of wood and the success it had already met in using coal for other heat-based industries. Iron was the last to yield, and it soon turned out that not all ore could be successfully reduced in the manner Darby demonstrated. More important, the iron produced was not as generally useful—fine for castings but not as convertible to malleable iron. Partly for these reasons Darby's process was not immediately applied elsewhere. Not until the 1780s did coke ore reduction begin to dominate the scene.

Fig. 4–8. Fitch's 1785 Newcomen engine design

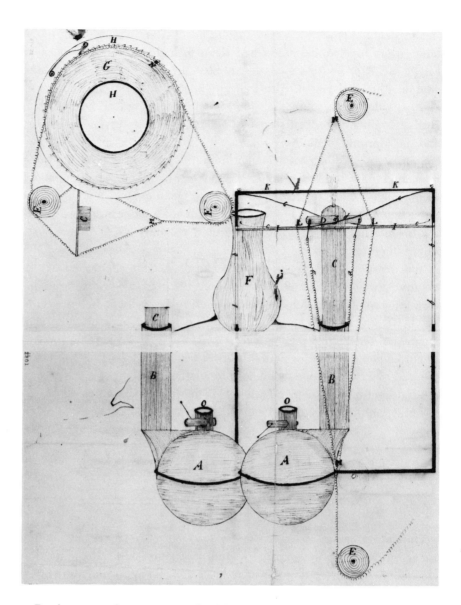

By then two other processes had begun to have a major impact on iron production. These were puddling and rolling, more mechanical methods of converting pig to bar iron, that is, to malleable, workable iron. Both processes were first patented in 1783 but had come into use earlier. Together with coke ore reduction, they gave England a clear advantage over its competitors in iron production.

Why did the American colonies and the new United States not move quickly to gain these advantages? To begin with, the mother country had encouraged the production of raw, pig, and bar iron in the colonies. England offered a good market with no duties. On this basis, a large iron industry grew in America, using the plentiful wood supply to make the charcoal required for ore reduction. By the Revolution, when the colonies were producing more iron than the mother country, Britain put to use its new techniques for making iron more cheaply—and the new United States lost its advantage of duty-free exports. British iron was imported, despite the high cost of transporting so heavy a product. American iron production declined as a result of falling exports, and no immediate incentive or financing was available for introducing the new techniques.

Not until about 1815 did conditions change sufficiently to encourage the importation of the English advances. By then American industrial needs had diversified sufficiently that different sorts of iron were needed. Also bituminous coal became available for coking near Pittsburgh, where the changes first succeeded. Coke iron was less generally satisfactory, but because it was cheaper and could be used just as well for some needs, an American market began to emerge. Knowledgeable British immigrants, working with American innovators, transferred puddling, rolling, and coke ore reduction—but not nearly as early as they might have been imported had those changes been needed.

REVERSE TRANSFER

The transfer of technology became a two-way street. As Americans modified English machines, they immediately began to invent similar and related devices and put new techniques into use. Some of these and some wholly American ideas were in turn transferred to Europe and adopted there. An individual American contribution to British technology was a result of Jacob Perkins's emigration to England in 1797 and his introduction of his nail-making machine there (figs. 4–9, 4–10). This was a device that cut and headed nails in a single mechanized machine. Such machines became important in both countries.

Of more continuing importance were the many American inventions related to textile production, which began very shortly after 1790 but became noticeably significant between 1814 and 1830. Because inventions previously patented in the United States might also be patented in Britain, virtually all transfers of important American developments before 1815 were made by patenting and selling them abroad. Afterward, however, British patents became less essential.

Among the many transfers, two related ones had particular significance: the cap spinner of Charles Danforth of Ramapo, New York (fig. 4–11), and the ring spinner of John Thorp of Providence, Rhode Island (fig. 4–12). Both were patented in the United States in 1828, Thorp's two months after Danforth's, and in Britain in 1829. Each repre-

Fig. 4–9. Nail-making machine,
Bridgeton City Park, Bridgeton,
New Jersey

Fig. 4–10. Nail-making machine
drawing

sented a similar and significant improvement over the flyer used on the standard spinning frame spindle for the purpose of increasing the speed of the spindle—a constant American effort. The replaced flyer was an inverted U-shaped arm that rotated around the bobbin on the top of the spindle in order to twist the yarn. The cap was a continuously spinning, inverted metal cup; the ring was stationary but ran the yarn through a small metal loop that spun continuously around the ring to twist the yarn. By 1815 the Americans had already speeded up their spinning frames more than the British. These two inventions took some years to be fully adapted and put into use, but they did displace earlier spindles in both countries.

The British were kept reasonably well informed of American textile technology, especially in the early years, because Americans and their British agents sought to turn their inventions to profit in Britain as well as in the United States. In other technologies, however, the British were less concerned about what was being done in the United States than Americans were about British developments. British manufacturers, with cheaper labor and a market conditioned to high-quality goods, did not respond to all the American labor-saving machinery that usually produced cheaper and coarser goods.

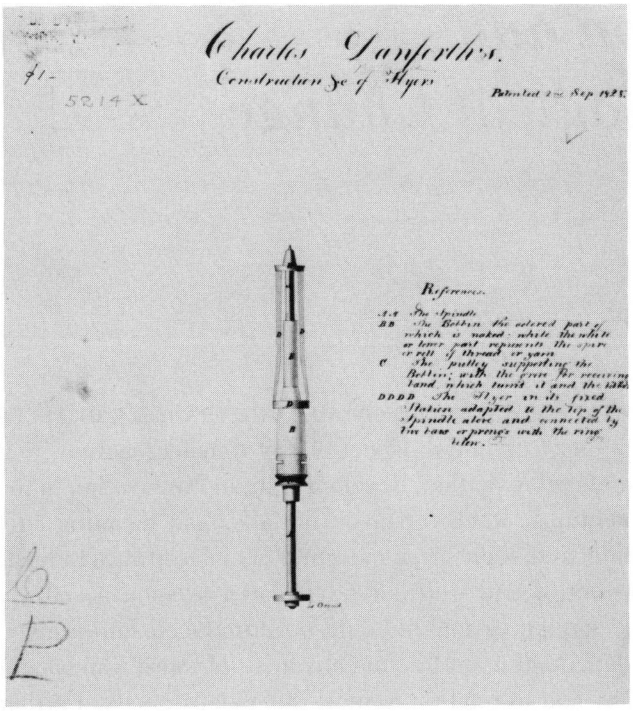

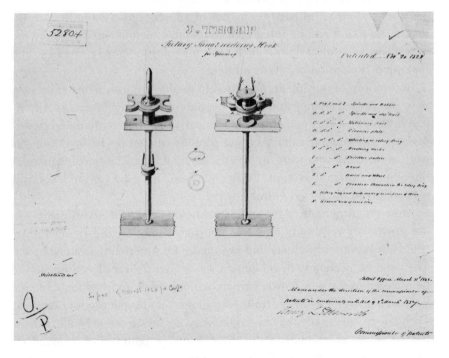

Fig. 4–11. *Danforth's cap spindle patent, 1828*

Fig. 4–12. *Thorp's ring spindle patent, 1828*

Invention and Technological Change

AMERICAN ADAPTATION ALWAYS ACCOMPANIED THE TRANSFER OF TECH-nology and was the most essential aspect of any transfer; moreover, it paralleled and stimulated invention, development, and innovation in the United States. Inventions, wherever made initially, had meaning only when integrated into a specific economic and social setting. Indeed, they usually came out of and were already related to such a setting. Whether a specific foreign invention could be introduced into a given community often depended upon the inventiveness of those who sought to introduce it. They had to relate it to new, indigenous needs. Further invention was often needed to accomplish this. In any event, what is called invention, the initial workable form of a new technological idea, has to be followed by a period of development.

Development is primarily a matter of adapting and extending an invention so that it can be integrated into both a technological system and a business and cultural system. It calls for continuing inventiveness and invention. Invention begets invention.

Innovation, or putting an invention to productive use, is the third step in technological change and as much a part of applying foreign as American inventions. This is the ultimate objective of all invention and development. The life and labor of those directly related to the invention, as well as of many who were indirectly affected, were altered by innovation. Successful innovation always involved unhappy by-products and was not given unalloyed enthusiasm.

After the American Revolution technology enjoyed attention it had not previously received. This was spurred in part by the rising Industrial Revolution in England, but even more by American circumstances. The need for economic development was evident. New directions had to be pursued in the new nation, which had gained more freedom of choice but had lost credit sources, trade advantages, and some production aids. Technology, especially the new technology, seemed to some to offer means for bypassing shortcomings in developing new patterns of production, financing, and marketing. Certain Americans grew enthusiastic as they perceived that the introduction and development of emerging technologies offered personal profit as well as an improved American economy.

Most agreed that economic improvement would benefit from technological change, that invention would benefit the nation. Those who did not agree were largely opposed to engaging in new enterprises and sought instead to encourage agriculture and the kind of trade that had produced prosperity in the colonial era.

A much exaggerated emphasis came to be placed on invention, and the process of invention was personified to an unreal degree. Not only technological change but the complex process of producing new industries was often oversimplified and represented as the result of a single invention. Questions of labor conditions, management, marketing, finance, and social meaning were but little pursued. In considering canals, steamboats, railroads, the telegraph, mechanized textile production, and the interchangeable parts method of manufacturing, the contemporary focus of attention was on mechanical processes.

Nevertheless, invention and continuing inventiveness are essential to all technological change and were especially fundamental in the American Industrial Revolution. The manner in which new mechanisms and mechanical improvements are devised and carried through has recently become more clear. Designing a machine requires good visual or spatial thinking. It requires mental arrangement, rearrangement, and manipulation of projected components and devices. It usually requires a trial construction of the machine, or at least of a model of it, and then more mental manipulation of possible changes in order to bring it to an effective working condition. Robert Fulton understood the process with unusual clarity. He wrote, "The mechanic should sit down among levers, screws, wedges, wheels, etc., like a poet among the letters of the alphabet, considering them as the exhibition of his thoughts, in which a new arrangement transmits a new Idea to the world."[1]

INVENTION AND THE PATENT SYSTEM

Invention was celebrated as the creative origin of new processes, of individual wealth, and of national well-being. It was seen as an individual achievement and as the cause of the great technological and economic changes that took place in the period before the Civil War. This understanding was accompanied by the expectation that every technological change not only was the result of specific invention, but was the product of a known and identified inventor. Invention was thus personified, and inventors became eponyms by whom the inventions credited to them were known. Thus, to mention the lightning rod was to recognize Benjamin Franklin; the steamboat called up Robert Fulton, the sewing machine Elias Howe, the reaper Cyrus McCormick, the revolver Samuel Colt, and the telegraph Samuel F. B. Morse.

This view of invention and technology celebrated inventors as heroes, as benefactors of the nation and the world. Christian Schussele painted in 1863 a famous view of outstanding American inventors that he called *Men of Progress* (fig. 5–1). Two versions of the oil painting survive, plus many prints of engravings. The copies were widely distributed, hung in many homes, and influenced Americans who saw these heroes as more responsible for their improved quality of life than politicians and government leaders.

Schussele represented prevailing attitudes reasonably well, but he

ENGINES OF CHANGE

was not a scholar, and the concept of "one man, one invention" usually exaggerated the contribution of the man pictured and included some for their less important inventions. Most of those pictured were both inventors and entrepreneurs who had carried their work to varying degrees of innovation.

Schussele ranked his heroes by putting models or drawings of their inventions beside the most honored. Samuel F. B. Morse has the most prominent position, sitting beside his telegraph recorder on the central table. Cyrus McCormick is in second place, standing at the left front, beside a model of his reaper; Charles Goodyear, third, facing Morse with a pair of rubber overshoes beneath his chair; Richard Hoe, fourth, talking to Morse, with a drawing of his rotary press on the middle of the floor; and Elias Howe, fifth, at the extreme right, sitting behind his sewing machine.

Benjamin Franklin, often viewed as the godfather of all inventors, is represented by a painting on the wall. Franklin, of course, was a scientist as well as an inventor, and only one of the others represented within the room could also sustain that claim. This was Joseph Henry, sometimes seen as a successor to Franklin in the study of electricity. Henry's work underlay the electromagnetic telegraph; indeed, he transmitted a signal by electricity before Morse conceived his telegraph. Henry is shown standing behind the table, and, strikingly, a straight line drawn from Franklin, through Henry, would point to Morse in the place of honor. Morse was no scientist, but his telegraph has been asserted to be the first science-based invention, and in fact, it would have been impossible before the work of Ampère. This little connection reveals a contingent article of faith. New science had very little to do with invention and technological change in this era, but there was a widespread belief that it should and that, in the future, it would.

The United States patent system reflected most of these attitudes. More important, it did much to perpetuate and consolidate them. Patents were intended to encourage technological improvement and the economic growth of the country. They did this by identifying and acknowledging individuals in a process that opened them to rewards.

Patents, of course, had long been a part of the British system. They had been granted by individual colonies since the seventeenth century and by separate states since independence. Patents were, fundamentally, term monopolies granted to inventors for the sale of devices that were believed to be useful to the public. They encouraged invention by offering inventors the sole right to profit from sales for a stated number of years. They then encouraged economic growth by opening to everyone the sale and use of patented devices as soon as the period of monopoly ended.

Fig. 5–1. Christian Schussele, Men of Progress, *1863. From left to right, the inventors pictured are: Dr. William Morton (discoverer of the use of ether in surgery), James Bogardus (cast iron architecture), Samuel Colt (revolvers), Cyrus McCormick (reapers), Joseph Saxton (mint machinery and coast survey apparatus), Peter Cooper (locomotives and steel), Charles Goodyear (rubber), James Mott (iron), Joseph Henry (the science of electricity), Eliphalet Nott (anthracite coal stove), John Ericsson (screw propellers and ironclad ships), Frederick Sickels (steam engine improvements), Samuel F. B. Morse (telegraph), Henry Burden (horse shoe machine), Robert Hoe (rotary printing press), Erastus Bigelow (carpet loom), Isaiah Jennings (friction matches), Thomas Blanchard (copying lathe), and Elias Howe (sewing machine)*

The United States Constitution of 1787 included a patent provision. Combining patents with copyrights, it gave Congress the power "To promote the progress of Science and useful Arts by securing for limited Time to Authors and Inventors the exclusive right to their respective Writings and Discoveries."[2]

As in most of its provisions, the Constitution did not spell out in detail or answer key questions about how the patent system should be designed and administered. For example, British patent law offered patents for the introduction of foreign inventions that might already have been patented in another country, a direct means of encouraging the transfer of technology across national boundaries. George Washington favored following this practice, but others disagreed. In his first message to Congress, Washington did not even mention the copyright question, despite his interest in encouraging "science and literature." His primary vehicle for this encouragement was a national university, which he advocated in several contexts. He was, in all his approaches, more concerned with the need for invention than with original literary works.

The Patent Act of 1790 established the American patent system, providing a fourteen-year monopoly for patented products. It made no provision for patenting foreign inventions. It also deviated from British practice by requiring a careful examination of every patent application. It defined as patentable "Any useful art, manufacture, engine, machine, or device, or any improvement therein not before known or used."[3] To this specification of utility and priority, the requirement of originality was added by implication. The Act called for specifications, drawings, and where feasible, a model. Three cabinet members were designated as the review panel, but in practice, Thomas Jefferson, Secretary of State, administered the system.

The initial patent act was unsatisfactory. Most of the sixty-seven patents granted were inconsequential. Important ones, such as Eli Whitney's cotton gin and Oliver Evans's automated mill, produced bitter complaint from the inventors that they were not well served by the patent system. A long controversy among steamboat inventors had preceded the patent act and indeed was a major spur to its enactment. However, the patents granted for steamboat inventions only confused the issue further by failing to decide on specific priorities and by overlapping one another.

There was also an intrinsic problem that remained unresolved. Jefferson took the provision for examination of each application seriously and set up committees of informed people to test each. The process was time-consuming to a point that would have been impossible had there been a larger number of patent applications. The result was a new law in 1793, which eliminated the examination requirement and provided little more than registration of each patent claim. The whole burden of resolving conflicting claims was left to the courts.

This too was a failure, not resolved until 1836 when a third patent act finally established the basis of the system that has continued. It provided for a patent office that would award patents on the basis of originality, novelty, and utility through a corps of patent examiners. Court conflicts continued, but confidence in patents returned, leading to a continuing increase in the number of applications. The 23,000 patents granted in the 1850s represented a fourfold increase over those awarded in the preceding decade, and the curve kept going up. The following list shows the pattern of patent registrations during the period covered in this book.

Patents Issued, 1790–1860					
1790	3	1814	210	1838	531
1791	33	1815	173	1839	414
1792	11	1816	206		
1793	20	1817	174	1840	477
1794	22	1818	222	1841	511
1795	12	1819	156	1842	500
1796	44			1843	512
1797	51	1820	155	1844	510
1798	28	1821	168	1845	502
1799	44	1822	200	1846	644
		1823	173	1847	576
1800	41	1824	228	1848	643
1801	44	1825	304	1849	1,050
1802	65	1826	323		
1803	97	1827	301	1850	986
1804	84	1828	368	1851	859
1805	57	1829	447	1852	914
1806	63			1853	956
1807	99	1830	544	1854	1,847
1808	158	1831	573	1855	1,992
1809	203	1832	474	1856	2,438
		1833	586	1857	2,822
1810	223	1834	630	1858	3,530
1811	215	1835	752	1859	4,314
1812	238	1836	700		
1813	181	1837	433	1860	4,588

Source: *Historical Statistics of the United States: Colonial Times to 1970* (Washington, D.C. 1976), part 2, pp. 958–59.

The monopoly granted by a patent was intended to reward the inventor, but the second purpose of the patent was the reverse of a monopoly. This was to make available to everyone the details of the patent after the term of the monopoly had ended. The new technology would be diffused widely to the benefit of the nation. Patent models, which continued to be required, served as important vehicles in this process. They could not be duplicated and distributed, and measured drawings were not made widely available until later. As a result, visits to the patent office became useful to mechanics seeking to make use of released patents. Unfortunately, a fire in 1837 destroyed the early models and most of the written patents. Thereafter, the collection continued to grow, and many models have survived.

CELEBRATED INVENTIONS

Each invention has its own individual story and realm of influence. Some preceded the patent system, and some were never patented or patented only after they had succeeded. Benjamin Franklin's lightning rod became an almost legendary invention, both because it was successful and because it had symbolic significance. Franklin had been studying electricity imaginatively, with no utilitarian objective—although with the admitted hope that something useful might turn up. The lightning rod has as good reason as the telegraph to be called a science-based invention; it came out of studies that were then at the forefront of science. It did prevent lightning damage.

Although relatively simple, the lightning rod evoked many variations. It produced immediate controversy, especially in Britain, over whether it should be tipped with a point or a ball. American patents continued to be issued for "improvements" to the lightning rod, dramatizing the usual sequence that followed an important invention in which many contingent patents were issued (fig. 5–2).

Franklin the inventor became a model to emulate, a model supporting the hope that Americans would excel in invention. His attitude toward invention had wide influence. He believed that social progress was forwarded by invention. But because inventions were so beneficial to society, he believed that they should be placed above the reach of personal profit. In harmony with this position, he conspicuously declined to receive any profit from his own inventions, specifically from his "Pennsylvania Fireplace," which he turned over to a friend, Robert Grace, to build and market for his own advantage. Few inventors followed Franklin's practice. Joseph Henry was an exception in his motivation to keep science above the personal profit that moved most inventors.

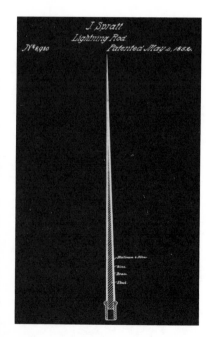

Fig. 5–2. J. Spratt's 1852 lightning rod patent

The first patent granted under the Patent Act of 1790 went to Samuel Hopkins for an improvement in manufacturing potash. This response to chemical technology was very atypical. Although several successful patents were issued for salt making, distilling, and other chemical production processes, mechanical technology long received the major attention. Hopkins's improvement involved a new "Apparatus and Process," the essence of which was a furnace for burning the wood ashes before boiling them. Hopkins published a paper on the invention but found himself unable to sell very many people on it. The process proved relatively ineffective.

Eli Whitney's cotton gin was patented under the Act of 1793 on March 14, 1794 (fig. 5–3). This device was exceedingly successful as a mechanism; it has been credited with turning cotton production into a prosperous business and with fastening slavery upon the South. Some have even charged it with responsibility for moving the nation toward the Civil War.

There had been gins before Whitney's, but none could handle the short staple cotton that could be raised most easily in many of the southern states. Whitney's could. It offered major labor savings over the costs of hand separation of seeds from the cotton fiber.

The patent did not bring wealth to Whitney, however, despite the immediate and wide application of his gin. The problem was that the device was too easily copied. Men who understood the basic design could reproduce and sell it without needing a model or measured drawings in hand. They did not pay Whitney his required royalties, nor did individuals who made their own gins. Whitney tried to take the violators to court, but he used up all his profits in fighting their patent infringements. Although a very simple and successful invention, the gin was a patent failure.

The Smithsonian Whitney cotton gin model was made very early, but it is not a patent model (fig. 5–4). It was used to demonstrate the gin. The hand crank moved the cotton to the sawtooth wheels, which pulled the fiber through the wire slots, separating it from the seeds that fell to the bottom of the gin. The function of the brushes was to move the cotton and to clean it off the sawteeth (fig. 5–5).

Working gins were larger, of course, often about three feet square and sometimes powered by steam rather than hand operated. They became an integral part of cotton production, perhaps the most conspicuous new technology in agricultural production and processing that was American in origin. The Georgia gin was initially built before 1860 and powered by a horse whim on the level below the gin. Its rough appearance contrasts sharply with the well-finished Smithsonian gin model and offers a more realistic sense of ginning in the old South (fig. 5–6).

Fig. 5–3. Eli Whitney

Fig. 5–4. Whitney's cotton gin, demonstration model

Fig. 5–5. Whitney's gin, close-up view

Fig. 5–6. Antebellum Georgia cotton gin

The first steamboat patents failed just as badly, but in a more complex manner. Steamboat inventors and promoters became vociferous during the writing of the United States Constitution and remained so while the 1790 Patent Act was written and the first patents granted under it. Members of the Constitutional Convention and the early congresses were sensitive to the steamboat question, which influenced their actions. Steamboat advocates kept pressing for an effective patent system.

The result was not what any of them sought. Within the first year the two leading contenders, John Fitch and James Rumsey, each received a patent, John Stevens got three related patents, and three more were granted for seemingly related improvements to the antique Savery engine. Fitch's patent ostensibly covered steamboats in general; in fact, it conflicted directly with Rumsey's, which gave him specific protection for water and air jet steam propulsion. Before these were issued, Rumsey had gone to England where he obtained a British patent; afterward Fitch went to France and got a French patent. Fitch's 1790 boat, the *Perseverance,* which ran over 2,000 miles on commercial schedules between Philadelphia and Burlington, incorporated the design its inventor later submitted for both his American and French patents (fig. 5–7). Stern crank and paddle propulsion was the key element of the design.

Both Fitch and Rumsey died defeated, convinced that the United States patent system had injured them and was, at least in some measure, responsible for their failures. While their primary difficulties certainly came from other sources, their patents, both American and foreign, contributed no help. More important, the experience of the two men led others to doubt the utility of filing for patents.

Robert Fulton had studied the history of steamboat building very carefully before he arranged to bypass the patent system entirely (fig. 5–8). He formed a partnership with Chancellor Robert R. Livingston of New York State, who had been pursuing steamboating for several years. Officially, Livingston was judge of the court of chancery, but unofficially, he was second only to the governor as a state leader. He was able to obtain for himself and Fulton a twenty-year monopoly of steamboat service on New York waters—if they could run a boat at four miles an hour. They did not have to prove that they had invented anything or to conform to other patent requirements. In 1807 Fulton ran his *Steamboat* or *North River Steamboat*—later known as the *Clermont*—from New York City to Albany, the beginning of steamboating in the United States. Not until 1809 did he seek and obtain a patent, using the *Clermont* and his work on it as the basis of his claims (fig. 5–9). Fulton's bypassing of the patent system was, for him, a great success.

After the Patent Act of 1836 the system worked more as intended, but because economic development broadened and so many more patents were granted, the variety of problems actually multiplied. The sewing machine represented a major technological change, with major social and economic accompaniments. It rested on the patents of several inventors, no one of whom can be reasonably designated as *the* inventor.

The fact that this invention can be credited to no single person emphasizes a characteristic of most inventions. Only the least complex are attributable to a single individual—and even those have grown from roots planted by others. The sewing machine was typical, too, in that most patents succeeded the manufacture of the first commercial machines.

Fig. 5–7. Fitch's 1791 patent drawing

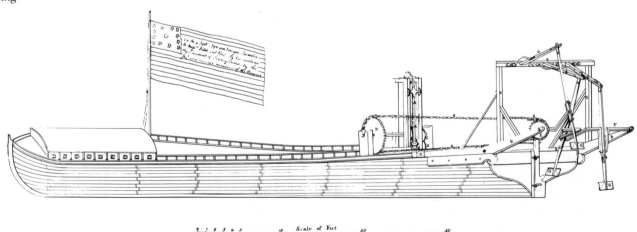

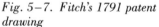

Because the sewing machine was quickly recognized as an important development with extended impact, a need arose to identify *the* inventor, and Elias Howe, Jr., was most often chosen. His patent, issued on September 10, 1846, used an eye-pointed needle and a shuttle to form a stitch. The machine, however, was not a practical success; it could sew only a short, straight seam under very limited conditions. For many years Howe did not attempt to manufacture commercial machines but collected a fortune through royalties and payments from frequent infringement suits.

Isaac Singer was not suggested as the primary sewing machine inventor, but he is identified with the greatest success and diffusion of the sewing machine. His patent of August 12, 1851, described the now familiar vertically reciprocating needle that stitched horizontally held cloth. Little about it was original, but it did represent a substantial improvement over existing machines. More basically important, Singer went on to achieve resoundingly successful commercial production based on his patent in combination with others. The patents were fundamental, but alone they were only a beginning. Singer's success was a matter of combining his own inventiveness with others and concentrating on good organization, financing, production, and marketing.

Fig. 5–8. Robert Fulton

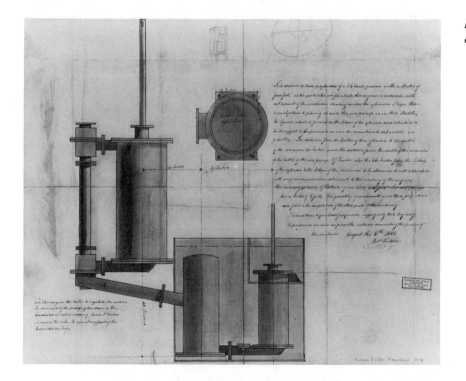

Fig. 5–9. Fulton's 1809 patent drawing (the Clermont*)*

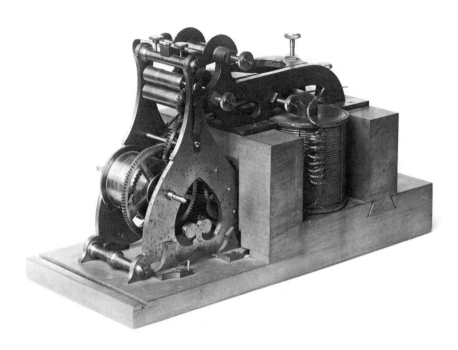

Fig. 5–10. Morse telegraph recorder replica, 1844

Samuel F. B. Morse's telegraph patent requires special attention, because it seems so much more effective in bringing wealth to the patentee and in diffusing the telegraph widely. The identification of Morse as the inventor of the telegraph looks, at first glance, less complicated than it is. His first patent of June 20, 1840, followed a period of development of the electromagnetic telegraph, which he had initially conceived in 1832. That conception was based on new scientific knowledge, especially that of Ampère, and its development into a working device followed input from Joseph Henry, Leonard Gale, Alfred Vail, and others. It was paralleled by the development of electric telegraphs by others, most notably by Charles Wheatstone in England.

The most critical action, however, in turning the telegraph into a commercial innovation was the $30,000 grant by Congress in 1843 for a trial of the telegraph between Washington and Baltimore. Conducted the following year, the trial was a technical and public relations success. It occurred when the presidential nominating conventions met, both of them in Baltimore. Morse was able to use his telegraph to report the nominations to the sitting Congress before any other news of them arrived. Thereafter, the telegraph spread rapidly (fig. 5–10).

This time, the patent worked very well to enrich the designated inventor. It protected Morse and his partners, Gale and Vail. It permitted them to set up a series of companies for running the telegraph between different centers, assigning themselves a number of shares in each company, based on the patent rights. It brought the Morse telegraph to dominance in the United States and in most of the non-British world.

Morse's surviving "canvas stretcher telegraph" model is not a patent model but the actual telegraph he built in 1837 (fig. 5–11). It is made from an artist's canvas stretcher of the sort Morse used for his oil paintings. It memorializes the fact that Morse was neither a scientist nor a mechanic but an artist—indeed the first art professor in the country, at New York University. The art-technology connection was not as bizarre as it might seem; Robert Fulton also began his career as a painter, and John Fitch, among other things, produced art works of silver.

Fig. 5–11. Morse canvas stretcher telegraph, 1837

The telegraph story represents a great patent success, but at the same time, it underscores a need patents did very little to satisfy. It is one thing to conceive and put together a new working device. It is quite another to develop it to a point where it is commercially useful and to convince those who might use it that it is worth their investment. The patent opened the door to profit for every inventor, but that individual was then on his own, without any financial support, for converting his idea into an innovation. This process was always difficult and usually expensive. Morse was almost unique in being able to convince Congress to pay for this imperative need.

The United States government and state and local governments played varied and continuing roles in encouraging technological change and industrialization. What government could do was limited by its poverty more than by consistent opposition to intervention in the economic process as is sometimes believed. The patent system was its most direct means for encouraging technological change. Many of the other actions to aid technology and forward industrialization were more complex in their goals and in their effects.

TARIFFS AND OTHER GOVERNMENT SUPPORT

The Constitution gave Congress powers, in addition to the patent power, that permitted further encouragement of manufacturing and industrialization. Most internal matters were left to the states, while Congress was given the power "to regulate Commerce with foreign Nations,"[4] and although the states were barred from levying either import or export taxes, Congress was given the very important import tax, or tariff power.

The tariff became the federal government's most important means for encouraging manufactures. It was, however, not totally clear-cut, because much of the motivation behind tariff legislation was to raise revenue, although raising revenue in that manner immediately produced controversies. Merchants, especially those engaged in foreign trade, opposed tariffs, because they would raise prices and reduce international commerce. The southern states opposed tariffs also, because the South was most successful in exporting farm products and did not want to increase the price it paid for manufactures. The conflict between merchants and manufacturers grew with the War of 1812, and the multilayered sectional conflict grew into a major crisis during this period.

Most tariffs were levied against the importation of manufactures, British industry being able to produce cheaper goods, primarily because of lower labor and capital costs. The threatened American iron industry emerged very early as an advocacy group. The "infant industry" argument, that new industries needed tariff support until they reached a competitive level, became important in urging tariff support for new manufacturing efforts—such as the expanding production of textiles. How useful tariffs were is exceedingly difficult to determine. The decade of the fifties is generally viewed as the most decisive decade in the development of manufacturing, but tariffs then were at lower levels than 1828 and 1832. But even by 1860 most American imports were still manufactures.

The tariff became a political issue, present in almost every campaign and dominating some of them. It was just one of several issues that related to technological change and industrialization. A few were combined in what came to be known as "the American system" (fig. 5–12). The American system was a phrase introduced by Henry Clay when, in defending the tariff, he combined it with internal improvements (primarily of canals and roads). The purpose was to reduce the dependence of the United States on overseas sources by encouraging both manufacturing and domestic trade. The American system became more complex after its introduction in 1824, but it continued to distinguish those favoring manufactures and internal development from those who benefited from external commerce and the export of raw materials.

Initially, it was not clear how much support the federal government was permitted to offer industrialization; it was even less clear how much it might decide to offer. One early attempt at direct leadership and direct support was the Society for Encouraging Useful Manufactures, usually called SUM. It was established in 1791 with the support of Alexander Hamilton, Secretary of the Treasury, and his assistant, Tench Coxe, in Paterson, New Jersey, at the falls of the Passaic River. Factories were proposed to produce textiles, iron, paper, glass, and other products.

Government support, primarily from the state, came in several forms. SUM was given permission to run a lottery and to sell stock. It was exempted from property taxes for ten years, given powers of eminent domain, and its workers were exempted from state tax and from military duty. It did not succeed, the usual reasons given being bad management, dishonest officials, and inadequate skilled labor. An important technical reason was the fact that the falls yielded only one-tenth the horsepower available at the later, resoundingly successful location of Lowell, Massachusetts, on the Merrimack River. The opposition that had arisen to SUM, emphasizing its unfairness to competing enterprises, ensured that its failure would not be followed by similar efforts. Federal support thereafter was confined to broader actions such as patents, tariffs, and general financial order.

State and local governments were in a position to exercise more direct efforts in favor of manufacturing, and some did so. Sometimes they bought stock in desirable enterprises, they exempted corporations from taxes, and on occasion they provided limited liability for investors in

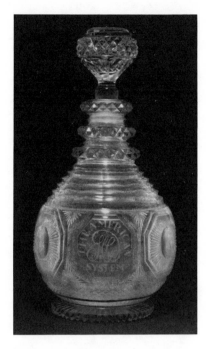

Fig. 5–12. Glass decanter, engraved "the American system" and "HC," thought to have belonged to Henry Clay

certain industries. Others gave premiums to encourage industry. South Carolina, for example, offered rewards for the first person to put into operation saltpeter, sulphur, iron, steel, and salt works.

Yet state as well as federal support was limited. Leadership in specific enterprises was left largely to individuals, to profit motivation, and to voluntary organizations. All sorts of plans and proposals arose, some seeking and some obtaining state tax advantages; overall, however, they depended upon private funding. In addition to personal profit, these ventures projected a variety of goals: teaching skills, employing the poor, and decreasing dependence on overseas imports. Many of the specific projects failed, but some of the active organizations continued to flourish.

VOLUNTARY ORGANIZATIONS

Voluntary organizations to advocate various objectives were very much a part of the American scene; some turned to the promotion of industrialization. The first learned society in the country, the American Philosophical Society, emerged during the period of agitation before the American Revolution (fig. 5–13). It was formed "to Promote Useful Knowledge," specifically including what was then described as "Ameri-

Fig. 5–13. Philosophical Hall on Independence Square, 1785

ENGINES OF CHANGE

can Improvement." Science was central to the Society, but it also published accounts of inventions and improvements and occasionally made awards for them.

By the 1820s more limited and specialized organizations arose, dedicated to the promotion of technology and material development. The Franklin Institute, founded in Philadelphia in 1824, combined business leaders and University of Pennsylvania professors in an effort to encourage and train mechanics. It tried to improve technical education and to publicize invention and industrial needs in its journal. The American Institute, founded in New York City in 1828, followed the direction of Clay's American system after the tariff controversies of that time.

The Franklin Institute held fairs every two years and the American Institute every year to display competing products and inventions. Winning participants were awarded premiums, often medals, and sometimes cash payments. Fairs proved a successful means for promoting invention and production. Winners advertised the medals they received, and visitors often gained from observing good collections of the newest designs in a variety of products (figs. 5–14, 5–15).

Similar organizations were founded in other leading cities, but the pattern veered toward mechanics institutes in which the participants as well as the promoters were primarily working mechanics. A number of these also held fairs, and even more introduced lectures and courses to improve the education of mechanics. All of those involved were advocates of material improvement.

Fig. 5–14. American Institute gold medal, 1842

THE CONTROVERSY

The whole country, however, was not equally convinced that technological change was a good idea, and there was significant disagreement, especially about industrialization. The advocates were more obvious and more vocal than were the dissenters. Businessmen, manufacturers, politicians, inventive mechanics, and others saw benefit to themselves as well as to the country. Merchants, southern planters and leaders, small farmers, and sometimes the work force of operatives were less enthusiastic or even negative. A debate ensued after the factory system became prominent.

Thomas Ewbank, enthusiastic Commissioner of Patents, was almost unrestrained. In 1842 he asserted, "Science and the arts are renovating the constitution of society. . . . Does an author wish to introduce characters who have left permanent impressions of their genius on the world? Where can he find them in such variety as in the race of inventors? . . . Let him detail the circumstances that led to the conception, and accom-

Fig. 5–15. *Franklin Institute gold medal, 1845*

panied the improvement of those inventions and discoveries that have elevated civilized man above the savage."[5]

The *Scientific American*, perhaps the greatest advocacy periodical of the time, expressed a deep belief in progress through invention. Published after 1847 by Munn and Company, the leading patent firm in the country, it encouraged inventors to invent and then led them through the maze of required steps to obtain a patent. Of the *Scientific American*, Munn and Company asserted, "All the most valuable discoveries are delineated and described in its issues; so that, as respects inventions, it may be justly regarded as an *Illustrated Repertory*, where the inventor may learn what has been done before him in the same field which he is exploring, and where he may bring to the world a knowledge of his own achievements."[6]

Edward Everett, one of the greatest orators of the day, praised mechanization and material advance without restraint. "We live in an age of improvement," he wrote. "What changes have not been already wrought in the condition of society! What addition has not been made to the wealth of nations and the means of private comfort by the inventions, discoveries, and improvements of the last hundred years!"[7]

He too attributed much of the success he saw to American freedom: "It is the spirit of a free country which animates and gives energy to its labor . . . makes it inventive, sheds it off in new directions, subdues to its command all the powers of nature, and enlists in its service an army of machines, that do all but think and talk."[8]

Those who sought to counter the effects of all this enthusiasm did not concern themselves with invention but with the people they felt suffered from industrialization. Jabez Hollingworth, himself a textile worker, followed well-worn paths in depicting farming as preferable to factory manufacturing. He asserted: "Manufacturing breeds lords and Aristocrats, poor men and slaves. But the Farmer, the American Farmer, he, and he alone can be independent. He can be Industrious, Healthy, and Happy. I am for Agriculture."[9]

Some pictured factory life as the destruction of American freedom. Thomas Mann wrote in *Picture of a Factory Village* (1833):

> *For liberty our fathers' fought*
> *Which with their blood, they dearly bought,*
> *The factory System sets at nought.*
> *A slave at morn, a slave at eve,*
> *It doth my inmost feelings grieve;*
> *The blood runs chilly from my heart,*
> *To see fair Liberty depart;*
> *And leave the wretches in their chains,*

To feed a vampire from their veins.
Great Britain's curse is now our own;
Enough to damn a King and Throne.[10]

The focus was nearly always on the factory worker, not on the consumer, not on the general public. Intellectuals saw beyond the direct problems of workers to the deadening effect of factories. William Ellery Channing, a literary clergyman, wrote that factory labor was a "monotonous, stupefying round of unthinking toil"; that it confined operatives to "the heading of pins, the pointing of nails, or the tying together of broken strings."[11]

There were at least two sides to the big question, and many could see both sides. Ralph Waldo Emerson noted, equivocally, "machinery is good, but mother-wit is better. Telegraph, steam and balloon and newspaper are like spectacles on the nose of age, but we will give them all gladly to have back again our young eyes." Again, forgetting the balance, he expressed a common fear of determinism. *"Things are in the saddle,* and ride mankind."[12]

The negatives remained and indeed grew faster than they could be reduced—but the enthusiasts were dominant. Life was improving for most people, whatever the cause. For those not squashed by them, invention, technological change, and industrialization were exciting developments that appeared to have something to do with making the world more interesting, with opening more options, and with improving the quality of life.

VI Farming and Raw Materials Processing: Causes and Effects of Mechanization

THE PRODUCTION AND PROCESSING OF RAW MATERIALS, INCLUDING farm output, were closely tied to mechanization and industrialization. Agriculture is often seen as an activity in opposition to industrialization, and agrarians are usually pictured as a political force opposed to manufacturing and technological development. This view is not totally untrue, but the reality is more complex. The biggest truths are that farming expansion and prosperity constituted a foundation on which industrialization rested, and that technological change became important in farming development itself.

FARM PRODUCTION

Most Americans were not meticulous farmers. The plenty of land and the continued opening of new farmlands offered an opportunity that ran counter to good, careful farming. Colonial immigrants and those who moved into farming from other pursuits found that it was better to forget about yield per acre. More money could usually be made by doing things quickly and crudely. Careful plowing, appropriate fertilizing, and crop rotation were known at an early point to increase yield, but many Americans were correct in concluding that it was not worth their effort. If they soon depleted their soil, the cheapest solution might be to move on to new acreage.

The great increase in food and fiber production that released farm workers for factory labor—as the Industrial Revolution proceeded—depended mostly on bringing more acres of rich farmland under cultivation. This development also rested on commercial as opposed to subsistence farming; American farming was overwhelmingly commercial from an early point. Improved tools, increased mechanization, and better farming techniques contributed to increasing production—but not as much as has been assumed. They pointed to the shape of future more than to immediate improvement.

Of course, some farmers did prosper by intensive farming. Colonial German immigrants sought out the most fertile land available and cultivated it with the same intensity they had learned in Europe. Even where land was plentiful, this approach proved successful for them. A little later, during the early days of the Republic, American leaders and well-to-do farmers introduced the techniques then being advocated in England. They experimented with and publicized marling, liming, and fertilizing soils, the use of seed drills, new plow designs, crop rotation, and planned animal breeding. Still, few "dirt" farmers followed the lead either of the Germans or of the advocates of new techniques.

Europeans and particularly the English encouraged the improvement of farming implements and mechanization, as well as improved breeding and crop rotation practices. The London Society of Arts gave more premiums for inventions of plows and farm implements than for any other category. Many European patents were taken out for machines to perform farming or processing operations. By the 1820s mechanical reapers, threshers, grass cutters, and seed drills were numerous. Change was in the air, but few of the devices worked very satisfactorily and they were not much used.

American efforts to mechanize agriculture reached an effective point about the same time as the new technology of the Industrial Revolution. Elkanah Watson was most responsible for finding an effective way to introduce the new agricultural techniques, beginning with his fair at Pittsfield, Massachusetts, in 1811. His parade at the fair celebrated both American agricultural implements and a spinning jenny and loom. Other leaders in agricultural improvement also frequently combined farm improvement with the mechanization of technology—as did Robert Livingston in New York, whose promotion of agriculture is less remembered than his role in steamboating.

The Berkshire movement, as it became known, spread the Watson type fairs widely, first over New York State and then over much of the nation. County fairs and state fairs became features of rural America, especially in the North. They succeeded so well because they attracted farmers, brought them together in competition over their own produce, and informed them by showing new implements in operation. Farmers responded in a way they had not greeted the first agricultural societies, which, from 1785 on, had offered little but published advice and written accounts of new techniques. The written word alone reached very few farmers.

In addition to demonstrations and plowing contests, a periodical literature began to grow, and some farmers began to respond to farm journals. Most of them, however, long continued to read very little but farmers almanacs. Agricultural societies published their own proceedings.

The results of using the new implements and of applying the new chemical knowledge that rose from the 1840s were reported. New techniques were described and debated. Farming changed, but slowly.

As more land was opened to cultivation, farms in the North increased in size just as plantations did in the South. Output grew rapidly, but the number of farmers did not. Between 1820 and 1870 the northern population grew about 4.5 times, the number of people on farms only 2.9 times, and the urban population 14.5 times. National policy succeeded in distributing land to farmers and in encouraging farm expansion. The growth of population, the increase of farm acreage, and the proportionate decrease in numbers of farmers made possible the industrial growth that paralleled these developments.

Improved farm implements, production technology, and farming techniques accounted for the smaller part of this change. These developments did help, however, and their contribution continued to increase. Ever since the colonial period, efforts had been made to import the best implements and techniques. This process, plus the continuing influx of immigrants from widely different backgrounds, introduced a variety of ways of farming. Some German, Dutch, French, Irish, Scottish, and English methods were introduced, and at points American Indian and slave techniques were added as well. This resulted in some sharply differing communities but, overall, in uniquely American patterns.

Until the establishment of the new nation, Americans contributed very little to improved implements—except through evolution. That was how the shovel plow used in shallow sandy soils in the South and the deep plow in the North developed from design changes that had moved in opposite directions. Occasional individual inventions, such as Jared Eliot's seed drill of 1743, had been recognized. After 1790, however,

Fig. 6–1. Old Colony strong plow, a deep plow, 1840

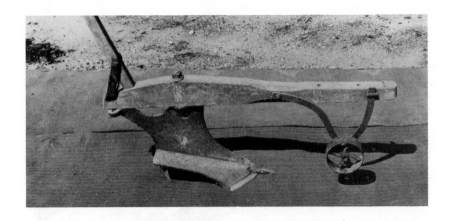

agricultural patents quickly took the lead over those granted for other mechanical devices (figs. 6–1, 6–2).

In the United States many farmers made their own plows of wood or mostly of wood. The moldboard, a curved, trapezoidal plate that turned the soil over, was nearly always made of wood. Wooden plows were inefficient because of their drag (or resistance) as they were pulled through the soil, and because they could not maintain a sharp edge to cut the soil. The answer to the second difficulty had long been understood—the plowshare or coulter placed in front of the moldboard could be made of iron, preferably wrought iron, and given a sharp edge. The moldboard presented more of a problem, which Thomas Jefferson sought to solve by designing a "moldboard of least resistance" (fig. 6–3).

He understood correctly the need to reduce the drag created by soil adhering to the plow and sought, "mathematically," to design a moldboard with less resistance. He published his recommendations in an article in which he explained how such a plow could be constructed. It was tried in this country, and models were built and put to the test in Paris. Unfortunately, however, it did not work well enough to take hold. Jefferson's contribution was to identify and call attention to the need.

The signs of real improvement came with the introduction of metal plows, most of them protected by patents. In 1797 Charles Newbold designed a cast iron plow that gained some usage. Jethro Wood's 1819 iron plow had interchangeable parts. A variety of succeeding patents led to John Deere's 1837 plow with a steel cutting edge and wrought iron moldboard (fig. 6–4). Its great advantage was the self-scouring nature of the moldboard, which depended far less on its shape than on its surface. Because the soil did not collect and clog it up, it sailed cleanly through the soil and with reason was dubbed "the singing plow." By the 1850s seed drills came into general use. Perhaps more prescient was the revolving horse-drawn hay rake, which became commercially available in the 1820s and by the 1850s was displacing older forms.

Fig. 6–3. Jefferson moldboard of least resistance plow (replica)

Fig. 6–4. John Deere plow

Full mechanization was attained in harvesting and threshing wheat. Before mechanization, threshing was a hand operation usually with a flail, although treading was still sometimes used. Winnowing or cleaning the grain was a slow process; fan mills were known early but did not become prominent until the 1830s and 1840s. Threshing machines were known before 1820, too, but they came into use only after John and Hiram Pitts's 1837 patent (fig. 6–5). This combined threshing, separating, and fanning. In the 1840s and 1850s combined machines of this sort came into widespread use.

The mechanical reaper represents a more complicated story than the medal awarded to Cyrus McCormick at the 1851 Crystal Palace fair would suggest. There were many reapers before McCormick obtained

ENGINES OF CHANGE

his patent in 1834, and still more years passed before his reaper was developed into a commercially useful product (fig. 6–6). Until the 1850s the cradle scythe prevailed as the common implement used in harvesting. From the 1820s on several inventors experimented with their own designs for harvesters. Obed Hussey's 1833 reaper was the first to attain commercial success (fig. 6–7). McCormick's did not become very good until several improvements, including Hussey's cutter sickle, were combined in his 1855 model. By the mid–1850s at least four firms offered a self-raking reaper; by then the reaper was clearly here to stay. It is striking that not only the reaper came into widespread use in this period, but the thresher and a variety of seeding, hay mowing, and other machines were generally accepted at the same time.

Other changes in farming techniques also bloomed around the 1850s, notably improved soil care. Neither manure, lime, and gypsum nor crop rotation came into wide use until long after they had first been suggested. Manure was scarce at the beginning when cattle raising was very limited, and collecting and spreading manure continued to be costly because it was labor-intensive. The serious chemical study of soils by Justus Liebig was first published in 1840, containing the recommendation of guano, or seafowl excrement found mostly on ocean islands, as a soil fertilizer. Increasing amounts were then imported into the United States. With lime and gypsum, guano became important, but only in specific places. Regional differences remained enormous, as they did in rotation. Rotation of crops was adopted early at occasional locations, such as southeastern Pennsylvania. In the 1840s and 1850s that practice, too, came into more general use.

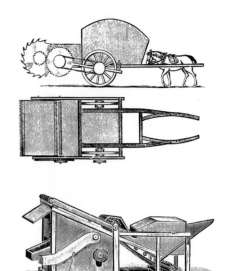

Fig. 6–5. Pitts thresher, 1838

FOOD PROCESSING

Most food processing was initially carried out on the farm or in the home, but commercial food processing started very early and continued to grow. Meat salting and packing, baking, cheesemaking, and brewing rose to importance in export and ship provisioning trades. These operations were also carried out in cities for the local market, while farmers continued to do this work on their own. Butchering was done on the farm as well as in abattoirs in cities.

One of the most essential operations was the milling of grain, which was done in one of two types of mill: the country mill and the commercial mill. The country mill was often operated seasonally by a farmer and part-time miller who ground grain for other farmers, taking a small part of the meal as his payment. The commercial mill bought the grain from the farmer and often sold the meal for export; commercial mills sometimes had bakeries associated with them. Mills, powered by water or less often by wind, represented mechanized food processing production that had not changed much in hundreds of years. They were familiar to everyone.

Gristmills, of course, represented an early and very important mechanization of food processing which dominated the American scene, but they were not essential. The hand grinding of grain had preceded mills, and it was still practiced in nineteenth-century America. Indians continued to use stone mortars and pestles, and Americans sometimes ground grain by hand in what was called a quern (fig. 6–8). This consisted of two flat millstones, each "dressed" on its grinding surface with cut slits; the top millstone was rotated by hand.

Machine milling had long since become usual in the United States and in Europe. It made use of the same sort of waterwheels and windmill sails as those in sawmills, and the gearing was much the same. The millstones were made of different materials: limestone, marble, or French burr stone—regarded as the best (fig. 6–9). As milling became increasingly specialized, the stones had to be dressed differently and sometimes designed differently. Most mills produced wheat or corn flour, but oats and buckwheat called for specially dressed stones. Still more different were the stones for grinding gypsum, dyes, phosphate, apples, and cork. Mills were in operation throughout the country, and in most areas there are surviving examples (fig. 6–10).

The automation of flour milling was one of the earliest and most basic

Fig. 6–6. McCormick reaper, 1834 (model)

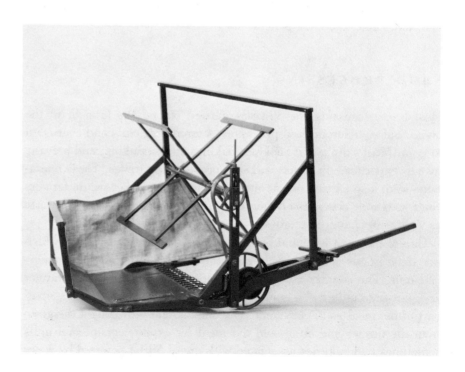

ENGINES OF CHANGE

Fig. 6–7. Hussey reaper

Fig. 6–8. Quern

Fig. 6–9. Wheat millstones

American contributions within the context of the Industrial Revolution. This was accomplished by Oliver Evans, who built a flour mill of his design on Red Clay Creek in Delaware in 1785 (fig. 6–11). Evans was an inventive and imaginative millwright who somehow caught the spirit of mechanization and carried it through to great technical success, both in this effort and later in steam engine design. He obtained a Maryland patent for his mill in 1787 and the third patent granted by the United States in 1790.

The basic mill function was not altered. Millstones were used as they had always been, powered by waterwheels, which Evans studied carefully but did not alter. His changes were all in the direction of using machines to replace humans in carrying out every required operation. This was a matter of moving grain and ground meal from one place in the mill to another and of moving it about in a single location (fig. 6–12).

Evans's patent claim was based primarily on the total mechanization of milling, by putting together a discontinuous sequence of operations using technological devices that had long been known. The human presence was reduced from four men and a boy to two men—and they had little to do but to set the waterwheel in motion, stop certain motions, put others in operation, and move the barrels out as they were filled with flour. Evans introduced three important mechanisms, only one representing a new invention in itself. The upward movement of grain and meal was accomplished by what he called an elevator. This was a long-known chain of buckets. As Evans applied it, it was an endless belt of leather or canvas to which wooden cups were affixed to carry the grain or

Fig. 6–10. Philipsburg Manor mill, Tarrytown, New York

ENGINES OF CHANGE

meal up. Metal buckets were soon substituted. Moving grain and meal horizontally he accomplished primarily by what he called a conveyor, an Archimedean screw device that moved the grist along as it rotated. Evans made the spiral screw out of small flat pieces of wood.

In addition, one of Evans's devices deserves to be accepted as a separate invention. This was the hopper boy, so named because it took the place of a boy who had previously performed the function (fig. 6–13). The hopper boy mechanically raked out freshly ground flour to cool and dry it. It then raked it up again into a hole at the center of the device so the dried flour could be moved on. Although the most original of the components of the Evans mill, the hopper boy was the component least used by those who adopted his system of milling.

Fig. 6–11. Oliver Evans

Evans entered a long and only partially successful attempt to publicize his mill and make his patent financially profitable. He provided information on how to build his mill and licensed its use at a reasonable rate. Initially, he had little luck in getting it adopted, because millers were prospering without it. Gradually its advantages became clearer, and by 1792 he had licensed his invention to more than a hundred mills. Still, he had to defend his patent rights continually and came to feel badly injured by the patent system.

Evans was particularly antagonized by Thomas Jefferson, who made a point of the well-known nature of the components Evans had used to design his automated mill. Jefferson said that he admired Evans but did not regard his mill as deserving a patent. In this position he was wrong, because nearly all patented machines were composed of previously known components.

The use of Evans's mill was limited largely to the wheat-producing areas of Delaware, Maryland, Virginia, Pennsylvania, and New Jersey. The milling business was booming at this point. Profitable and employing many people, it was the most important industry in Delaware. Much of the flour was shipped overseas, especially to the West Indies. Indeed, the large overseas trade of merchant mills caused them to stop grinding small parcels of grain for local families. Delaware residents, however, succeeded in getting their state legislature to enact a law requiring that mills set aside some time each week for local needs.

Evans was surprised to find absolutely no response to his mill in England. In the United States, mills often were operated continuously, day and night, for seasonal periods, particularly when the West Indies trade demanded flour for export. Apparently, neither the advantages of continuous operation nor the labor-saving aspects of his automated mill offered much appeal to English millers, who generally ran small mills intermittently.

The great contribution of Evans's mill was the introduction of continu-

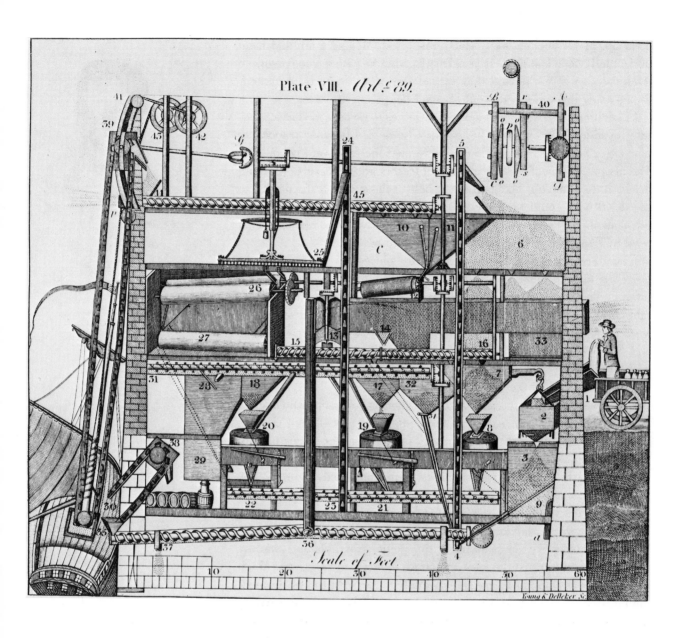

Fig. 6–12. Evans's mill. Evans's mill mechanized all the work that had to be accomplished in a mill, from receiving the grain to grinding it and pouring the flour into barrels. The drawing shows grain being poured in from a wagon on the right and being raised from a ship on the left. The chain of buckets, constituting the elevator, is raising the grain from the ship (35) to the top floor of the mill (39). There it is shown dropping to the left end of the horizontal conveyor, an Archimedean screw, which moves it to the right (10). The hopper boy is located to the left of (25). Three sets of millstones are shown operating at (8, 19, and 20). Many mills were built using components just as they are shown in this drawing.

ous processing, in which raw material was introduced at one point and the finished product removed at another. Ultimately, this early form of automation spread widely, but a number of years passed before even the milling process was further developed. In 1841 Joseph Dart, a Buffalo miller, applied Evans's chain of buckets to fill grain elevators. He also gave new life to the Evans mill two years later when he improved it and added steam power to the process. The automated mill and the elevator system became an expanding part of milling. The further centralization of storage and milling reduced costs, gave better prices to farmers, and encouraged the growth of a world market.

Other improvements in food processing began to proliferate. Canning became significant in the 1820s, moving increasingly from jars to tin cans. In 1856 Gail Borden began canning condensed milk. By 1860 more than five million cans of food had reached the market. Although the use of ice had grown somewhat, the introduction of controlled refrigeration appeared only after canning began. Most of this development was related to the transportation of perishables, to which ice was applied in iceboxes. When a uniform rail gauge was achieved in the North in the 1850s, long-distance transportation, especially of meats, became increasingly profitable. Mechanical refrigeration was attempted but did not succeed until after the Civil War.

Agriculture experienced fundamental changes in the period between 1790 and 1860, including those resulting from the mechanization of farm production and processing. More influential were economic changes that interrelated directly with agriculture. The importance of newly opened rich land, especially in the Midwest, of immigration and inter-

Fig. 6–13. Reconstruction of an Evans hopper boy, Colvin Run Mill, Fairfax, Virginia

nal migration, and of urbanization determined much of what happened to farmers. Industrialization grew in a symbiotic relationship with agriculture. It helped to produce the cities that put great demands, and restrictions, upon farmers. Industrialization depended on increasing farming productivity in order to free labor for the factories. Farming depended on industrialization to provide the transportation, the new and mechanized farming and food processing implements, and the markets for farm products upon which the whole pattern of change rested.

COAL AND IRON

Coal and iron were the most important extractive mineral industries for the Industrial Revolution and also for farming. Iron has been correctly dubbed "the right hand of industry in all its forms," but it could not fill that role in the United States until the price of iron dropped to a point that made it widely accessible. Through the colonial era and into the national period, wood was more used as a material than iron and more used as a fuel than coal. Iron was sometimes used to bind or strengthen wooden construction, but it was expensive and, compared with wood, more difficult to work. As a fuel, wood was more widely available than coal and in frontier and certain rural areas virtually free of cost. Special needs had to arise before coal could become important and the use of iron could be much extended.

Americans did not quickly follow the English lead in new modes of iron production, rolling, puddling, and the use of coke, for reasons that are less obvious than they seem. The United States continued to have an ample supply of wood for charcoal, which inhibited the introduction of coke; in addition, charcoal iron was superior for most uses to coke iron. Yet, rising transportation and other costs raised American iron prices at the same time that the new English efficiency and productivity brought their prices down, especially in wrought iron. The importation of English iron rose, and American iron production languished. Not until industrial needs increased and became more complex, calling for large quantities of differing sorts of iron, were the English improvements in iron production introduced. The beginning of change was intimately tied to coal production.

Even as late as 1830 the United States produced iron overwhelmingly on the basis of traditional methods, using charcoal and waterpower. A large part of the problem was that coke was made from bituminous coal, which was not accessible in most of the United States. Only in Pittsburgh were large quantities of bituminous available, and there the coke reduction of ore, puddling and rolling, and the use of the steam engine began to grow from 1815. In the Midwest the greatest demand for iron rose out of agriculture, but in the East it was highest for industrial needs—and higher overall. There the solution was the opening of the anthracite coal fields of eastern Pennsylvania (fig. 6–14).

The wide use of anthracite coal depended on the building of railroads and canals to serve the mines. By the 1830s and 1840s the widespread use of cheap coal had many ramifications. It brought an expanding use of steam power and increasing factory production of sugar, spirits, beer, chemicals, glass, earthenware, and India rubber. It followed the development of the "hot blast" method of iron reduction with anthracite, not coke. Anthracite iron boomed. By 1845 more than two million tons of anthracite were shipped from Pennsylvania mines. By 1855 steel-

CONNER & PATTERSON'S.*

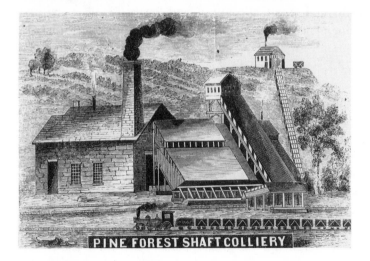

PINE FOREST SHAFT COLLIERY

Fig. 6–14. Coal mine vignettes

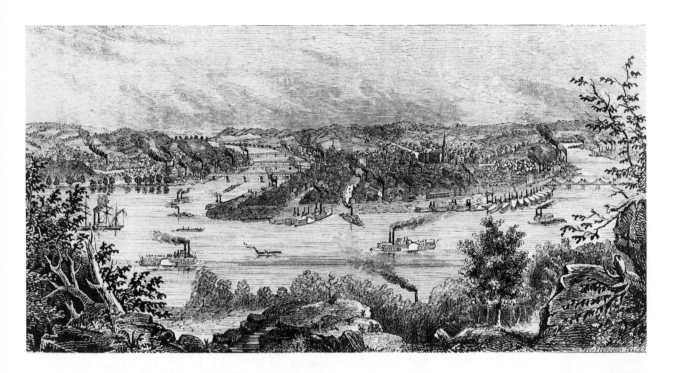

Fig. 6–15. Pittsburgh ironworks and furnaces

makers had shifted to anthracite smelting. The high sulphur content of Pittsburgh bituminous slowed the increase of coke reduction there, so that even by 1860 anthracite still dominated the production of iron (fig. 6–15).

Agriculture was a beneficiary of these major developments that tied coal, iron, and steel production to industrial growth. Iron and steel towns arose and fed industrialization, with important indirect effects on farmers and the need for farm products. Directly, they brought iron and steel into use for farm tools and machines. Steel plows became standard. Seed drills and planters, reapers, and harvesters all came into general use coincidentally with rising availability of malleable iron and steel.

The Industrial Revolution involved many, complex interrelationships. Coal and iron mining, production, and use were closely intertwined—but not inseparable. Coal was fundamental for steam engines used in newly mechanized manufacturing plants and, in time, in steamboats and railroads. It also came into increasing use for space heating and various chemical processes. Iron was increasingly the critical material needed in mechanized manufacturing and transportation—as well as mechanized agriculture and food processing. Agriculture was directly related, both as a causative factor and as a factor affected by mechanized manufacturing and transportation. Very little of what happened in any of these areas followed a one-to-one, cause-effect line. The Industrial Revolution was dominated by a multiplicity of causes and effects.

VII Transportation and the Need for Invention

INTERNAL TRANSPORTATION WAS FAR MORE IMPORTANT TO THE UNITED States than to European nations. It was more important because distances were so much greater in America and existing transportation facilities were so inadequate to needs, especially as the needs multiplied with independence. Not only were the population centers in Britain and France more concentrated, but most were clustered close to one another. Ocean transport served the port cities of those nations well, and rivers had been improved and canals added to reach into their interiors. Roads were in the process of being improved. By contrast, the United States emerged into nationhood with a colonial economy that had never faced the unmet needs for better transportation. It had bypassed them by concentrating on external trade and food and fiber production on farms.

The American pattern of trade and production differed from that of the leading European nations. Agricultural and forest products remained the primary exports; even by 1860 manufactures accounted for only 10 percent. All the large American cities were ports, built primarily upon international trade. Great distances separated a widely dispersed population, more than nine-tenths of whom were initially engaged in agriculture; individual families often remained very much on their own. Their purchases were few and their cash crops small. Internal trade was constricted, expensive, and undeveloped. To move from such a sparse, colonial economy to one more similar to Britain's and France's and one more encouraging to industrialization, much change was required.

Improved internal transportation was a prime requirement. The deficiency had long been recognized, but it was not easy to solve. Road improvement rested on local governments, but what was called for was far beyond their ability to finance. Not only were the roads mostly unsurfaced, even in the cities, but the many rivers and inlets that interrupted passage between major cities were unbridged and had private ferries only at the most travelled points. Fords were possible only where the water was abnormally shallow; even then, they became impassable in periods of high water (fig. 7–1).

Fig. 7–1. Roads and navigable rivers, 1790

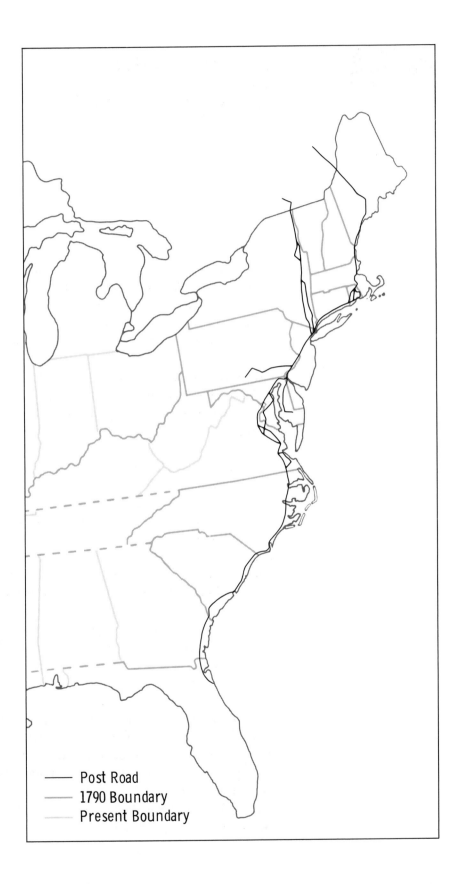

Post Road
1790 Boundary
Present Boundary

RIVER TRANSPORTATION

Rivers and lakes offered another form of transportation, but the large lakes were distant from most settlement and rivers ran toward the coast. By contrast, most early traffic ran parallel to the coastline rather than toward the interior. As the country developed, river routes toward the interior became more travelled, but they had another serious problem. It was easy enough to go with the current down the large rivers, but going against the current was difficult. On much of the Hudson, the Delaware, and the Chesapeake, sailboats were able to move upstream, but in smaller rivers they often could not.

For carrying freight up and down rivers, new boat designs were developed in an anonymous, evolutionary manner. The Durham boat emerged on the Delaware River about 1750, a long narrow boat that could carry fifteen tons of cargo. It had a mast and two sails but depended heavily on four or five crew members whose job was to push the craft forward with poles or oars. Slightly modified, it became known on the Mohawk River as the Schenectady boat (fig. 7–2). The Hudson River sloop was also a freight boat but was able to rely on sails alone to move against the current and even against the wind on the broad and deep Hudson (fig. 7–3).

Fig. 7–2. Pole boat and Schenectady boat

Fig. 7–3. Hudson River sloop

Fig. 7–4. Stagecoach

Fig. 7–5. Stagecoach advertisement

ROADS

Roads were heavily used, and stagecoaches provided regular transportation between major centers (figs. 7–4, 7–5). A new approach to road improvement was the turnpike system, which depended on private initiative but often with state support. Promoters collected fees from everyone using the road, expecting to turn a profit. They had to maintain the turnpikes in good condition in order to attract and retain users. This led them to follow the lead of France and England in improving road engineering and construction. The first American turnpike was built in Vir-

Fig. 7–6. National Road at
Fairview Inn, Maryland, 1827

ginia in 1785. The most famous was the Lancaster Turnpike, completed
in 1794, connecting Philadelphia to Lancaster and contributing to the
increase of east-west traffic. Lancaster opened access not only to western Pennsylvania but to the Great Valley that ran between the Blue
Ridge and the Alleghenies—through Virginia and the Carolinas to
back-country Georgia. The success of the Lancaster Pike stimulated
much more turnpike construction.

Roads improved slowly, if at all, and a conflict arose within the federal government about both the constitutionality and the desirability of
supporting road construction. In 1803 a plan was launched for building
the National Road from the Potomac River in Maryland over the moun-
tains to Wheeling, now West Virginia, and ultimately to St. Louis (figs.
7–6, 7–7). Although begun, it was never finished, stalled by those who
regarded it as unconstitutional and by the turnpike and canal builders.
By 1856 its completed segments had been turned back to the individual
states.

Fig. 7–7. National Road mile marker

CANALS

Canal building arose to parallel road improvement efforts (figs. 7–8, 7–9). Americans had planned and surveyed canal routes before independence, but the first to be completed was the Santee Canal in 1800, connecting Charleston with Columbia, South Carolina. The states became increasingly involved in canal projects of their own, and several key routes were completed in the 1820s and 1830s. The great achievement was the Erie Canal, opened in 1825 between Albany and Lake Erie. It was 363 miles long and served as an important training ground for American engineers who went on in the next fifteen years to build 3,300 miles of canals at a cost of $125 million. It not only opened communication to the West but proved a major factor in making New York City the national metropolis.

The country became crisscrossed by canals, which, combined with

Fig. 7–8. Canal boat

Fig. 7–9. View of canal lock

road construction, played an increasing role in economic development. The power source was the same, horses and mules, which were more reliable than sailing vessels could ever be. Sailing ships at sea were problem enough when bad weather might damage or sink them and lack of wind could hold them becalmed for long periods. They fared still worse on inland waters where gusty and uncertain winds were frequent, and narrow passageways might require wind from a specific sector. But the river highways were so impressive in the United States, especially after the enormous Mississippi River system came into use, that men continued to seek means for using them effectively. Furthermore, roads and canals remained expensive and limited in their capabilities.

STEAMBOATS

The answer became a major American contribution to transportation technology: the steamboat. Why should the United States, which began with a colonial economy and lacked the technological development of either England or France, have passed both in bringing the steamboat to a point of utility? Several European trials of steamboats had been attempted before the Americans entered the field. The United States lacked the capital, the skills, and the experience the English had had in producing commercial steam engines. The one thing Americans did have, however, was a compelling need that the Europeans lacked. Indeed, when the English first tried to introduce steamboats, they used them in a very different way from the Americans. They used them in canals and as tugboats instead of for river and lake transport. Even the earliest American steamboat inventors had their eyes on the Mississippi, and in due time that river with its tributaries became the richest realm of steamboating in the world. The steamboat converted the Mississippi into a national highway system.

The earliest American steamboat efforts were important, not for changing transportation patterns but for the technology involved and for pointing toward the future. The ultimate failure of both John Fitch and James Rumsey to carry the steamboats they built to continuing success should not obscure the importance of their contributions. Each man went through a lot of heartbreaking developmental problems, magnified by difficulties in getting support and in finding mechanics who could handle the required work. Fitch formed three successive companies as he pursued his objective, and his *Perseverance* of 1790 ran with few breakdowns and provided regular income—though never enough to make it profitable. Fitch was fortunate in gaining the aid of a German-born and -trained clockmaker, Henry Voight, who made fundamental, creative contributions. Rumsey won the support of Franklin as well as Jefferson, who called him the most brilliant mechanic he had ever known. He solved the need for good workmen by going to England, where he bought a Watt and Boulton steam engine and used English mechanics for his work.

Fitch designed many different engines, boilers, and propulsive schemes, aided at key points by Voight, whose boilers were especially impressive (figs. 7–10, 7–11). Fitch built a boat model with an endless chain of paddles and sketched out jet propulsion and twin propeller schemes, in addition to the crank and paddle boats he put into operation. Rumsey stuck to the jet propulsion Franklin had urged, but there made an important advance. He coupled his steam engine directly to the piston and cylinder water pump, used for squirting the jet of water out the stern, by placing the engine directly on top of the pump and using

Fig. 7–10. Fitch steamboat, 1785 (model)

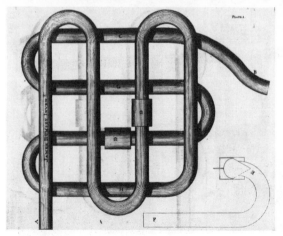

Fig. 7–11. Voight water tube boiler, 1788

the same piston rod for each (fig. 7–12). Years later, in 1840, that idea was separately patented and effectively used.

The range of ideas considered and tested was remarkable. Many of the concepts were later carried to fulfillment. More basically important, not only did Fitch and Rumsey convince themselves during their competition that steamboating was feasible and desirable, but many others accepted the great possibility and some were driven by it.

John Stevens was a fascinating promoter infected by the "steamboat mania." Not himself a mechanic, he was a well-to-do land owner, political figure, and proponent of technological and economic change. He hired the best mechanics he could find and in 1804 got a small steamboat, the *Little Juliana*, running out of Hoboken, New Jersey, where he lived (fig. 7–13). His boat has special interest because it used twin screw propulsion (fig. 7–14). There was nothing new about propellers, but Stevens actually put them to work. He also introduced an interesting boiler design, dubbed the "porcupine boiler," because it had water tubes that projected like sticks into the fire chamber.

Although time passed Fitch and Rumsey by, Stevens kept going and others entered the fray before Robert Fulton returned to the United States in 1806 and worked with his partner, Chancellor Livingston, toward his landmark success. Fulton had examined a trial steamboat in England and built a rather unsuccessful one in Paris. He experimented himself, especially on hull forms, but the fact that he contributed no clear-cut invention has led too many to discount Fulton's role in bringing the steamboat to fulfillment (fig. 7–15). The problem in part is the view held then that invention was the only important factor in technological change. It never was. In fact, by Fulton's day there were enough inventions in hand to carry the steamboat through after the other needs were met.

Fig. 7–12. Rumsey jet steamboat, 1788

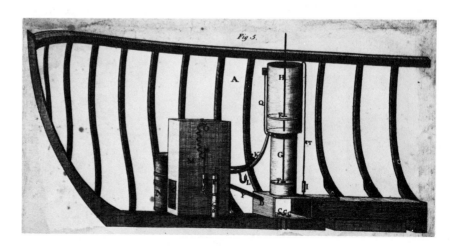

ENGINES OF CHANGE

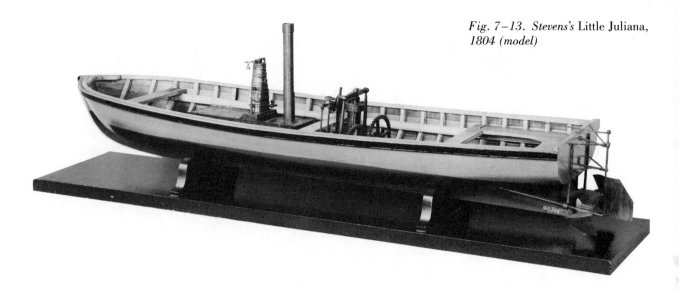

Fig. 7–13. Stevens's Little Juliana, *1804 (model)*

Fig. 7–14. Little Juliana *engine*

Fig. 7–15. Fulton's Chancellor Livingston, *1815 (model)*

Livingston solved the problem of obtaining a monopoly without having to worry about a patent. Fulton solved the engine problem, which had absorbed an enormous amount of effort on the part of other builders; he bought a Watt and Boulton engine, after obtaining a special license to permit its export. The third critical solution was beginning on the Hudson where, because of distances, poor roads, and terrain, land transport could not compete effectively.

Fulton established steamboat commerce on the Hudson and in Long Island Sound in a manner that was both technically and financially successful. He inaugurated steamboating on the Mississippi and was projecting on the Chesapeake a development similar to that in New York when he died in 1815. Others took over, and steamboat traffic burgeoned in most of the developed and developing inland waters.

A major American contribution that became an integral part of Mississippi steamboating was the high-pressure engine (fig. 7–16). This was invented by Oliver Evans, virtually simultaneously with Richard Trevithick's similar engine in Britain. It did not use a condenser as the Watt engine did, and it was simpler and more compact. Because it vented steam to the atmosphere, it required high quantities of water, which was no problem when operating in fresh water (fig. 7–17). The plentiful supplies of wood in America also reduced the large fuel demand to a minor problem.

With the introduction of steam, inland waterways became a great resource. They offered cheap transportation for freight and for individuals. Many population centers and extensive areas of the country were well served by steamboats, but the application of steam to ocean travel was less successful. Despite the *Savannah*, a ship with auxiliary steam power that crossed the Atlantic in 1819, the Americans did not take a

Fig. 7–16. Evans's drawing of his high-pressure engine

Fig. 7–17. A Mississippi River boat, the Buckeye State, *1841 (model)*

similar lead in developing ocean steamships. In fact, they excelled throughout the period in building wooden sailing ships, most dramatically the clipper ships. The United States reached a point where it carried more cargo with a smaller merchant marine than Great Britain.

But, good as inland steamboats were, they had severe limitations. They were operable only on rivers, lakes, and bays, and neither roads nor canals proved adequate to supply the increasing need for transportation in areas that steamboats could not serve. The answer proved to be the railroad, the application of steam power to rail transportation—a combination that was not inseparable. Indeed, rails without steam were an old and well-known method for moving materials, especially in mines where humans pushed ore carts on rails. This was another European technology that was not transferred to the United States, because without deep mines it was not needed.

From the beginning, overland transportation had seemed preferable to water transportation, and railroads to steamboats, but railroads involved many additional, complex problems. John Fitch's first dream of the application of steam power to transportation was not of a steamboat but a steam carriage. As he told the story, he was walking on a dusty road near Neshamini, Pennsylvania, in 1785, when he was passed by a horse and carriage. The thought struck him suddenly: why not dispense with the horse and apply "the force procured by Steam" to run the carriage? He realized the difficult obstacles to such a plan when he began to draw up designs. The curves, steep grades, muddy roads, and fords would be hard for a steam carriage to manage. Because of that he became an "inventor of steamboats": propelling a boat on a flat body of water eliminated all the civil engineering required for overland transport. Although he realized it less clearly, the mechanical engineering was easier, too.[1]

Other inventors also tried their hand at steam-powered land transportation, although the inventive energy of most steam engineers went into water rather than land transportation. One exception was Oliver Evans, whose *Oruktor Amphibolos*, a combination steam wagon and steamboat, rumbled through the streets of Philadelphia and into the Delaware one day in 1803 (fig. 7–18).

John Stevens, builder of the steamboat *Little Juliana*, one of the foremost proponents of steam power in the United States, was a great advocate of railroads. His 1812 *Documents tending to Prove the Superior Advantages of Rail-ways and Steam Carriages over Canal Navigation* calculated the comparative costs of railroads and canals and presented evidence that railroads would be no more expensive than canals and vastly more useful. Stevens included in his pamphlet the replies of correspondents who denied the possibility and economy of railroads. Some said the friction of the wheels on the track would be insufficient to move the train, or that the track could not be built strong enough to stand the weight of the engine. Moreover, they said, railroads were too expensive; canals were the appropriate transportation for the new nation. Stevens managed to obtain a state charter for a New Jersey railroad connecting Philadelphia and New York City but was unable to fulfill the opportunity. He was able to build a small locomotive that ran on a circular track in Hoboken, New Jersey, in 1825, to demonstrate the possibilities of steam railroading—the first steam locomotive to run on rails in this country.

In the 1810s and 1820s canals continued to boom. With the exception of small, special-purpose horse railroads used to connect mines with canals or seaports, railroads were not even attempted, held back by cost and technical problems. An early canal/railroad compromise was built

Fig. 7–18. Evans's Oruktor Amphibolos, *1803 (model)*

in the 1820s to connect Philadelphia with Pittsburgh and the West. Because of the Appalachians a direct canal route patterned on the New York Erie Canal was not possible, and, instead, Philadelphians turned to a canal/railroad combination. The Pennsylvania system was a remarkable design. The canal had 174 locks, a 900-foot tunnel, several aqueducts, and, in one thirty-two-mile stretch, ten inclined planes where canal boats were pulled uphill by steam engines, alternated with eleven nearly level stretches where steam locomotives were used.

Steam railroading could not be successfully introduced until steam locomotives had undergone considerable development and track design and construction had been improved. More compact engines and boilers producing more horsepower per pound were required for locomotives. The American terrain demanded a great deal of grading and bridging, and it took a long time to develop trackage that was both reasonable in cost and sufficiently strong and enduring.

As in earlier technologies, England led the world in railroad development. The English began with many advantages: a flatter terrain and denser population, availability of capital, mechanical skills, good management, and steam engine experience. Still, although the first steam locomotive was built in 1803, it was not until 1825 that the founding of the Stockton and Darlington Railroad began effective railroading. By this time American technology was highly developed and in certain fields—notably river steamboating and some areas of textile production—led England and the rest of the world. Railroading had been introduced and surely could have been carried through to success without further external input. However, there was a clear advantage to bypassing much development work by importing English locomotives, which had proven effective. This was a pivotal step that did not lead to long extended importation but to the manufacture of American adaptations based on the English prototypes. The most critical import was that of the *John Bull* in 1831, built by Robert Stephenson and Company and bought by the Camden and Amboy Railroad.

Transportation comprised a much more important aspect of mechanization and industrialization in the United States than elsewhere. It was pursued so vigorously because of the need, because distances were so great and existing transportation so inferior. The need was never fully satisfied, but the many approaches all improved American technical capabilities and influenced American life. The rising mode of transportation was railroading, which reached the level of leadership following the import and adaption of the *John Bull*.

The John Bull *and the*
Rise of American Railroading

MORE THAN ANY OTHER MODE OF TRANSPORTATION, THE RAILROAD epitomized American technological and commercial development. And more than any other new machine, the locomotive symbolized the Industrial Revolution. Literally and symbolically, it was the American nation moving across the continent and into the future. "The whistle of the locomotive," wrote Nathaniel Hawthorne, hearing it break the silence one day in 1844, "tells a story of busy men, . . . men of business; in short of all unquietness . . . since it brings the noisy world into the midst of our slumbrous peace."[1] The railroad was a symbol of a new way of life founded on machines and factories. To Americans of the nineteenth century, it represented progress (fig. 8–1).

The United States had a seemingly unlimited need for transportation. Atlantic port cities wanted fast, cheap connections with the booming trans-Appalachian West. Small towns wanted a mercantile connection with large cities. Everywhere, there seemed to be commercial advantage in cheaper, faster transportation. Roads, steamboats, and canals met some of the need, but all had their limitations. Roads were slow. Steamboats were useful only on navigable rivers. Canals, too, had geographic limitations, and some froze in the winter. Neither roads, canals, nor steamboats filled the expanding need in the United States for inland transportation.

Meanwhile, in England, railroads were beginning to be planned and built. The Stockton and Darlington, the first railroad for general transportation, began operation in 1825. As English engineers solved the technical problems, Americans began to plan their own short-run railroads. Businessmen in large cities turned to railroads to gain in competition with their rivals. Baltimore projected the Baltimore and Ohio to compete with Philadelphia and the Pennsylvania System, and even with the Erie Canal. Boston planned the Boston and Albany to compete with New York City. The Charleston and Hamburg Railroad was the first to start scheduled passenger service with a steam locomotive. In a short time, towns and even projected towns decided that they needed railroads.

Fig. 8–1. Currier and Ives, Across the Continent: "Westward the Course of Empire Takes Its Way," *1868*

The railroads were planned mostly by private commercial interests, though often with local or state government assistance. States helped the new railroad companies in a variety of ways, granting the right of eminent domain, monopolies on certain routes, exemption from taxes, or lottery or banking privileges. Some state governments bought stock or loaned money to railroads; others required that private banks purchase railroad stock before the banks could receive a state charter. And some states, including Pennsylvania, Virginia, and Georgia, built and owned railroads themselves. The federal government, too, provided aid. Railroad owners convinced the government to reduce tariff duties on imported track, and many made use of army engineers to survey tracks.

The first problem that confronted American railroad builders in the 1820s and 1830s was motive power. Horse power was one alternative. Horses pulled the cars on most of the small railroads serving mines. They were slow, though, and many inventors thought about applying the steam engine to land transportation. Early attempts were completely unsuccessful. Not until the early 1830s did American attempts to build locomotives obtain even partial success. Peter Cooper built the *Tom Thumb* for the Baltimore and Ohio in 1830, and the West Point Foundry in New York built the *Best Friend of Charleston* for the South Carolina Railroad in 1831 (fig. 8–2). Both engines worked, but both also made visible the great need for development and improvement. The public became aware of some of the problems with these early locomotives when the *Tom Thumb* lost a race with a horse.

As with many other technologies, the British led the world in locomotive design. The first steam locomotive was built in England in 1803. In 1829 came the most dramatic turning point in locomotive design and construction, when the Liverpool and Manchester Railroad held the Rainhill trials to pick the locomotives it would use. These trials were won by George Stephenson's *Rocket* (fig. 8–3). The *Rocket* was the first locomotive of modern design, with a multitubular boiler and a direct, gearless drive. "She set the basic pattern for all subsequent main-line steam locomotives"[2] and made Robert Stephenson and Company the world's leading locomotive builders.

In 1829 the Delaware and Hudson Canal Company imported four colliery locomotives from England, the first locomotives in North America. Only two months after the *Rocket's* victory at the trials, the Carbondale and Honesdale Railroad in Pennsylvania bought a locomotive from

Fig. 8–2. The Tom Thumb *(model)*

Fig. 8–3. The Rocket *(model)*

Robert Stephenson and Company. The *Stourbridge Lion* was not very successful—because its track was too light, not because of the locomotive—but it opened the door to an important new approach to the equipping of American railroads.

The second problem for railroad builders to solve was track. Early on, engineers had to choose from a wide variety of types of track and roadway. The short early railways had used wooden tracks with an iron strap on top, mounted on stone blocks. This system worked reasonably well in England but not in the United States, where the stone blocks had to be put back into place after each cold winter's frost heaves pushed them out of line. Some railroads tried building their track on pilings. Others replaced the stone blocks with wood ties, an important application of a known technology that soon became standard. Ties came to be mounted on crushed stone or gravel roadbeds, which not only absorbed the pounding of the train but, more important, allowed water to drain off the roadbed. Because iron straps had a tendency to come loose from wood rails, railroads experimented with solid rails. Track gauge—the distance between the rails—was also an open question. Each railroad picked the gauge it thought most suitable, a practice that sometimes resulted in major bottlenecks where railroads of one gauge met those of another.

Track location, as well as track design, required early decision. Large cities, the termini of the rail lines, wanted the track to run straight between them, ensuring the shortest, fastest service. Small country towns often wanted the tracks to come near them, for a station could mean prosperity and growth. Farmers had mixed feelings about the new railroads; track through a farm could be detrimental to livestock and crops but might represent an opportunity to gain new markets. Politics was of critical importance in determining track location.

The details of location were dependent on geography. Hills and valleys had to be avoided as much as possible, or balanced, so that material taken from a cut through a hill could be used to fill in a valley. Straight track allowed greater speeds than curved. Here technological limitations and a second set of economic considerations, the cost of building track, came into play. American railroads, many of them undercapitalized, took shortcuts on track construction, building their tracks with steeper grades and sharper curves than did British railroads.

Finally, the engineering and economic decisions completed, the road was built. Track laying was an extremely labor-intensive process in the nineteenth century. Thousands of cubic yards of dirt had to be moved, thousands of stones had to be cut, and miles of track carefully aligned on the stone. This was done mostly by muscle power. Many an Irish immigrant worked with pick and shovel to build the early American railroads.

THE CAMDEN AND AMBOY RAILROAD

On July 14, 1831, a "locomotive steam engine" built by the firm of R. Stephenson and Company was loaded onto a ship in Liverpool, England, bound for Philadelphia. There it was to be received by "Edwin A. Stephens for the Camden and South Amboy R. Road & Trans Co." The *John Bull*, as the locomotive was to be named in honor of its place of birth, is today the world's oldest operable locomotive, a living symbol of the Industrial Revolution in this country (fig. 8–4). Its importation and adaptation to fit American conditions is a good example of the transfer of technology to America and the changes, technological and social, that the new machinery brought about. The story of the *John Bull* and the Camden and Amboy Railroad is, in a small way, the story of the American Industrial Revolution.

The trip between New York and Philadelphia, the two largest cities in North America, was not easy in the early nineteenth century. Although the two cities had been connected by road since 1682, in 1800 the trip could take as long as eleven hours on a good day, more than twenty hours on a bad day. The New Jersey legislature, eager to reduce the cost and time of the trip in order to increase trade, investigated possibilities for improvement.

In 1829 the legislature undertook one of its periodic investigations. Some of its petitioners favored a canal: a cross-Jersey canal, they argued, would become "the most important and productive link in the whole of the great chain of internal navigation along the Atlantic coast." They suggested that it would pay for itself in no time, its profit freeing New Jerseyites from taxes. Others opposed the canal, calling it a "burthen and vexation to our citizens," arguing that it was more likely to raise taxes than reduce them. The canal, they said, was "altogether unnecessary & uncalled for." [3]

A railroad was another possibility. Railroads had met with some success in England by this time, and there were plans afoot in several cities to build railroads. Meetings were held, and petitions were sent to the legislature arguing in favor of a New Jersey railroad. Proponents of the railroad agreed with those favoring the canal about the need for internal improvements but suggested that railroads were the wave of the future.

The committee studied the options. Canals were proven; the example of the Erie Canal, which had greatly increased the commerce and prosperity of New York City, weighed heavily in its deliberations. The only advantage they saw in railroads was their year-round operability—an advantage neutralized when the water froze at either end of the route between the cities, immobilizing the connecting water transportation. Against this advantage was a range of disadvantages, cost being the most important. Moreover, a railroad would be a monopoly: on a railroad people would have to depend on equipment owned by the company, while on a canal any farmer could use his own horse and boat.

The New Jersey legislature considered the proposed canal—the Delaware and Raritan—and the proposed railroad—the Camden and Amboy—at its 1829–30 session. Lobbyists presented every case. Some argued for the railroad, others the canal; some for private ownership,

Fig. 8–4. The John Bull

others for public. So furious was the competition that prominent supporters of each side felt it necessary to walk about the streets of Trenton armed at night, for fear of attack.

The legislature, faced with strong arguments on both sides, evaded decision by issuing two charters. Both the canal and the railroad would be built, parallel to one another, and both would be privately owned, although the state would have the right to buy out either after thirty years. Each corporation would give the state $100,000 in stock and pay a transit tax for all passengers or freight carried.

The Camden and Amboy $1 million stock offering was fully subscribed on the first day it was put up for sale. Its directors bragged that "Public opinion had, by this time, taken so strong a direction in favor of railroads, as a more cheap and expeditious mode of communication and transportation than canals, that the greatest of difficulties were experienced in regard to the canal."[4] The canal proprietors, fearful that they would not be able to raise the capital they needed, decided to build a railroad as well as a canal.

The threat of two competing railroads led the legislature to pass the "Marriage Act," combining the two companies. This act extended the charter for another twenty years, set rates for both railroad and canal, gave the new company the right of eminent domain, and, most important, guaranteed it a monopoly on the New York-Philadelphia route. In exchange, the company agreed to pay at least $30,000 a year in transit taxes and gave the state additional stock worth $100,000. The "Joint Companies," as the firm came to be known, successfully completed both railroad and canal.

It was not unusual for a state to grant a monopoly in order to encourage transportation within its boundaries. New Jersey had long given monopolies to companies running carriages on the New York-Philadelphia route. Few monopolies, though, were as far-reaching as that granted to the Joint Companies, which made it illegal to build any other railroad between New York and Philadelphia in New Jersey, or to compete with the railroad in any way. The grant of monopoly served its purpose; the Camden and Amboy got off to a fast start and before long was paying taxes to the state.

As soon as the state charter was granted and funding ensured, the board of directors of the Camden and Amboy turned its attention to building the railroad. As usual, the first problem was the motive power—horse or steam—that would pull the cars on it. The performance of steam locomotives then in use in the United States was not encouraging. None had met with great success. The directors of the Camden and Amboy decided that "the merits and capacities of the locomotive engines were matters of experiment and mere newspaper rumour. . . . These were questions that could not be solved in this country,"[5] and so they

Fig. 8–5. Robert Stevens

ordered Robert Stevens, president of the company, to investigate civil engineering and locomotive design in England (fig. 8–5).

Stevens had grown up among the latest advances in steam technology in America. Not only was he the son of John Stevens, a long-time supporter of railroads, but he was familiar with the steamboats run on the family's Union Line between New York and Philadelphia. Stevens had two goals in mind for his trip to England. He wanted to examine railroads, deciding which features were to be emulated and which improved, what was appropriate for an American railroad and what needed to be changed. And he wanted to examine locomotives and to study their features; might ordering a locomotive and having it shipped across the Atlantic be the answer?

Stevens visited all the important railroads in England. With the help of the English railroad owners, he "possessed himself of all the information that can be obtained on the subject."[6] One of the railroads he studied was the Liverpool and Manchester, where Stephenson's *Rocket* was in successful operation (fig. 8–6). The Liverpool and Manchester was the best-built railroad in England and, from its opening in September 1830, a model for other railroads. It was, a British writer wrote in 1832, "*the* experiment which was to decide the fate of Rail-ways."[7]

Stevens did decide on the Liverpool and Manchester as the model for the Camden and Amboy but recommended shortcuts to decrease the cost of the track and bring it within the resources of the company. These shortcuts, which became typical of American railroad engineering, were to have a great influence on American locomotive design, for when the railroad civil engineering was changed, the locomotives that ran on it had to change as well.

Just a few weeks before Stevens arrived, Stephenson and Company had delivered a new locomotive to the line. The *Planet* was the best locomotive yet built (fig. 8–7). Its firebox was incorporated into its boiler and the cylinders separated, giving greater efficiency. Power was transmitted to the wheels by means of a crank axle. Impressed by the *Planet*, Stevens went to visit Stephenson's locomotive factory.

Robert Stephenson and Company had been established in 1823 by George Stephenson, Robert's father, a civil engineer responsible for many important early bridges, tunnels, and railroads. The firm became

Fig. 8–6. The Liverpool and Manchester Railroad, 1831

Fig. 8–7. The Planet

the world's foremost designer and builder of locomotives. Some 400 workmen labored there, using mostly hand tools to build some of the most advanced machines of the day (fig. 8–8). A visitor described the factory:

In 1837 there were no small planing or shaping machines—there was only one slotting machine. . . . Steam hammers were of course unknown, and only hand labour was available for the ordinary work of the smith's shop, with the exception of the punching and shearing machinery. Riveting by machinery . . . was unknown. . . . There was not a single crane in Robert Stephenson's shop in 1837. And the only steam-engine in that which was the most important locomotive shop in the world of that day, was a vibrating pillar engine. . . .[8]

The success of the shop depended on the design skills of Robert Stephenson and the metalworking skills of his employees.

Stevens decided to order a locomotive for the Camden and Amboy from Stephenson. He considered his options. He liked the *Planet;* he liked even more the *Samson,* Stephenson's next locomotive, built to haul freight. He also wanted incorporated into his locomotives some of the features of the locomotives built for the Liverpool and Manchester by Edward Bury of Liverpool, one of Stephenson's rivals. Stevens and Stephenson drew up a memorandum outlining the design of the locomotive (figs. 8–9, 8–10). The memorandum reveals both Stevens's understanding of and beliefs about steam engines and the extent to which he acknowledged the superior expertise of the builder.

The locomotive, to be named the *John Bull,* was built, disassembled, and shipped across the Atlantic. It arrived in Philadelphia in late Au-

Fig. 8–8. Robert Stephenson and Company locomotive works

gust and was taken to Bordentown, New Jersey. There to receive the cargo was Isaac Dripps, mechanic for the Camden and Amboy. Dripps had never before seen a locomotive, but, though only twenty-one, he was well prepared for this moment. Born in Belfast, Ireland, in 1810, he had come to the United States as a child. At sixteen he was apprenticed to Thomas Holloway, Philadelphia manufacturer of marine steam engines. Within two years he had become foreman of the shop. When the Union Line's steamboat *Swan* was sent to Holloway's shop for repairs, Robert Stevens was so impressed with Dripps's work that he persuaded him to join the Camden and Amboy as chief mechanic.

It took ten days for Dripps and his crew to put the *John Bull* together. Stevens came to Bordentown to see the completed locomotive and to make final adjustments. By November the *John Bull* was ready to be shown off (fig. 8–11). It was a time for celebration: the local newspaper announced, "The Railroad company gives a fête to-day . . . . A locomotive engine and its cars are to make a trip over a portion of the road."[9]

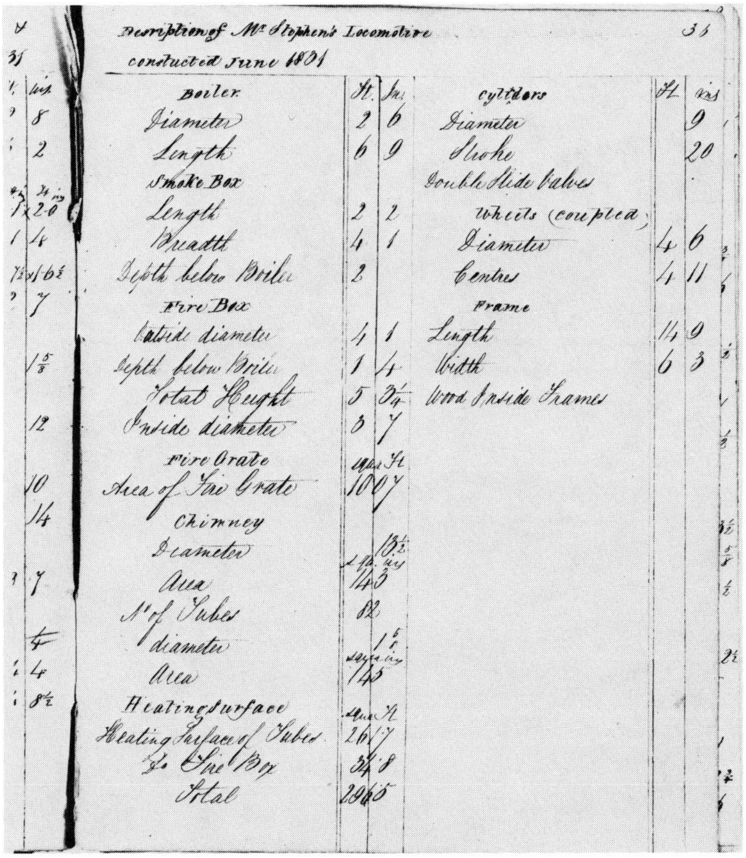

Description of Mr Stephen's Locomotive constructed June 1831

	ft	in		ft	ins
Boiler			Cylinders		
Diameter	2	6	Diameter		9
Length	6	9	Stroke		20
Smoke Box			Double Slide valves		
Length	2	2	Wheels (coupled)		
Breadth	4	1	Diameter	4	6
Depth below Boiler	2		Centres	4	11
Fire Box			Frame		
Outside diameter	4	1	Length	14	9
Depth below Boiler	1	4	Width	6	3
Total Height	5	3¼	Wood Inside Frames		
Inside diameter	3	7			
Fire Grate	sq ft				
Area of Fire Grate	10	07			
Chimney					
Diameter		13½ in			
Area	1	43			
No of Tubes	62				
diameter		1 5/8 in			
Area	1	45			
Heating Surface	sq ft				
Heating Surface of Tubes	261	7			
do Fire Box	34	8			
Total	296	5			

Fig. 8–9. Stephenson description of the John Bull

"There was a great assemblage of people there," an observer wrote, "and all wanted a ride. The legislature was invited and attended in a body, and a great many of the best people in New Jersey."[10]

The *John Bull* was put in storage while the Camden and Amboy track was prepared. Major John Wilson, of the U.S. Army Corps of Topographical Engineers, who had surveyed the routes of several canals, was hired to determine the best location for the track. Central New Jersey was flat, presenting few geographic obstacles. Wilson's solution to the balance of economic and geographic factors was a track that ran on almost a straight line between Camden and Amboy, following closely the existing highway between the two cities. The company decided to build only a single track—a decision that saved money but would be responsible for some horrendous train wrecks.

Following Stevens's suggestion, the Camden and Amboy's track was modeled on that of the Liverpool and Manchester (fig. 8–12). Over most of the route, rails were laid on stone blocks set on a foundation of broken

Fig. 8–10. Plan of the boiler of the John Bull

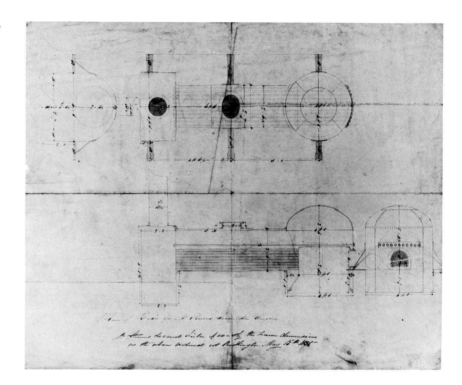

Fig. 8–11. The John Bull and cars as they looked in 1831

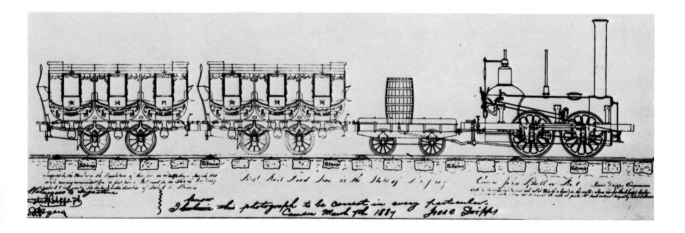

stone. On embankments, where earth would settle, the track was laid on wood to allow easy adjustment. Although the company claimed that "the road is of the best and most permanent construction,"[11] it quickly replaced the stone blocks with wooden ties.

The rail was Stevens's own invention. He decided not to use the Berkenshaw rail used on English railroads, because it required an expensive iron rail chair to hold it—not suitable in the United States, where skilled metalworkers were scarce. On board the *Hibernia* sailing

*Fig. 8–12. Track of the Camden
and Amboy Railroad*

to England, Stevens had considered the proper shape for the rail, carving models from scraps of wood to visualize the forces it would have to withstand. Trial and error led him to a rail that resembled a T, the shape that became the standard pattern for railroads throughout the world. On arrival in England he distributed a plan for the rail to several ironworks (fig. 8–13). Only the Dowais Iron Works, in Wales, bid on the project, for the rail was heavier than English rail, and few ironworks wanted to risk their rolling machinery on the project. The rails were shipped beginning in spring 1831.

The track was built and opened in sections, the first on September 19, 1832. Fifteen months later the final section was opened. Track was only the most visible part of the railroad's capital investment. The list that appears on page 139 suggests the amount of infrastructure necessary to run trains over sixty miles. These structures and the track cost about $3.2 million. The single largest expense was for the iron rails, about $500,000. Almost as much was spent preparing the roadbed, and $370,000 went for real estate. Steamboats and wharfs for the river part of the route cost about $500,000. The line's seventeen locomotives, by comparison, were cheap, only $124,000; the cars, $141,000.

The Camden and Amboy Railroad and Transportation Company emerged as one of the largest corporations in the country. In 1834 it

Fig. 8–13. Stevens's T-rail plan

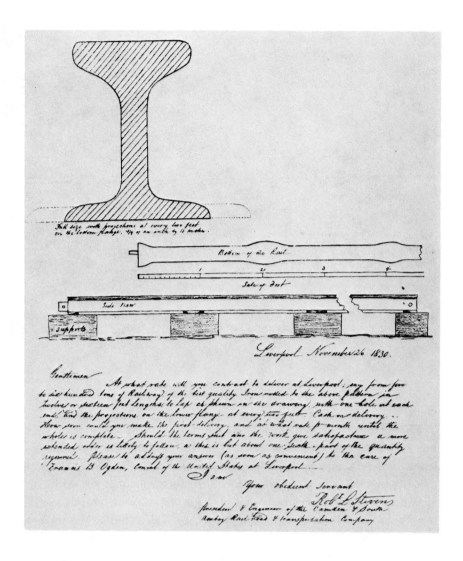

carried 105,000 passengers and almost 8,400 tons of freight. From the very beginning the railroad was profitable; in 1833 it had receipts of almost $500,000 and expenditures of only $287,000. Its investment in people, track, locomotives, rolling stock, and political power paid off well.

THE INVENTION OF THE AMERICAN LOCOMOTIVE

In the United States in 1831, the *John Bull* was one of the most complex, technologically advanced machines. The Camden and Amboy's first *Annual Report* expressed wonder and delight at the usefulness of

Camden and Amboy Railroad Inventory, 1840

17 locomotives

64 passenger cars (including 2 with rocking chairs)

7 baggage cars

64 freight cars

24 dump cars, used in repairing the road

12 snow scrapers

11 car houses, for repairing and storing cars

9 "transportation houses" (passenger offices, etc.)

9 engine houses, for repairing locomotives

8 shops, including 3 carpenter's shops and 3 blacksmith's shops

5 woodsheds

12 water tanks, including one with a tide wheel to raise water

3 wharves

3 taverns

47 houses for workmen

2 superintendent's houses

the technology: "The surprise and gratification experienced . . . from the rapid motion of the locomotive engines, has been more than equalled during the present season by its wonderful capacity for propelling ponderous loads. It [is] a power which has almost annihilated time and space."[12]

Railroads spread throughout the United States in the following years, requiring a rapid development of locomotives, track design, and railroad organization. While it was not in the forefront of technological improvement, the Camden and Amboy participated in many of these developments.

Following the example of the Camden and Amboy, other American railroads imported British locomotives. Over the next twelve years, about 120 were imported from England, but it was not long before Americans began to build their own locomotives. By 1841 British imports constituted only one-quarter of the almost 500 locomotives in service in the United States.

The Camden and Amboy made use of both British and American shops for its locomotives, which were modeled on the *John Bull.* They were built in local machine shops, except for the cylinders and other precision parts, which were ordered from R. Stephenson and Company.

Nine locomotives were built at the Stevens machine shop in Hoboken, where the Stevens steamboats were also built and repaired; others were made in the New York machine shops of Ezra K. Dodd and Henry R. Dunham, both makers of steam engines for ships. New York was already a center of machining skills; American factories were ready to produce locomotives as soon as a demand for them existed.

By 1840 ten American locomotive builders were in operation. Although they modeled their earliest designs, including *Old Ironsides*, on British imports, American locomotive design soon began to diverge from that practiced in England (fig. 8–14). The interchange between economic and social demands and railroad technology determined the initial modifications and continued to condition development. Because American roadways and roadbeds were built as cheaply as possible, with steeper grades and sharper turns than English railroads, they required more powerful locomotives. English locomotives had a hard time holding the track.

The primary answer to that problem was the bogie truck. This was a set of four leading wheels that swiveled independently, following the track as it curved and preventing the locomotive from derailing. Although first patented in England in 1812, it was not much used there. In 1831 John Jervis reinvented the bogie truck and installed it in his *Experiment*, later renamed the *Brother Jonathan* (fig. 8–15). This was one of the great American innovations in locomotive design.

The *John Bull* needed a similar device. As imported from England, the *John Bull* was, in technical terms, an 0–4–0; that is, it had no guide wheels, two sets of powered wheels connected together, and no following wheels. It did not hold the track well. Dripps and Stevens mounted a two-wheeled truck in front of the locomotive, attached to the front axle, and disconnected the power drive to that axle. They enlarged the hole that fastened the front axle to the frame of the locomotive, allowing it to pivot slightly. The *John Bull* was thus converted to a 4–2–0; the two front pair of wheels served as a four-wheel pilot, turning with the curves of the track, and the rear set of wheels served to transmit power (fig. 8–16). This improvement was probably made in 1833, just after Jervis had introduced it.

The standard American locomotive emerged by 1850. This was a 4–4–0. That is, it had a swivel or bogie truck in front, then four rigidly coupled drive wheels, and no rear truck. The four drive wheels were outside connected to horizontal cylinders, forward of the wheels. The engineer and fireman stayed on a cab at the rear of the locomotive, just behind the boiler. American locomotives tended to be wood burning, not coal burning, for the United States still enjoyed a plenty of wood. That required spark-arresting stacks, for wood sparks and burning fragments

Fig. 8–14. The Old Ironsides
(model)

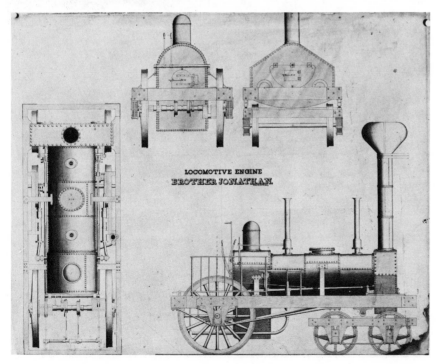

LOCOMOTIVE ENGINE
BROTHER JONATHAN.

Fig. 8–15. The Brother Jonathan

quickly developed a reputation for starting fires along the route. Large numbers of patents were granted for different stack designs. Wood was stored in a tender immediately behind the locomotive. At the front of the locomotive there was usually a cow catcher designed to push impediments out of the way; American railroads were unable to fence off their tracks, and most farms remained unfenced. Usually both a bell and a steam whistle were incorporated—to warn people off the track—and a lantern was placed on front for night travel (fig. 8–17). The Camden and Amboy continued to modify its locomotives to keep up with the latest American inventions. By 1860 the *John Bull* looked more like an

Fig. 8–16. Detail of the John Bull'*s pilot truck*

Fig. 8–17. The Baltimore and Ohio Railroad's No. 232, *built by William Mason and Company, Taunton, Massachusetts, in 1858, was a typical locomotive of the day.*

American locomotive than like the British locomotive it had originally been (fig. 8–18).

As the number of American railroads increased, and as American machine shops developed their abilities to produce large, complex mechanisms like locomotives, more and more railroads bought their locomotives from American manufacturers. American builders produced 35 locomotives in 1835, 200 in 1845, and 500 in 1855. By the 1840s some American builders were exporting locomotives to the Continent and even to Britain. At the same time, American engineers began to build railroad systems overseas (fig. 8–19).

THE RISE OF AMERICAN RAILROADS

Railroads, like all the new business enterprises of the American Industrial Revolution, were more than simply the new technology of which they were built. The businessmen who ran them needed to do more than simply put the technology in place; they had to find a work force to run the machinery, managers to manage the workers and the machines, and a public to buy their product. Railroads drew upon the example of earlier transportation systems to organize their operations, but because they had a much larger work force and because the speed of trains demanded a closer management of that work force, railroads led in the development of managerial control of their workers. They developed systems of accounting, scheduling, and timing to enable them to keep the trains moving safely, and on time.

As one of the first large American railroads, the Camden and Amboy

Fig. 8–18. The John Bull, *1877*

LOCOMOTIVE "JOHN BULL,"

The John Bull *and the Rise of American Railroading*

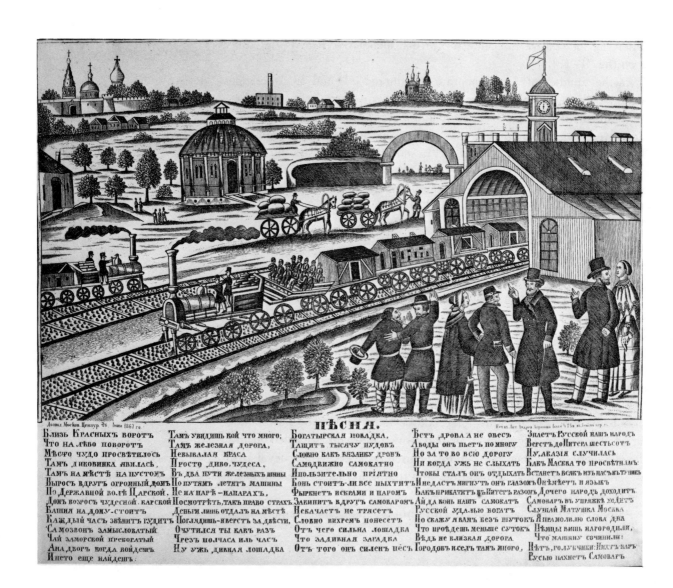

Fig. 8–19. Railroad built by Americans in Russia

was in the forefront of solving these organizational problems. A trained work force was one of its first requirements. The job titles shown on the following page indicate some of the skills employees needed to keep the railroad operating. Working for the railroad paid well; it was skilled work. In 1845 locomotive engineers received $40 a month, firemen $32 a month, for a six-day week; a day's work was one round trip between Camden and Amboy. (They received a bonus of two or three months' pay at the end of the year.) The men worked hard for their pay. The boiler demanded the constant attention of the fireman, and the engineman needed to keep a close eye on the mechanisms of the locomotive and on the track ahead. Both stood on an exposed, open platform while the

Camden and Amboy Railroad Job Titles

superintendent	switch tender
engineer	conductor
bar keeper	brakeman
ticket agent	depot agent
baggage master	steward
bridge tender	mechanic
telegraph operator	woodcutter
guard	transportation
division road superintendent	storekeeper

Fig. 8–20. Conductors on the Michigan Southern and Northern Indiana Railroad, 1864

train ran down the tracks at about thirty miles per hour. Conductors had responsibility not only for passengers but also for ensuring the timely running of the trains (fig. 8–20).

Strictly enforced rules were a second element of railroad organization. On the Camden and Amboy, rules covered the varied systems of baggage checks, when one train should wait for another, which train should back up when two trains met, the speeds for various parts of the line (often a matter of city and state law), rules for ticket sales, schedules, signals, work rules, statistics to be kept, and many other tasks. A system of fines for negligence or for failure to follow the schedule enforced discipline.

Managers, the third element of railroad organization, made certain that each employee knew his job and carried out the rules. Managerial hierarchy was one of the important contributions of railroads to the Industrial Revolution. Although factories and farms had long had managers, it was the railroad, with its large number of employees distributed over a large area and its need for precise timing with the possibility of catastrophe from any error, that demanded a strict system of management.

RAILROADS AND THE AMERICAN INDUSTRIAL REVOLUTION

Railroads became the most important means of transportation in the United States, although roads and river transport continued to grow and canals only slowly lost their support. Everywhere, railroads boomed. By 1840, 3,300 miles of track had been built in the nation, equaling the national canal mileage; by 1850, 8,900 miles. In 1850 the federal gov-

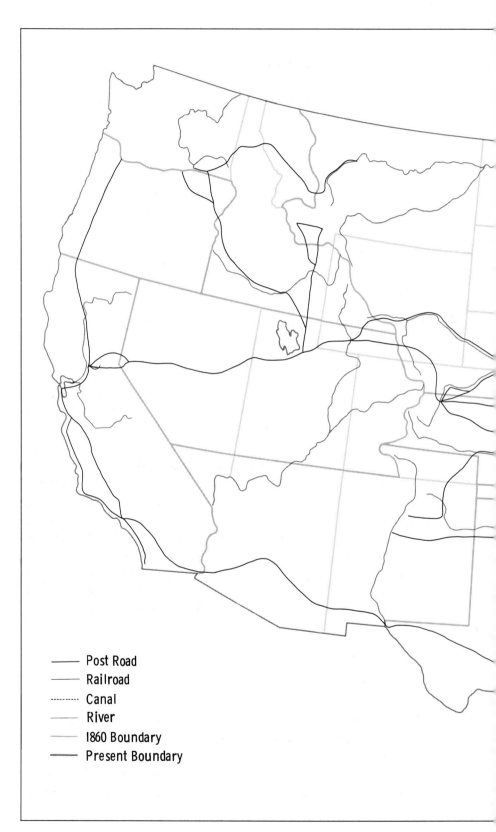

Fig. 8–21. Rivers, roads, canals, and railroads in 1860. Improved transportation was a major cause of American growth to 1860. Roads multiplied, construction and bridging improved, and although paved roads were rare, road travel was important. Steamboat development permitted the use of great river systems, especially the Mississippi. Canal building peaked about 1836, but canals remained important. Railroads grew rapidly. In 1860, more than 30,000 miles of track tied together much of the country, especially the Northeast and Midwest.

— Post Road
— Railroad
-------- Canal
— River
— 1860 Boundary
— Present Boundary

ernment began to encourage construction by giving land grants in the Midwest to railroad companies. By 1857 forty-five railroads had received some 18 million acres. By 1860 more than 30,000 miles of railroad interlaced the North and Midwest (fig. 8–21).

Railroads had fundamental influences on the economy. The claim has been made that railroads created a national economy; certainly they helped it move in that direction. By 1860 railroads had produced interrelated regional economies and had begun to knit these economies together. Cheaper transportation meant greater specialization, for markets of increasing size could support producers who appealed to a small following. The American market became large enough to support an ever-increasing industrial base.

The growth of railroads had a major influence on the growth of industry. Railroads, because they required unprecedented quantities of iron and steel for rails, made the production of iron, steel, and coal into major industries. Iron and steel proved to be the materials, and coal the fuel, required to mechanize and industrialize many lines of production.

Agriculture also was fundamentally changed by the rise of cheap overland transportation. Cheap, large-scale transportation allowed farm-

Fig. 8–22 (a and b). Travel times, 1790 and 1860. The time required for travel continued to decrease with new technologies and continuing construction.

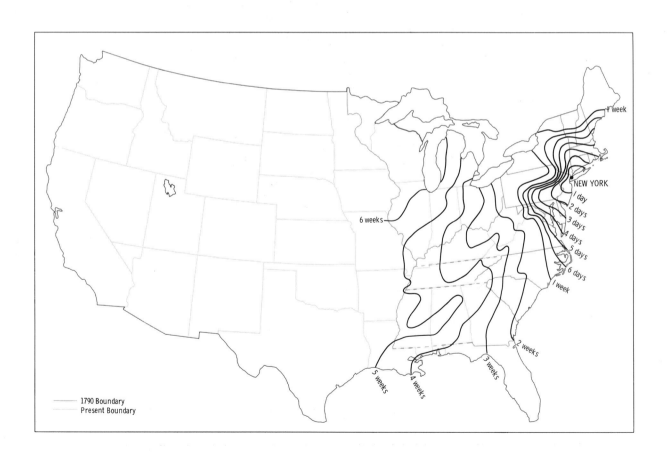

ENGINES OF CHANGE

ers increasing specialization, for they could sell their goods to a large market over great distances.

Railroads brought extensive social and cultural changes to the United States. Cheaper travel permitted more people to travel, tying the country together first into regions and then into a nation. Travel time continued to decrease (fig. 8–22). The growth of cities and towns became increasingly determined by, and oriented toward, the railroads. Cities like Chicago boomed as new territory was colonized along railroad lines. Railroads became powerful political organizations. New Jersey was known as the "Camden and Amboy state" because of that railroad's political influence.

Along with trains came the train crash. Railroad accidents were not common in the earliest years of railroading, for the few trains in use ran slowly. By the 1850s, though, accidents had become all too common: "Everyday the record of mortality is continued. Now it is a collision; now the explosion of a locomotive, and then again the sudden precipitation of an entire train down a steep embankment or perhaps into some river. . . . Every man or woman who steps out of a railway car unhurt does so with a feeling of sensible relief."[13]

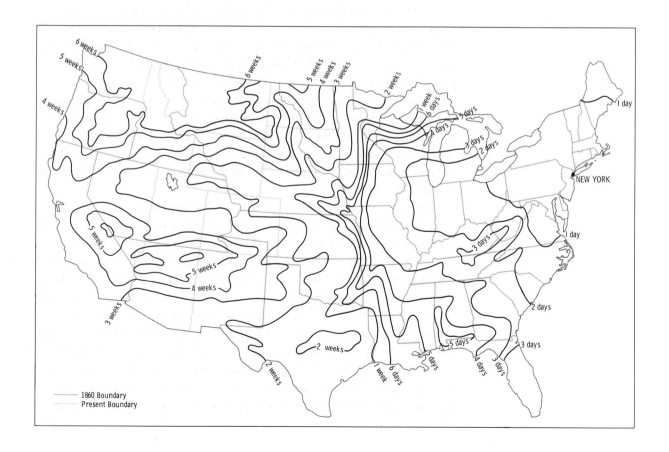

Fig. 8–23. Accident on the Camden and Amboy, Burlington, New Jersey, 1855

The Camden and Amboy had one of the worst records in the country. In 1855 a disastrous accident occurred, killing twenty-four passengers and injuring more than eighty (fig. 8–23). Already unhappy with high prices and poor service, the result of the Camden and Amboy's monopoly, the traveling public was outraged when the company's report on the accident made no apologies and suggested no changes in operations. A pamphlet reflected "the unanimous judgement of the community that the regulation of the Camden and Amboy Company, in the running of their trains, need revision."[14] The president of the railroad responded in a letter to a Philadelphia newspaper. What right, he demanded, did a mere citizen have to set his word "against the experience and knowledge of those who have devoted the best part of their lives to the consideration of railroad subjects"?[15]

The accident and the letter emphasize a continuing dimension of the Industrial Revolution. The *John Bull* conveys most directly the excitement of technological advance and the beginnings of affluence and material plenty. At the same time, however, that it stands as a symbol of greater speed, lower costs, and great benefits to consumer as well as entrepreneur, it also stands for monopoly, privilege, and corruption, and the rise of a technological and corporate elite. Along with new machines came new social arrangements and attitudes. The balance between individual profit, power, and advancement, prime motivations for technological change and industrialization, and the social changes they brought represented an unending struggle. Some groups and individuals were unjustly injured or destroyed as a result of the pursuit of profit in

ENGINES OF CHANGE

Fig. 8–24. George Inness, The Lackawanna Valley, *1855*

industrial development. Still, the benefits were the most evident and universal result.

By 1860 railroads were an accepted part of the American commercial and physical landscape. The country's economy was knit together by the trains that had become a part of everyday life. George Inness, hired to paint the new roundhouse of the Lackawanna Railroad, showed the buildings and tracks as part of a rustic landscape (fig. 8–24). The smoke from the locomotive echoes the cloud behind the church. The machine had become a part of American culture. Railroads were central to the new industrial America.

The Business of Production

"THERE IS NOTHING THAT CAN NOT BE PRODUCED BY MACHINERY,"[1] Samuel Colt, the American arms manufacturer, bragged to the British Parliament in 1851. A few years earlier Daniel Webster had told the Society for the Diffusion of Useful Knowledge in Boston how machinery might best be organized to make things. "Corporations, . . . [a] union of many to form capital," he said, were the best way of "carrying on those operations by which science is applied to art, and come in aid of man's labor in the production of things essential to man's existence."[2]

Machines and businesses were both important parts of the American Industrial Revolution. Mechanization allowed men and women to do more things, in less time, than they could do before. These improvements in technology, the sort of advance recognized by the patent office and recorded in American history as "Yankee ingenuity," rarely took place in a vacuum. Most inventors wanted to make money from their work, and so most inventions were made in response to the needs of the American economy. The interaction of machines and the American economy came increasingly to be mediated by business firms.

EARLY AMERICAN INDUSTRY

The relatively unstructured society of the United States caused American industry to develop differently from its English counterparts. While the latter were often set in their ways, with tradition essential to everyday operations, American business was less constrained by legal and economic precedent. Americans were, in general, more ready to accept new technologies; the British were more likely to make use of specialized workers. One of the foremost British historians of British industrialization has labeled as "Americanisms" the thoughts and deeds of the most enthusiastic technologists and the most energetic and industrious entrepreneurs and workmen of Victorian England.[3] Even in the early nineteenth century Americans were admired for their "get up and go," their willingness to try new things in new ways.

The contrast between British and American industrial styles is apparent in a brief examination of the differences in the development of one industry. English pin manufacture was industrialized long before it was mechanized. In his *Wealth of Nations*, published in 1776, Adam Smith described the extensive division of labor of the British pin industry (fig. 9–1). As many as seventeen people worked on each pin, each performing a single small task with simple tools. In the United States, this degree of specialization was unknown. The more favored approach to production was mechanization. Several Americans invented powered machines that performed all the operations. One of the most automatic machines was invented by John Howe, of New York City, in 1842; it took in brass wire and cut, headed, and pointed it into pins (fig. 9–2). Ironically, the efficiency of a system based on division of labor was a major drawback to the inventing of machines to produce pins, for it required a very great advance in mechanization to compete with a factory producing pins cheaply by specialized hand labor. The American pin industry initially had to ask for tariff protection from the unmechanized British pin industry.

Fig. 9–1. The British style of pin making

Although many industries were established around improvements in machinery, some were not: the garment industry is one example. Some businesses were mechanized in some places and not others: hand looms were common in Philadelphia long after they had been replaced by power looms in Lowell, Massachusetts. Some improvements in mechanization did not lead to industrialization. Some inventions were undertaken specifically to avoid the factories that were part of most American industrialization. And occasional incidents of Luddism—the destruction of machines—occurred when their introduction seemed likely to put people out of work. In general, though, Americans accepted technological change and industrial development. They looked to mechanical invention to make their work easier and improve their standard of living.

One result of the easy acceptance of change that characterized American entrepreneurs and working people was the constant state of flux of American business. Most American entrepreneurs did not specialize in one industry or trade but were ready to take on any commercial enterprise that might make them money. American mechanics did not consider themselves bound to one trade but were willing to shift their energies into new areas of work. In the early years of the United States, most industrial enterprises had low barriers to entry. It was common for craftsmen to drift easily into and out of business: one year working for a master, another year farming, the next year setting up their own shop or factory, only to go bankrupt and head for the cheap land of the West a year or two later.

The American commercial and legal systems encouraged the flexibility necessary for forming a new industrial society. Merchant capitalists traditionally undertook every aspect of their business: buying and selling, wholesale and resale, owning and insuring ships, and banking and insurance enterprises as well. When they invested in industrial undertakings, they were sufficiently flexible to deal with the many surprises of a new environment. The banking system too, though rudimentary, was flexible. Perhaps in part because capital was scarce, entrepreneurs found many ways to raise it, from formal means like bank loans or investment to means as informal as lotteries. The flexibilities of the American legal system allowed companies to fall into and out of bankruptcy, taking advantage of the ease with which creditors could be escaped. In 1857, the first year for which statistics are available (and

Fig. 9–2. Howe pin machine

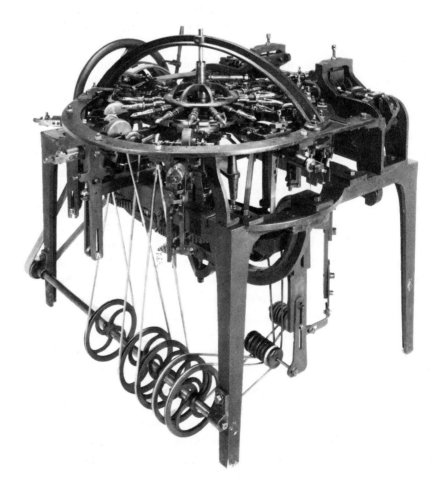

a depression year), business failures averaged 2.42 per 100 firms—a high rate they have never approached since. This flexibility showed other disadvantages as well: it was in part responsible for some of the depressions that racked the country in the antebellum years.

Capital—money—is usually the central need of a new industrial enterprise. In nineteenth-century America an entrepreneur could raise money in several ways. The most common source of funds, especially for small firms, was the entrepreneur's or his family's own pocketbook. Often a journeyman craftsman would save up his earnings to allow him to go into business for himself, moving to a new town to open a shop. Sometimes friends or relatives would put up the needed money. Sometimes a mechanic could rent a mill or factory and then buy it with the money he made from its operation. An 1841 Philadelphia newspaper outlined the alternatives:

A mechanic, without money, wishes to buy leather for making shoes. What are his resources? His intelligence, industry and integrity, which will surely procure credit with the tanner and dealer in leather. . . . A merchant or mechanic would establish a manufactory, and has not sufficient means. What is his expedient? Union with others in a partnership, combined with credit founded upon their intellectual and moral capital.[4]

Once in business, an entrepreneur relied on an extensive network of debt and credit. Banks, though more common in the United States than in England, were of only secondary importance in funding industry, for they usually preferred to lend to merchants rather than manufacturers. In fact, small manufacturers often attacked banks, accusing them of lending only to the rich, and driving small competitors out of business and forcing formerly independent workers to become "mere laborers, mere operatives."[5] Most credit for businesses came from suppliers. Banks played the role of expediters of trade, offering credit for bills drawn by distant customers on out-of-town banks.

While the typical small firm required little capital and could depend on individual or family money, larger firms usually required more money than an individual could supply. This became more true toward the end of the antebellum era, when factories needed more machinery and larger work forces. The solution to the increasing need for capital was a partnership joining the skills and capital of a small group of people, or a corporation, a legal arrangement for the firm in which many individuals invested in one company. The corporation allowed larger firms, and, as important, it allowed the development of professional management.

The corporation had its start early in the American colonies. Some corporations, among them the Virginia Company and the Massachusetts Bay Company, were chartered in England for settlement and trading purposes. Other companies, for example the Proprietors of Boston Pier, were chartered to provide services to towns. Originally, to receive the advantages of the corporate organization, it was necessary that the corporation serve the public interest in some manner.

The industrial corporation was rare, however, even late in the eighteenth century. The Society for Encouraging Useful Manufactures, formed in 1791 to undertake diversified manufacturing at Paterson, New Jersey, was one of the first. Its failure, and the great outcry against its governmental connections, helped to dampen the enthusiasm for industrial corporations. Only in 1809 was a general incorporation statute passed in Massachusetts, and later in other states. These statutes allowed the easy formation of manufacturing corporations for private purposes. After 1820, when the Supreme Court ruled in the *Dartmouth College* case that corporate charters were protected contracts, the corporate form became increasingly popular.

The Waltham textile mills and the northern New England mills that followed were the first successful large industrial corporations in the United States. Railroads, with their great need for capital, also took the form of corporations. Despite opposition from farmers and small businessmen, many states granted stockholders in corporations limited liability in the 1820s and 1830s, freeing them from responsibility for the corporation's debts. This encouraged the corporate form of organization. By the time of the Civil War there were many manufacturing corporations, large and small, in the United States. The corporate form became more common in the United States than in Europe, where companies wanting the protections of incorporation had to make special application for it.

The basic advantage of the corporation was the increased capital it allowed a business. Companies with larger capital could invest in more machinery, and machinery was quickly perceived to be essential to industrial success. Another set of advantages of large enterprises stemmed from the greater specialization they made possible. Not only could they take advantage of increased division of labor, but they could also organize a managerial hierarchy. The Industrial Revolution saw the growth of increasingly large business firms.

Businesses both large and small invested heavily in machinery. An American ideology that favored mechanization, part of the democratic heritage of the nation, became widespread. Alexis de Tocqueville, in his 1835 analysis of *Democracy in America*, declared that Americans were addicted to practical science. They wanted to make money from their science, seeking "every new method that leads by a shorter road to wealth, every machine that spares labor, every instrument that diminishes the cost of production."[6] Ambitious men believed that the way to wealth was through mechanization, and that the way to mechanization was invention. The superintendent of the eighth census of 1860 restated common beliefs when he lauded the importance of invention:

The mechanic arts—particularly in our country, where they are most diffused, and all but universal—appear to contribute more directly than any others to the general comfort and improvement of the people. . . . The acquisition and diffusion of knowledge, the means of intercommunication and transportation, the comforts, enjoyments, and security of the fireside, and even the honor and integrity of the nation itself, are dependent upon the skill and enterprise of the manufacturer and the mechanician.[7]

Mechanization was encouraged by the economic resources of the United States. Waterpower and later steam power were cheap and available, and so American business turned to waterwheel and steam engine to drive machinery. Labor was scarce and thus expensive, and so machinery was substituted where possible.

The United States was well endowed with waterpower sites, and its supplies of wood and coal for steam engines were unsurpassed. Waterpower was used from the beginning of American settlement. Sawmills and gristmills throughout the colonies depended on waterpower, making use of the power of tides, streams, and rivers. Most counties had scores of mill sites. The 1840 census listed some 66,000 mills in the country: 23,700 gristmills, 31,650 sawmills, 2,600 fulling mills, and 8,200 tanneries—a ratio of one mill for every 245 people. Chester County, Pennsylvania, was a typical developed area. In 1810, when the county had a population of 40,000, the United States census found 390 waterpowered mills: 29 fulling mills, 11 paper mills, 1 gunpowder mill, 12 clover mills, 148 gristmills, and 189 sawmills. These mills, mechanical outposts in a rural countryside, were often the precursors of industrial development. In 1849, when the owner of one of Chester County's sawmills decided to sell the site, he advertised it as "one of the best for manufacturing purposes in Chester County and well worthy of the attention of capitalists."[8]

Waterpower was turned to useful work in several ways. Some mills used simple tub wheels, a horizontal wheel on a vertical axis that could be hooked directly to a millstone for grinding wheat. Undershot wheels were another simple way of making use of the power of falling water. Overshot wheels and breast wheels, though providing greater efficiency, required not only a greater fall of water but also more technical ability in design and construction.

Deciding which type of waterwheel was the most appropriate for a given site was the work of the millwright (fig. 9–3). He took into account a variety of considerations when he was hired to build a mill. Some were geographic: the amount of water in the stream, the height of the fall of water, the terrain. Others were technical: what he knew how to build, what materials were available, and how much power was needed. Still others were economic. Millwrights were among the most skilled craftsmen of early nineteenth-century America.

In the 1830s and 1840s the turbine gained wide use. The turbine made use of the force of the water either in impact (the impulse turbine) or as it exited (the reaction turbine) to turn a wheel with many blades at a very high speed. It developed from a combination of theoretical French investigations and practical American experimentation. The first successful turbine was invented by Benoît Fourneyron in 1827. Americans including Calvin Wing and Samuel Howd came to similar adaptations of the waterwheel in the 1830s. The French and American traditions culminated in the theoretical and experimental work of James B. Francis, chief engineer of the waterpower for the Lowell, Massachusetts, textile mills (fig. 9–4). By 1860 turbines, especially the Francis turbine, had begun to replace the waterwheel in providing industrial power.

The United States made wider use of waterpower than any other nation, in part because of the geography of the country and in part because of the popular inclination toward mechanization. Especially in the early decades of the nineteenth century, waterpower helped make American industry boom. The widespread availability of cheap waterpower had important effects on the style of American industry. Combined with the high cost of labor, the low price of power meant that machines were generally run faster here than in Great Britain. This helped to increase further the American appetite for mass production. The location of most waterpower sites in the countryside, far from commercial centers where workers lived, helped to reinforce the paternalistic tradition of American industry. Factory owners often felt that they had to provide housing and a company store when the factory was located out of easy reach of cities and towns.

In 1860 waterpower provided about one-half of all industrial power. While some mills and factories, especially on the frontier, used animal power, it was steam that presented waterpower's main competition. The steam engine became increasingly competitive with the waterwheel and the turbine. The rapid expansion of use of the steam engine was driven by economics; the price of coal dropped sharply in the 1830s when canals and railroads opened the Pennsylvania coal fields, and inventors increased the efficiency of steam engines.

Coal-fueled steam engines were much more flexible than waterpower. Factories powered by steam did not have to be built on streams and rivers but could be located in cities. Steam changed the geography of manufacturing in this country, for the old Northwest, deficient in waterpower, was well endowed with coal. In 1838 a government census

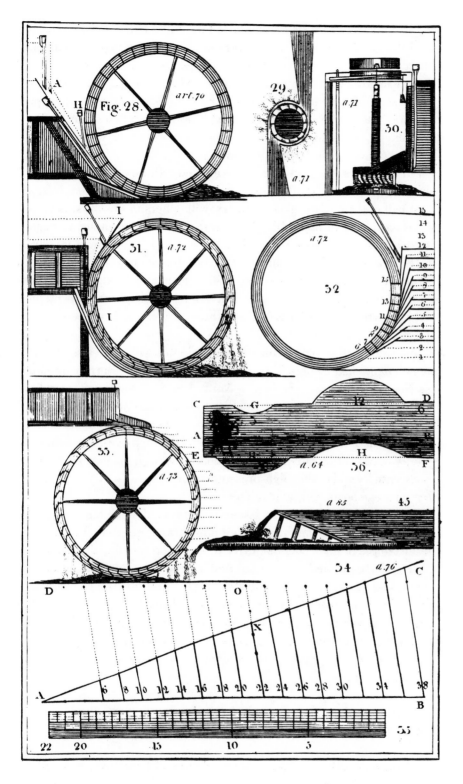

Fig. 9–3. The types of waterwheels, shown in Oliver Evans's The Young Mill-Wright and Miller's Guide: *28, undershot wheel; 29 and 30, tub wheel; 31, breast wheel; and 33, overshot wheel.*

counted almost 2,000 steam engines in the United States. The state that used the greatest amount of steam power was, surprisingly, Louisiana, where almost every sugar mill was equipped with a steam engine. The second-ranking state was Pennsylvania, where steam engines were used for all sorts of industrial enterprises. Even in New England, where waterpower was plentiful, water-powered factories installed steam engines as backups, for times when water was low or frozen or when it was so high it kept the wheel from spinning.

Pittsburgh was the first large American city whose industry was based on steam power. In 1838 steam engines in the city numbered 133, almost half of them in the glass industry, with others in sawmills, machine shops, and iron rolling mills. Pittsburgh was a center of steam engine construction as well as use. The F. & W. M. Faber Company, established in 1834, was one of many small engine builders in the city (fig. 9–5). In 1860 the company employed thirty-five men and produced $60,000 worth of steam engines and other machinery. Its shop, which contained eighteen lathes, three furnaces, and three forges, was itself powered by steam.

Innovations in steam engine design made this wide use possible. The steam engine had come a long way since 1753 when Schuyler imported his Newcomen engine, the first in North America. American steamboat and factory owners imported English low-pressure steam engines and constructed similar engines on their own. American inventors were in the forefront of the technological advance of the high-pressure steam engine. Worked out by Oliver Evans, among others, in the first years of the nineteenth century, the high-pressure steam engine was widely used, first on steamboats and later in factories.

Thousands of patents were issued to improve the efficiency of steam engines so that they might get more power from less fuel. Perhaps the best example of this economic drive to invention was the challenge that George Corliss issued to potential purchasers of his engines: he offered to give them away for free in exchange for the fuel savings his customers gained from his patented improvements! The machinery to capture the power of falling water, especially the turbine, improved too, but its efficiency did not improve nearly as drastically as did that of the steam engine. The steam engine soon became the dominant prime mover in American industry.

FACTORY MANAGEMENT AND LABOR

Technological advances like those exemplified by improvements in waterwheels and steam engines were essential to the American Industrial

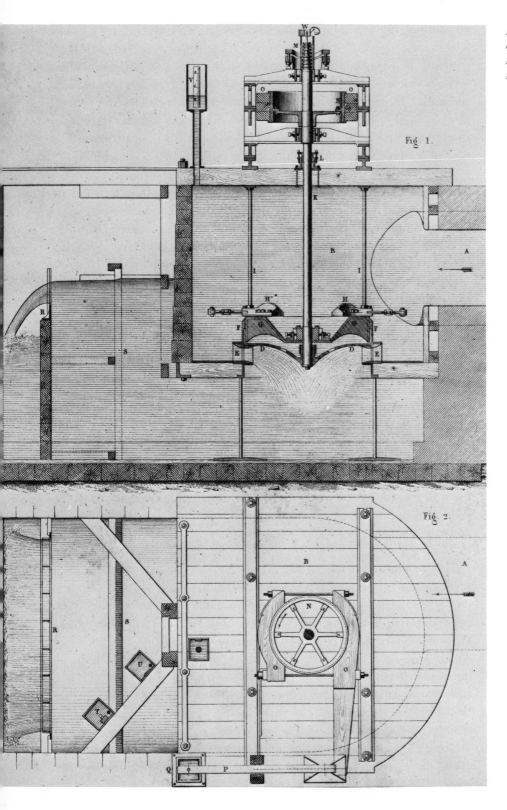

Fig. 9–4. Turbine at the Boott cotton mills in Lowell, Massachusetts, designed by James Francis

Fig. 1

Fig. 2

Revolution. Some early industrialists, though, made the claim that their success was due not to their triumphs of technology but rather to their triumphs of organization. Andrew Ure, an English authority on the factory system, wrote in 1835 of the founding father of the mechanized textile mill: "To devise and administer a successful code of factory discipline, suited to the necessities of factory diligence, was the Herculean enterprise, the noble achievement of Arkwright!"[9] Administration and discipline were as essential to the rise of industry as was machinery.

Small factories were generally managed by their owners, who were usually skilled workmen. When factories got larger, owners could no longer manage the work themselves and hired professional managers to fill that function. These managers scheduled and accounted for work, oversaw the daily activities of the labor force, and kept books showing the financial accounts of the factory.

New England textile mills were the first factories large enough to require full-time managers. In addition to salaried men responsible for the overall operations of the mill, other men were in charge of managing the mechanics who kept the machinery in operating order, and overseers handled the discipline and direction of the women who tended the machinery.

In the 1840s railroads, with their property and work force spread out over many miles, developed an increasingly elaborate managerial system. Any error in timing could result in a disastrous accident, so railroads were in the forefront in the rise of management. Each geographic division of a railroad had its own functional managers—an assistant master of transportation, a roadmaster, and a senior mechanic. Above them all was the master of transportation, the master mechanic, and the general superintendent. The current-day managerial structure of line and staff management was first established by the Pennsylvania Railroad in 1857.

This beginning of the managerial revolution did not occur without protest. Many owners of mills and factories hesitated to hand over authority to managers. Many artisans believed that factories with absentee ownership and hired managers could not but fail. The increasing hierarchy necessary for large industrial enterprises fired the wrath of some Americans, for it seemed to them that these new hierarchies, and the increased division of labor that usually accompanied them, would destroy the equality they had fought for and won in the victory over the British in the Revolution. The first century of the American Republic was the time when inventors, entrepreneurs, and employees worked out the balance of industrialization and mechanization. Each group influenced the emerging practices of management of machines, money, and labor.

Alexis de Tocqueville applauded the rapid acceptance of machinery in America but worried about the growth of the factory system. He thought that the democratic surge to industry would, paradoxically, lead America away from democracy and back to aristocracy, fearing that by creating a class of unskilled machine tenders on the one hand, and a class of "masters" who surveyed and directed the whole operation on the other, industry might eventually destroy democracy. How, he asked, could a man who spent all day heading pins be expected to help rule a nation? The owner of the factory was the "administrator of a vast empire." What sort of democratic relationship could he have with his workers? De Tocqueville warned against the growth of a "manufacturing aristocracy." [10]

American workers made bold use of what they saw as the tensions between democracy and industry. Adopting the rhetoric of the American Revolution, striking Lowell mill girls called themselves "daughters of freemen" and their employers "purse-proud aristocrats." [11] Workers in New York City held their craft parades on the Fourth of July. In speeches they combined the ideology of republicanism and craft tradition: Philadelphia shoemakers, responding to complaints that their organization was a "combination," or conspiracy, responded that "the Declaration of Independence was the work of a combination." Seth Luther, leader of the Workingman's Party in Massachusetts, used the rhetoric of the Revolution in his *Address to the Workingmen of New England:* "Let us be de-

Fig. 9–5. Engine built by F. & W. M. Faber, c. 1850

termined no longer to be deceived by the cry of those who produce *nothing* and enjoy *all*, and who *insultingly* term us—the farmers, the mechanics, and laborers—the LOWER ORDERS—while the DECLARATION OF INDEPENDENCE asserts that 'ALL MEN ARE CREATED EQUAL.'"[12]

Workers attacked the "luxury" of merchants and factory owners, which they saw as part of a European aristocratic tradition that opposed the freedom of the American tradition. They argued that the artisan was the basis of American democracy.

Part of their opposition to the new factory derived from the change that it brought about in the nature of work. Craft work differed from factory work. Preindustrial work culture was much less disciplined, much more irregular. Workers were used to working on their own initiative, and at their own pace. Periods of intense labor alternated with idleness. Drinking and eating on the job were accepted as part of the normal course of work.

Industrial work, with its powered machines and great capital investment, could not depend on this undisciplined work style. The pace appropriate to small shops was not suited to large factories. As the new philosophy of industry put it, time was money. In the course of the American Industrial Revolution, workers grew accustomed to the new standards, although new immigrants from unindustrialized areas of Europe had to be taught the same lessons when they went to work in American factories.

Workers responded to these standards in a variety of ways. Some accepted them; some simply quit their jobs and headed west. Some went to work in smaller factories where they had more control over their time, or saved up their money so they could buy their own shop and be their own boss. Others responded to the increasing size and hierarchy of American industrial enterprises by organizing workers to resist what they saw as the increasingly onerous demands of business.

The American labor movement grew out of labor guilds and benevolent societies founded to provide insurance and mutual aid. These craft unions occasionally struck for better pay and fewer hours' work, although until 1842 trade union activities were considered a conspiracy, and strikes were illegal. Unable to strike successfully, many workers turned to politics. Workingmen's parties had their origins in the late 1820s, when property requirements for voters and officeholders were removed. In big cities throughout the Northeast "mechanics" organized to support the ten-hour movement, free public schools, the abolition of imprisonment for debt, the protection of wages by lien laws, and the control of banks. For the most part, unions were concerned only with local issues, usually reacting to the actions of factory owners. No national labor unions emerged until after the Civil War.

The coming of organized labor, along with increased mechanization, the increased use of inanimate sources of power, and increased division of labor and greater managerial hierarchy, were reflected in the statistical snapshot taken on the eve of the Civil War by the eighth census of 1860. According to that census, the United States had more than 140,000 manufacturing establishments, with a total amount invested of just over $1 billion. These establishments produced almost $2 billion worth of goods, almost double that of 1850—a per capita production of $60.61. More than a million men and 250,000 women worked in these factories. For an average eleven-hour day, they earned, on average, about $1.00. (Men earned about twice as much as women.) The largest industry, by number of employees, was textiles; some 115,000 men and women worked at producing cotton goods, some 40,000 at woolen goods. Boots and shoes were second, with 123,000 employees, men's clothing third, with 115,000, and lumber fourth, with 75,000 employees. There were 1,562 banks in the country, with a capital of almost $500 million.

Compare these statistics with the state of American industry fifty years earlier, in 1810. Total production was about $115 million, a per capita output of about $16. (There was substantial deflation between 1810 and 1860: in 1860 dollars, 1810 production was $162 million, per capita production $22.60.) The four leading industries—leather goods, iron and steel, flour milling, and food products—each contributed about $14 million of that 1810 total. Other major categories of products were machinery, wood products, hats, and chemicals. Textiles did not make the list of major industries; most cloth production was still done in the home. The eighty-eight banks had a capital of only $23 million.

In the fifty years from 1810 to 1860, the United States had moved toward its role as an industrial nation. In 1860 it was second only to Britain in industrial output. It is important, though, to keep the figures in perspective. The population of the country in 1860 was over 31 million, the total work force just over 10.5 million. About half of the men and women who worked were farmers. The second largest group worked in the service industries. Manufacturing was third, followed by transportation and trade. Manufacturing enterprises comprised about 60 percent of the business concerns in the country.

These industrial establishments were spread throughout the country, with most of them in New England and the Middle Atlantic states. These states had about 70,000 manufacturing establishments, where some 900,000 men and women worked—almost two-thirds of America's industrial work force. New York was the most industrialized state, with more than 23,000 factories and more than 220,000 factory workers.

Pennsylvania was close behind, and Massachusetts was third on the list. At the other end of this tabulation, with the smallest amount of industry, were the new states of the West and Midwest and the southern states. The former were still frontier; the latter, mostly agricultural.

The differences in the ratios of capital to number of employees and number of factories are revealing of the differences in the industrialization of each of the states; they also cast light on the varying and complicated nature of industrialization and mechanization in America. Massachusetts and Rhode Island had the most workers per factory, each averaging twenty-seven. They also had the largest capital investment per factory. An average Rhode Island factory made use of an investment of over $20,000. Philadelphia and New York, every bit as industrialized as the New England states, had much smaller factories, averaging only about ten employees each. The average New York factory had about $8,000 invested in it.

These figures reflect, very loosely, not only the differences in the type of industrialization experienced by different sections of the country, but also the varying requirements of different industries. Rhode Island, for example, had many textile mills; New York had many garment shops; Pennsylvania had many small textile shops; Massachusetts had both textile mills and shoe factories. The varieties of factories reflected an economic, social, and cultural balance of labor, machinery, and management.

Geography partially explains the different directions and degrees of industrialization. The South depended heavily on its cash crops of cotton and tobacco and invested its capital in land and slaves. Skilled mechanics tended not to immigrate there, for little work was available to them. Northerners, on the other hand, were faced with less profitable agriculture and invested more heavily in trade. Trade demanded cities, where craftsmen could find ready markets for their skills. In the South, in part because of the predominance of tobacco and cotton farming, cities were less common. The lack of waterpower also discouraged industry in the South; its rivers did not provide the falls necessary for waterwheels.

The range of industry reflects the cultural diversity as well as the great variety of resources in the United States. At the start of the Civil War in 1860, the United States had undergone a vast range of industrial development, from heavily mechanized factories of New England to New York factories dependent on handwork, from iron plantations of Pennsylvania to craft shops manned by slaves in the South, from steam-powered glass works of Pittsburgh to still largely independent family farms of the frontier. Samuel Colt's promise that all work could be done by machines was made in good faith, but it remained a dream, not an accomplishment, in 1860.

Machine Shops: Machines to Make Machines

MACHINE SHOPS ARE CENTRAL TO THE STORY OF PRODUCTION, FOR ALmost every industry, every factory, mill, or home workshop required machines, which someone had to make. Machinists working in machine shops made the machines industry needed.

A machine shop contains hand tools and machine tools, a broad category of powered machines that cut and shape metal. It includes cutting tools—tools with sharp metal knives that cut away at pieces of metal; forming tools—tools that apply pressure to a piece of metal to shape it; and tools that employ a variety of other processes—grinding, scraping, and so forth. Machine tools are used in conjunction with a variety of hand processes to produce precisely shaped, accurately sized, and nicely finished elements of metal machines of all types.

Americans did not always have the abilities or tools needed to make machines of metal. Josiah Hornblower, who brought the first steam engine to America in 1753, was aware of the lack of machinery and skilled machinists in America. He brought with him not only several men to help him erect the engine but also duplicate and even triplicate parts of the engine, in case of accidents. Several times he had to send to England for replacement parts. No one in America could do the casting, forging, and machine shop work needed to produce the parts of a steam engine.

The lack of ability to make machines delayed American industrialization. In 1791 the owners of a cotton mill in Beverly, Massachusetts, claimed that "a want of skill in constructing the machinery" was the "principal impediment to our success."[1] When Samuel Slater wanted his textile machines built in the same year, even in an industrial town like Pawtucket there were no machine shops: he needed the services of a clockmaker, an iron founder, a blacksmith, a woodworker, and a hand card maker.

Americans quickly acquired the skills they needed to make machinery. Many British machinists emigrated here, to take advantage of new opportunities in America: between 1773 and 1775 some eighty-seven British machine makers immigrated to the United States, between 1824 and 1831 more than a thousand. By 1860 American machinists were among the best in the world. Few problems were beyond their skills. Specialized machine tools were available for many types of work. American machine tools were exported, even to England, long the leader in machine tool production.

The products of American machine shops, too, were exported to Europe. Among these products were railroad locomotives, perhaps the most magnificent product of the nineteenth century. In 1860 an American locomotive was a grand beast, standing twelve feet high, its machinery representing the peak of mechanical ingenuity of the day. Almost every inch of it, every pound of metal, every volume and every surface, was produced using machine tools. The story of the construction of a locomotive explains the work that went on in a machine shop.

A typical mid-nineteenth-century locomotive weighed about 44,000 pounds. About 2,700 pounds of the locomotive was wood, the rest metal. A locomotive contained about 24,500 pounds of cast iron, mostly in its cylinders, drivers, wheels, and fittings; 9,200 pounds of plate and sheet iron in its boiler and firebox; 12,000 pounds of roller bar iron; 7,500 pounds of hammered iron for frame, rods, and pins; 1,400 pounds of steel springs; 4,200 pounds of copper in the firebox, tubes, and tube sheets; and 500 pounds of other metals.

Altogether, a locomotive was built from about 5,000 separate parts. Each part of the locomotive was formed to a specific shape using a few basic methods. Some parts were cast; some were machined; some were forged; some were pressed. Each operation required special tools and skilled operators. Once formed on power machines, many of the pieces were hand finished, put into a vise and filed to an exact fit. Finally, all were fitted together, secured with bolts or rivets, and the locomotive was complete, ready to be delivered to the railroad that had ordered it (fig. 10–1). It took about one month—30,000 man-hours—to build a locomotive.

THE NORRIS LOCOMOTIVE WORKS

The Norris Locomotive Works in Philadelphia was one of the premier locomotive builders of mid-nineteenth-century America (fig. 10–2). In that company's five buildings, one of the largest industrial complexes in the city, some 600 men used a vast range of machine tools to build sixty-four locomotives there in 1855.

The first step in making a locomotive, or any piece of mechanism, was to draw up plans for each of the parts. Each piece of metal in the engine,

Fig. 10–1. Amoskeag
Manufacturing Company locomotive
and tender, 1851

whether of brass or iron, was drawn to scale, or full-size on a chalk
board. Pieces that needed strength in compression—that supported a
lot of weight resting on them—were cast (fig. 10–3). The first step was
to make them three-dimensional in full-size wooden patterns. Next,
these wooden patterns were reproduced in metal. To do this, each pattern was carefully embedded in special sand contained in a wooden box.
After the sand was pounded so as to catch every detail of the pattern, the
box was opened and the pattern removed. Molten iron was poured into
the mold in the sand left by the pattern. When the iron cooled it solid-
ified, reproducing in exact detail the original wooden pattern.

Casting was only one of several ways that metal parts were given their
initial, rough shape. Parts that needed to be extremely strong, or that
were subject to pulling forces—for example, the frames and the axles of
the locomotive—were not cast. They were forged. Blacksmiths pounded
iron with hand hammers or held pieces of iron beneath a giant steam
hammer that pounded the metal into shape (figs. 10–4, 10–5).

From the foundry or the forge the castings or forgings were taken to
the machine shop, the heart of the Norris Locomotive Works (fig. 10–6).
It was an enormous building, packed with every type of machine tool. A

Machine Shops: Machines to Make Machines

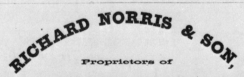

RICHARD NORRIS. HENRY L. NORRIS.

RICHARD NORRIS & SON,

Proprietors of

NORRIS' LOCOMOTIVE WORKS

BUSH HILL, PHILADELPHIA.

Established in 1831.

HEAVY

FORGINGS,

IRON

AND

BRASS

Castings

CHILLED

ENGINE

AND

Car Wheels,

WROUGHT

IRON

Car Wheels.

View of Works on Seventeenth and Hamilton Streets, Philadelphia.

THESE WORKS, having been greatly enlarged, and supplied with new and approved Tools, are prepared to execute orders to any extent, for

LOCOMOTIVES,

Of any Arrangement, Capacity or Weight Required.

In Design, Materials and Workmanship, the Engines produced at these works are offered in comparison with any others made in this country. Also

HEAVY FORGINGS,

From tough Scrap Iron, drawn under Steam Hammers, to any form required, and to any size, under 24 inches, Square or Round.

The facilities possessed by these works for furnishing heavy forged shapes, are believed to be unsurpassed. Special attention given to the Forging of

LOCOMOTIVE FRAMES,

With Pedestals welded in; AXLES, CONNECTING RODS, and other similar Locomotive shapes, all of which will be accurately Forged to sketches or patterns, and warranted in soundness and strength.

Wrought Iron Railway Wheels,

For Locomotives, or Express Passenger Cars, and of any size or weight required.

Chilled Engine and Car Wheels,

Of any size, and of Plate or Spoke Form. These Wheels possess an important improvement in the provision made for equal contraction in cooling, whereby the Wheel suffers no strain in any part.

IRON & BRASS CASTINGS,

To any weight or pattern, and from the best American Stock.

LOCOMOTIVE TIRES,

From LOWMOOR IRON, bent and welded to any specified diameter; and to fit accurately without boring.

A Norris First-class Passenger Engine.

A Norris First-class Freight Locomotive.

From the magnitude of their Establishment, and with a larger extent of Shops and equipment of Tools and Machinery than any other Works, they are enabled to meet demands for their work commensurate to their facilities, which are fully equal to THREE COMPLETE LOCOMOTIVES every six days. LIBERAL TERMS extended, and WORK GUARANTEED.

The whole number of Locomotives constructed at these Works up to January 1, 1856, was EIGHT HUNDRED AND FORTY-THREE, of which number ONE HUNDRED AND SEVENTEEN were on foreign account, having been shipped to the following countries:—England, France, Austria, Prussia, Italy, Belgium, South America, Cuba, &c. Except in a single instance of one engine only, the NORRIS' WORKS is the only establishment in the New World that has furnished motive power for their elder brethren on the other side of the Atlantic.

[For further particulars, see letter-press.

Published by A. J. PERKINS. (34) Printed by HENRY B. ASHMEAD.

Fig. 10–2. Advertising card, Norris Works

Fig. 10–3. Foundry at the Norris Works

Fig. 10–4. Nasmyth steam hammer, shown in the Smithsonian Institution's 1876 exhibition

Fig. 10–5. Forge shop at the Norris Works

Fig. 10–6. First story of the machine shop, the Norris Works

steam engine at one end of the building powered the shafting that ran down the center of each room near the ceiling. From pulleys on the shafts, leather belts stretched to pulleys attached to each machine tool. The overhead shafts ran all the time during working hours; each machine tool had a clutch that served as an on-off switch. To turn on a machine, the machinist pushed on a lever that slid the leather belt from an idler pulley to a pulley that turned with the shaft, thus joining the machine with the power of the steam engine.

In the machine shops the castings and forgings as well as round and square stock pieces of iron (produced in rolling mills, where hot iron was squeezed into shape by rollers) were cut to size and their surfaces smoothed. Round pieces—wheels, cylinders, pistons—were mounted on a lathe (fig. 10–7). The lathe spun the piece of metal; a sharpened steel cutter applied to the edge produced a perfectly cylindrical finished product of exactly correct size. A cutter applied to the inside produced a finely finished interior cavity. Lathes were the most common machine tool. The Norris Works had seventy-three lathes, more than all other tools combined.

Fig. 10–7. A slide lathe

A planing machine did for flat pieces what the lathe did for cylindrical ones (fig. 10–8). These machines—Norris had eight of them— cut flat items like engine frames, crossheads and crosshead guides, and air pumps to the proper size, and gave them the necessary smooth finish. Instead of being turned, as on the lathe, the castings were fastened to a bed that moved back and forth beneath a cutter. In each cycle the blade removed a small scraping of iron. An automatic mechanism then moved the blade slightly to take off another scraping. Before planers became common in the 1830s, this sort of work was done by hand by skilled workers using chisels, scrapers, and files.

Fig. 10–8. Planing machine with revolving tool box

Lathes and planers were the essential machine tools of a mid-nineteenth-century shop. The Norris Works' other tools were special-purpose items, or items used for more detailed work. In addition to its eight general-purpose planers, Norris had specialized planer-like machines: slotters and shapers. A shaper was similar to a planer, except that the tool and not the work moved; it was used to cut strap joints, cranks, and other uneven surfaces. A slotter was nothing but a shaper stood on end, so the tool moved vertically; it cut keyways and other details on the frame of the locomotive (fig. 10–9). Gear cutters and screw-cutting machines reduced the enormous labor of making those parts using only general machine tools or hand tools.

Fig. 10–9. Large slotting engine

Most machine tools were self-acting. That is, they worked largely on their own, requiring attention only to be set up, to be stopped, or to have the work or tools changed. The cutter was attached to a drive screw or a chain mechanism that moved it along the work at the correct rate. Even though largely automatic, each machine was closely attended by a machinist. He carefully chose the cutting tool and set the cutting speed and depth of cut. While the tool was working he watched it, occasionally lubricating the tool at the point where it cut the metal. He then measured the finished product, to make sure that the part was cut to the exact dimensions needed.

The self-acting machine tools were the heart of a machine shop, but they were not its head, or its soul. Tools in the hands of a skilled work-

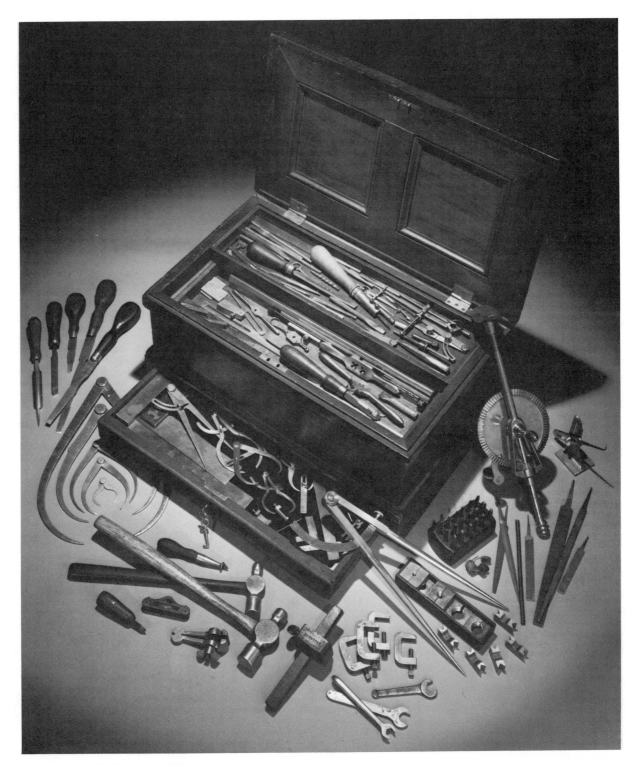

Fig. 10–10. Machinist's tool chest

man were essential in every aspect of the work. The skills of the machinist were reflected in his tools, and the final products of the shop were a direct outcome of the handwork of the machinist. His tool chest was a machinist's most prized possession: the tools in it made possible the precision work necessary to shape metal (fig. 10–10). A machinist's tools included dividers, calipers, and rules for measuring, hammers, hand drills, and scrapers and files for smoothing and fitting.

Exact fit was essential to the work of the machinist. A machinist spent much of his time filing roughly machined parts to fit; the Norris Works had some 200 vises used to hold work while machinists filed it for final assembly. The close fit of each piece with many others demanded accurate measurement. Until the 1840s, though, simple wooden rules like those used by carpenters were widely used in machine shops. Parts that needed extreme accuracy were measured with calipers, gauges, and models; the machinist took a measurement from a precise original, setting his calipers to the proper size, and then applying the calipers to the copy he was making. If multiple copies were needed, then gauges were used. The machinist held these accurately shaped pieces of metal to the part to show him whether it was accurately dimensioned. Not until after the Civil War did machinists have micrometers and other measuring tools that allowed them accurately and easily to measure the work they did (fig. 10–11).

Not every part of a locomotive was finished in the machine shop. Some metal parts were cut to size with giant shears and forced into shape by heavy presses. The boiler shop at the Norris Works had shears that cut iron plates half an inch thick, punches that made holes for rivets, and brakes for forming the sheets to the proper shape (fig. 10–12). The boilers were then riveted together—a hard and noisy job.

An advanced system of management was required to hold a shop the size of the Norris Locomotive Works together and keep work flowing as it should. Like other factories, the Norris Works published rules for its employees (fig. 10–13). It also had complicated systems of paperwork that allowed the managers to give orders to employees working throughout the buildings. Most of the locomotives the Norris shop made were of a standard design. A master file was kept of the number, name, dimension, and character of each engine about to be built. From that description six printed forms were completed, one for each division of the shop. By means of these forms, a contemporary observer wrote, "each division, besides being furnished with the plans and specifications, is presented with the orders in which the exact size and dimensions of the most minute article is given in detail."[2] Even with such precise directions, the machinists who made each part had to know a great deal about the details of their work (fig. 10–14).

Fig. 10–11. Brown and Sharpe micrometer #1

Fig. 10–12. Boiler shop at the Norris Works

Some shops the size of the Norris Works depended on a system of inside contractors to manage the work. An inside contractor was a highly skilled machinist who contracted with the company to produce parts in the shop, using the company's machines and materials. He paid his subordinates out of the sum the company paid him. Because they made money by lowering their costs, inside contractors were responsible for many new tools and new ways of doing work.

SMALL MACHINE SHOPS

Most machine shops spent less effort on management than the Norris Locomotive Works, for they were much smaller. There were thousands of small machine shops across the country. Many of them were part of some industrial enterprise. Others were independent, doing work on contract for anyone who would pay for it. All of them used tools similar to (though usually smaller than) those at the Norris Works. Most important, like all machine shops, they depended on the skills of the men who worked in them.

Augustus Alfred, a machinist in Harwinton, Connecticut (in the

Fig. 10–13. Work rules at the
Taunton Locomotive Works, one of
Norris's competitors

RULES AND REGULATIONS.

TEN HOURS LABOR SHALL CONSTITUTE A DAY'S WORK from 7 A. M. to 12 M., and from 1 P. M. to 6 P. M. except Saturdays, when work will stop at 5 o'clock P. M. Every man will be in his place promptly at 7 A. M. and 1 P. M., and NOT LEAVE WORK until the time above specified.

WORKMEN FINDING IT NECESSARY TO ABSENT THEMSELVES will make application to their Foreman. When unexpectedly detained from work, notice must be sent to the Foreman immediately. Regularity on the part of all persons employed will be indispensable.

EVERY WORKMAN, WHEN HE HAS USED A TOOL SUFFICIENTLY, must immediately return it to its place. No person will be allowed to accumulate Tools designed for the general use of the shop in their drawers or boxes. The strictest care and economy in the use of Tools, Files, and material of every description is required. Old Files should be returned to the Tool-room before new ones are taken out.

WORKMEN WILL NOT TAKE VISITORS INTO THE SHOP without permission from the Office. Reading, Smoking, and unnecessary conversation during working hours is prohibited.

EACH WORKMAN WILL KEEP HIS OWN TIME on cards furnished by the Company, accurately, which shall correspond to time on cards accompanying the different pieces of work. He shall also give his time to the Time-keeper each day.

WORKMEN WILL RECEIVE THEIR PAY EACH THURSDAY, at five minutes past six o'clock P. M. They will form in line, each shop by itself, according to their number, as heretofore.

NO WORKMAN WILL CARRY FROM THE PREMISES any material belonging to the Company without permission.

WHEN TOOLS NEED REPAIRING, they must be taken to the Tool-room. The Tool Fixer will not repair such tools except they come from the Tool-room.

WORKMEN WILL NOT WASH BEFORE THE WHISTLE BLOWS, and must never use oil for washing purposes.

A STRICT OBSERVANCE OF THE ABOVE RULES IS REQUIRED.

THE TAUNTON LOCOMOTIVE MANUFACTURING CO.

mostly rural northwest corner of the state), owned a typical small machine shop. In addition to being a machinist, Alfred was a clockmaker and part-time farmer. Waterpower from the Naugatuck River, held back by a dam and channeled through a canal to a waterwheel, powered his machine tools. His shop was a traditional country shop (fig. 10–15). An inventory of Alfred's estate at his death in 1864 outlined the type of work he did. Other than personal items (including a violin) most of his estate was agricultural—animals, ploughs, and farming tools. In his machine shop he had one engine lathe (a large lathe), three turning lathes (smaller), and two pinion lathes (for turning clock parts). These six lathes together were valued at $115. The hand tools he used—screw

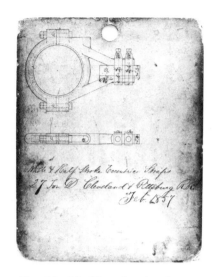

Fig. 10–14. Shop drawing from
the Baldwin Locomotive Works

plates, dies, files, drills, and so on—were valued at $250. In a small shop, even more than a large one, much of the work was done by skilled hands (fig. 10–16). In addition to hand and power tools for working metal, Alfred had specialized tools for making rifles, and carpenter's and blacksmith's tools.

A press Alfred built in 1855 for stamping small parts—possibly brass clock parts—survives (figs. 10–17, 10–18). Alfred may have made all of the parts in his shop, though some of the castings are large, maybe too large to have been made there. The base of the press is wood, a common feature of machines of this period.

The repair shop was a third type of machine shop. Larger than Alfred's shop and smaller than the Norris Locomotive Works, these shops were attached to factories that used machines in manufacturing. Every textile mill had a small machine shop to repair broken machines, make improvements on outdated ones, and try out inventions made by workers at the mill. Indeed, in the early 1800s, many machine shops were connected with textile mills, for they used more machines than any other type of factory. The shop at the Merrimack Manufacturing Company at Lowell, though larger than most, was typical. In the 1840s it had about two dozen machine tools, operated by six or seven men. Machinists were among the best-paid workers at the textile mill, making as much or more than overseers in the textile rooms.

Fig. 10–15. Alfred clock factory
and machine shop

Fig. 10–16. Conjectural
reconstruction of the interior of a
typical small machine shop of about
1855, at the National Museum of
American History

Fig. 10–17. Alfred press

Fig. 10–18. Detail, nameplate, Alfred press

Machinists were well paid by comparison with other trades, for it was not machines, but men skilled in the use of machine tools, that made up the critical element in machine shops. Paradoxically, when machine tools were originally invented in eighteenth-century England, they were hailed as a replacement for skilled labor. After all, it took less skill to shape a metal part using a machine than it did using hammer and chisel or a file. But as the parts made with machine tools became more complicated, the skill of the machinist became increasingly important.

American machinists were skilled in a variety of operations. Many of them, like Augustus Alfred, were jacks-of-all-trades, able to make a complex machine from scratch. Most were competent at running all of the machines in the machine shop, making anything for which they were given plans. Some could draw up the plans for a machine from suggestions of what was needed. The American machinist was a generalist, as English machinists were not. There, traditionally, the machinist was a specialist: he was a clockmaker or a cabinetmaker, a blacksmith or a tinsmith. The American machinist applied his varied experiences and skills to many different industries.

So important were the skills of the machinist that they became fundamental to the spread of the Industrial Revolution in America. Itinerant machinists diffused new ideas throughout the country. By moving from one industry to another, they transferred the knowledge that allowed the American Industrial Revolution to happen as quickly as it did.

The importance of machinists in the geographic spread of ideas within an industry is shown by the travels of one machinist. Isaac Markham was born in 1792 in Middlebury, Vermont. Markham was an inventive fellow, who as a boy had improved marble-cutting and wool-picking machines. In Middlebury he learned the machinist's trade from John Houghton, who had trained himself by building machinery for a cotton mill in New Hampshire. Houghton had been hired by David Page, the proprietor of a textile mill in Middlebury, to build machines. Page wrote a letter of recommendation for Markham that notes the wide range of skills of this itinerant machinist: "This may certify that Isaac E. Markham has worked for me . . . building cotton and woolen machinery. Mr. Markham has been the superintendent and draughtman of them. I consider him perfectly capable of doing every part of iron and brass work—after forged—and also honest, and entitled to the confidence of the public."[3]

Markham went from Middlebury to Waltham, Massachusetts, where he was hired as a machinist at the Boston Manufacturing Company. He stayed there a few years, learning about the machines and improving

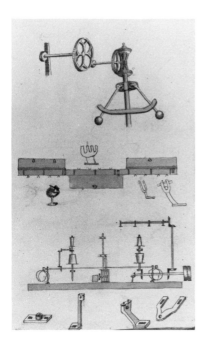

Fig. 10–19. Machine part drawings by Isaac Markham

them. From Waltham he went to Paterson, New Jersey, another textile mill town, where he picked up more knowledge of the machinist's trade. He drew pictures of machines that he saw at each of the places he worked (fig. 10–19). In 1825 Markham returned to Middlebury, bringing his skills and knowledge with him, and became the superintendent of a new cotton mill there. The spread of information about machines depended largely on just such machinists as Markham.

In their travels machinists spread not only ideas but also new tools and techniques. The milling machine, which uses a fast-spinning multiple-toothed cutter to remove metal from the piece being worked on, was the most important nineteenth-century American invention for the machine shop. Knowledge of this new machine was spread across the country in the heads and hands of machinists.

Simeon North of Middletown, Connecticut, was probably responsible for the invention of the milling machine, about 1816. He used it to produce pistols on contract to the United States government. The new tool's ability to cut irregular shapes to extreme accuracy, and thus replace a great amount of the hand filing previously necessary, attracted wide attention, and the superintendents of the government armories at Harpers Ferry, Virginia, and Springfield, Massachusetts, visited his factory. In 1816 North visited the Harpers Ferry Armory, where he met John Hall, head of the rifle works. Over the next ten years Hall improved the milling machine, making it more automatic and vastly increasing its usefulness.

Every important arms maker in the country visited Hall's rifle factory at Harpers Ferry, where they saw the milling machines. Some set up similar machines in their factories. In 1827 two of the principal workers left Harpers Ferry for Springfield, bringing the new tool and the techniques for using it.

The milling machine spread from Springfield to machine tool users throughout New England (fig. 10–20). It was adopted in armories first, because it eliminated most of the filing needed to produce the interchangeable parts demanded by the federal government. By 1860 it was beginning to gain wider use: sewing machine makers were among the first to take advantage of its speed and accuracy. Most shops, though, could not afford the high cost of these machines and the time required to constantly resharpen the many blades on the milling head. Not until the invention of new grinding machines, after the Civil War, did the milling machine gain wide, general use. Along with lathes, planers, and scrapers, the milling machine became part of the typical American machine shop by 1875.

Often, a shop equipped to make one sort of product branched out and made others, finding new uses for its machines and the skills of its work-

Fig. 10–20. Robertson milling machine, 1851

ers. The Lowell Machine Shop, one of the foremost textile machine manufacturers in the United States, not only made almost all of the machinery used at the many mills of Lowell but also sold textile equipment to mills throughout the country. The same tools used to produce textile machines could be used to make many other machines. When the market for locomotives developed in the 1840s, the Lowell Machine Shop manufactured them. In the same way, R. Hoe and Company, the foremost makers of printing presses in the United States, did contract work for a broad range of industries. The tools needed for building printing presses found use making everything from cannons to pin machines. The Hoe Company even expanded into making saws; the same machine tools used for making printing presses made saw-grinding machines.

Because of the versatility of machine tools and the wide range of skills of machinists, machine shops were central to the American Industrial Revolution. Almost every industry needed machines, and the skilled workers of the machine tool industry produced them. The presence of a powerful machine tool industry made possible the rapid expansion of American industry.

Textiles and the Styles of American Industrialization

CLOTHMAKING WAS THE MOST IMPORTANT INDUSTRY OF THE AMERICAN Industrial Revolution. It was important not only because of the value of the goods produced and the number of people who worked at looms and spinning machines, but also because in many ways it set the style of American mechanization, industrialization, and work.

It would be closer to the truth to say that the textile industry set the *styles* of American industrialization, for American industries developed in a variety of ways. Some depended on mechanized machinery, others on hand operations; some located in factories, others in small shops, others in the home; some industries employed unskilled laborers, others demanded the skills of highly trained workers. Large firms with much capital and paid managers comprised some industries; others were made up of smaller firms, run by their owners. All of these industrial styles can be found in the textile industry.

Before the production of textiles became an industrial venture, it was already an important American undertaking, a common household enterprise. The process of clothmaking was complex and required a variety of skills. To make linen, ripe flax was allowed to rot and then dried. Its fibers were then separated from its woody part with a flax brake, and the fibers swingled, or beaten by a wooden panel. This outside work was done by men. Women then took over. Their first task was to hatchel the flax; they pulled it through a hatchel, a device with many long spikes that combed the fibers and separated the short fibers from the longer ones, making it ready for spinning. Wool processing was similar to flax processing. Wool required more extensive carding before spinning to blend and align the fibers. It was a tedious process done by hand; a woman would hold a card in each hand, stroking the wool a little at a time and producing a continuous strand.

The fibers resulting from flax hatcheling or wool carding were spun into yarn on a spinning wheel. This process, unchanged since the sixteenth century, twisted and stretched the fibers into yarn and wound them onto a bobbin. Spinning was an essential household task. Almost

185

every household owned a spinning wheel, where women spent long hours spinning flax and wool into yarn to be woven into cloth.

Few women wove cloth themselves. Instead, they took the yarn to a professional hand-loom weaver who, for a fee, would weave the cloth. The weaver would wind the yarn that was to be the weft onto quills and load the quills into shuttles. Warp yarn was wound onto a warp beam. The warp beam was moved to the loom and each strand was threaded through harnesses onto a beam at the front of the loom. The harnesses were controlled by foot pedals so that they could be raised and lowered. The shuttle was passed back and forth between the warp strands, which were shifted with each pass so the warp and weft would be interlocked with each other and produce cloth. After weaving, the cloth would be cleaned and finished, the wool cloth fulled, or pounded, to thicken and compress it.

Most hand-loom weavers did not work at weaving full time. In Vermont, in 1810, the average weaver wove about 240 yards of cloth a year. This home-based, hand-powered method produced vast quantities of cloth. In nine months of 1791, for example, the women of Providence, Rhode Island, produced 25,000 yards of linen cloth, 6,000 yards of cotton cloth, and 3,000 yards of woolen cloth, as well as more than 4,000 pairs of stockings.

In the eighteenth century these hand operations began to be supplemented by powered machinery. Water-powered fulling mills were founded in many villages. In the 1790s machine carding became possible, and small water-powered carding mills were set up around the country, joining the fulling mills as common features of the rural landscape. By 1810 there were several thousand carding mills in the country, 413 in New York State alone. Women would take the wool to a nearby mill for carding and then take it home to spin.

EARLY FACTORIES AND MACHINES

Thus, though most textiles were produced in the home in the eighteenth century, important processes were done outside the home in mills using powered machinery. Even spinning had begun to move outside the home; textile factories were not unknown in America. From the early eighteenth century, many cities had found spinning a useful occupation for those whose poverty made them dependent upon government support. Running a spinning wheel not only helped to pay the city for expenses and helped to relieve shortages of cloth but also, it was thought, promoted good habits among the poor. These factories used traditional hand-powered spinning wheels and looms. The machines were gathered together into one building so that the work could be more easily supervised.

Among the earliest of these factories was the United Society for Manufactures and Importation, established in Boston in 1748. It employed several hundred poor women spinning and weaving linen. The entrepreneurs who sponsored the Society hoped that by teaching poor women to spin they would be able to support themselves. They also hoped to make a profit from the work and to lower the price of labor. Though both the city and the state government helped to underwrite the operation, the manufactory failed, perhaps done in by the multiplicity of its goals. Over the next half-century "houses of industry" with similar goals were established in Boston and other cities (fig. 11–1).

The Revolutionary War brought the first large-scale textile operations to Philadelphia. The United Company for Promoting American Manufactures, established in 1775, employed some 400 women spinners, most of them working in their own homes. The British occupation of Philadelphia put an end to the United Company, but after the war the Pennsylvania Society for Encouragement of Manufactures and the Useful Arts was established, supported by private investors and the state of Pennsylvania. The Society, like the United Company, attempted to use powered machinery—it offered a gold medal for the invention or importation of a workable powered loom—and like the United Company, was never successful. In 1790, just three years after its formation, the mills of the Society burned down—or, rather, it was thought, were burned down. Arson by hand-loom weavers was suspected.

None of the small textile factories that used hand machinery succeeded for long. One reason was that their employees were unused to the discipline of factory labor. A more important reason was that they

Fig. 11–1. House of Industry and House of Correction, Boston

competed with cloth manufactured in England. England could produce cloth more cheaply because a revolution had taken place there—the Industrial Revolution.

In 1770 James Hargreaves, an English mechanic, patented an improved spinning wheel, with multiple spindles. The spinning jenny, as he called his invention, meant vastly increased rates of production of yarn. A few years later, Richard Arkwright improved the jenny so that it would operate continuously and use waterpower. He incorporated it into a factory system, combining the new technology with new ways to discipline and manage workers. Hand weavers could not keep up with the output of the factories, and so ways were found to apply waterpower to weaving as well. By 1800 textile mills powered by water and steam were common throughout England (fig. 11–2).

Americans imported great quantities of cloth from England. Yet, especially after the start of the Revolution, many came to think that importing cloth was unpatriotic—as well as expensive. Economic independence was an essential part of political independence from Britain, and so patriotic Americans favored the wearing of American-made cloth: George Washington wore a suit of homespun at his inauguration. Throughout the country small textile factories began to appear.

These early factories and their British antecedents attracted much attention and no small concern. Americans debated the form the textile industry should take: Should it stay in the home or move into factories like those becoming widespread in England? Should the textile industry be encouraged, or should the United States continue to depend on British imports? Some, fearing the spread of the "dark Satanic mills" from England to this country, urged that factories be banned outright; some simply wanted government to do nothing to support the industry; and some wished its machinery redesigned so that the United States could produce the textiles it needed without factories.

Thomas Jefferson was one of the foremost proponents of home-based textile production. He wrote: "We have reduced the large and expensive machinery for most things to the compass of a private family, and every family of any size is now getting machines on a small scale for their household processes."[1] Jefferson and most of the others opposed to factories were not opposed to technology, and some of them backed up their philosophical position with inventions intended to keep the textile industry in the home and out of factories.

One of these machines was the domestic spinning jenny, a modification of the English spinning jenny, a factory machine, for home use (fig. 11–3). It spun thread faster and cheaper than the common spinning wheel. Moreover, the thread it spun was the proper material with which to clothe a democratic nation: made in the home, by self-sufficient fami-

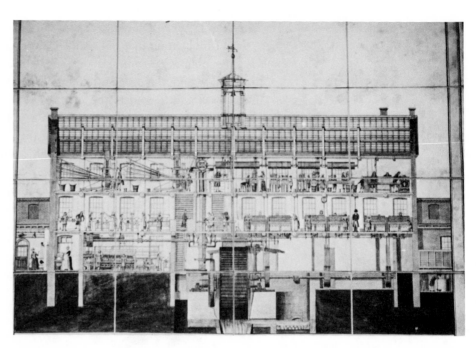

Fig. 11–2. Bedworth Worsted Mill, England, c. 1800

Fig. 11–4. Plantation spinner

Fig. 11–3. Domestic spinning jenny

lies, and not by a dependent class of factory workers. It was exactly the sort of innovation that delighted Thomas Jefferson.

The plantation spinner, or "spin-ginner," was another machine intended to take the processing of cotton out of factories (fig. 11–4). Plantation owners looked to the plantation spinner to free themselves from dependence on northern textile mills. A slave turned the crank that powered the machine's ginning, carding, and spinning mechanisms. A single machine could process enough cotton to make seven to ten yards of one-yard-wide cloth in one day.

The silk industry, too, saw the development of machinery for use in a family setting (fig. 11–5). Like the plantation spinner, this machinery brought all of the operations of silkmaking together into one hand-powered machine. It reeled and twisted silk from the cocoons, producing sewing silk or silk ready for twisting or weaving. Even with

Fig. 11–5. Home silk reeler

inventions like this, though, the domestic silk industry was never particularly successful, in part because a recurring blight destroyed the mulberry trees on which silkworms fed. Imported silk, and later silk made in large factories, proved to be cheaper than silk made in the home. While few of these innovations were successful, they are nonetheless important to the history of the American Industrial Revolution, for they give material reality to the philosophical debates about industry in America.

As ideologically appealing as it might be, the "family factory" could not compete with the economies of scale of large factories, especially when factory goods were easily and cheaply distributed by improved transportation systems. The combination of mass production and cheap distribution destroyed the hopes of the proponents of the self-sufficient family. The textile industry, and American industry generally, grew to depend on wage laborers tending machines for increasingly large firms. Textile firms were among the first American corporations, their work force among America's first factory workers. Textile mill operatives worked for wages under bosses who were themselves employees. They worked at the pace of the machinery, responding to its demands. The story of the textile industry in the first half of the nineteenth century serves as prologue to the story of American industry.

THE NEW ENGLAND MILL VILLAGE

The first successful textile mill using powered machinery in the United States was established in Pawtucket, Rhode Island, by William Almy and Smith Brown, American merchants, and Samuel Slater, an immigrant English cotton mill manager. Although the machinery and the way the mill was organized were new, it was by no means a complete break from the earlier history of manufacture in America. Textile machines and factories were not unknown. The mill fit into established commercial traditions (fig. 11–6). Only spinning was done at the Slater mill; weaving was still done in the homes of families throughout the area, as it had always been. Slater made sure that traditional family structure was reinforced in work at the mill. Although Slater brought with him from England both the secrets of the machines and the style of the English Industrial Revolution, he changed each to fit American ways.

The success of Slater's mill led to the expansion of the textile industry throughout New England. Not all of the operations took the same form as Slater's. The organizers of textile mills, responding to the chance to make a profit from the manufacture of yarn and cloth, set up their factories in several ways, depending on the local costs of labor, materials,

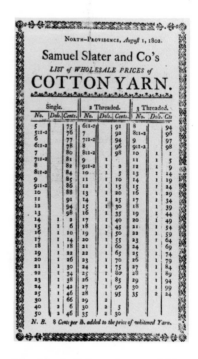

Fig. 11–6. Prices of yarn sold by Slater's mill

capital, power, and local cultural traditions. The varying effects of economics and culture on the formation of American industry can be traced in the varying organizational styles of the emerging textile industry.

Slater's mill was the first of many small textile mills built in Rhode Island and southern Massachusetts. The second mill was built in 1795, and between 1803 and 1807 twelve more were built. Following Jefferson's embargo of English goods in 1808, mills sprang up throughout New England. Moses Brown wrote to his son in 1810: "Our people have 'cotton mill fever' as it is called. Every place almost occupied with cotton mills . . . spinning yarn and making cloth is become our greatest business."[2] Between 1808 and 1812, thirty-six cotton mills and forty-one woolen mills were started. These small mills, located in small towns, produced yarn, which was "put out" to be woven by hand weavers in their homes.

Typical of these "mill village" mills were those located in Dudley and Oxford, Massachusetts, not far from Pawtucket. Small New England farming villages, these towns had in addition to farms the usual industrial shops: tanneries, sawmills, shoemakers, and so on. Oxford had some thirty-one of these small shops before the textile mills arrived. Samuel Slater established his first cotton yarn mill here in 1813, and a woolen mill two years later. By 1830 he and other mill proprietors owned twelve mills in the area, as well as extensive supporting operations.

Most of the employees who worked at the mill came from the surrounding countryside. In 1832 the dozen mills of the area employed 816 men, women, and children—an average of about 70 per mill. Most of the workers came to the mill in family groups.

Many of the adult men worked not in the mill but on farms owned by the mill owners. The men who worked in the mill, about one-third of the work force, were supervisors, mule spinners, hand-loom weavers, dressers, dyers, and machinists. These were skilled jobs requiring long training. A mule spinner, for example, operated a "mule," a type of spinning machine that spun fine yarn. He had to control the speed of the machine, keep it in good condition, and manage his "piecers," young children who worked for him, piecing together yarn when they broke. For this he was paid well, sometimes more than overseers at the mill. About 40 percent of the workers were adult women: they ran spinning machines and, when they were introduced, power looms. Finally, about one-quarter of the work force was children, mostly children of adults who worked in the mill. They assisted the mule spinners, helped out with the carding engines, and changed the spindles of the spinning machines when they were full (fig. 11−7).

By 1860 dozens of "mill villages" centered around textile mills could

be found in southern New England (fig. 11−8). These villages and their mills became a familiar part of the New England landscape, as well as an important part of its economic base. For all their number, however, they were not the dominant sector of the New England textile industry. Many more men and women worked in the large mills of the textile cities of northern New England.

Fig. 11−7. The weave room of a small mill

THE LARGE CORPORATE MILLS

The mills of Lowell, Massachusetts, attracted the most attention, for they were on a new scale, larger and more industrial than anything Americans had seen before. Americans applied an English metaphor:

Fig. 11–8. Webster, Massachusetts, a typical mill village

Lowell was the "Manchester of America." Lowell was a new industrial city, built from scratch by a group of Boston capitalists who have come to be called the Boston Associates. These men had earlier invested in the Boston Manufacturing Company, a textile mill Francis Cabot Lowell had founded in 1814 in Waltham, Massachusetts, about ten miles west of Boston. That mill was the first large-scale textile mill in America. It went beyond earlier American mills by including power-loom weaving as well as spinning. The mills at Lowell developed and extended the ideas experimented with at Waltham. In their size, corporate structure, and urban setting, these large textile mills set the style for much subsequent American industrial development.

The power loom was only the first step in creating an integrated textile mill (fig. 11–9). An entire system of machines, each machine producing a product suited for the next, had to be constructed. The new loom, for example, required yarn stronger than that used in hand looms, and therefore new types of spinning and sizing machines (fig. 11–10). The

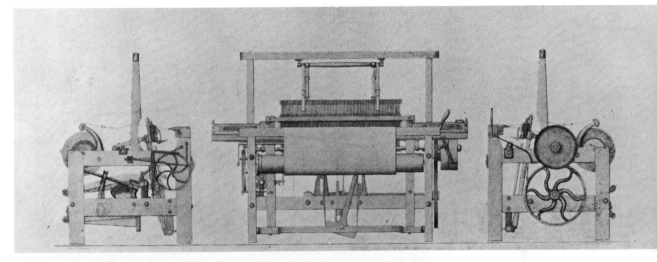

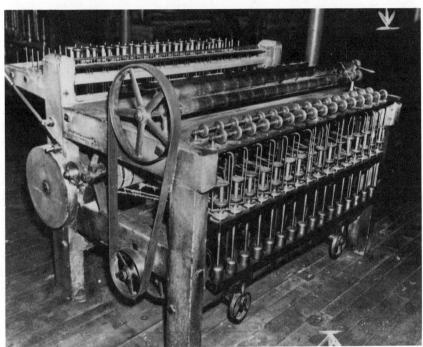

Fig. 11–9. An early Lowell loom

Fig. 11–10. Merrimack
Manufacturing Company throstle
twister

Boston Manufacturing Company made so many improvements in machinery that much of the firm's early profit came from selling patent rights to its inventions. But the biggest invention to come out of Waltham was the integrated factory itself—the idea of mechanizing all the processes of textile production under one roof.

The mill at Waltham was a great financial success, and a second mill was soon built. Demand continued to increase, but the two mills exhausted the waterpower available at the site, and the owners of the Waltham mill went looking for a new location. They found what was to be the site of the city of Lowell at the falls of the Merrimack River, near the confluence of the Merrimack and the Concord, about twenty-five miles north of Boston. A canal to carry shipping around the falls had been dug in the 1790s but was little used anymore. A few small mills used the waterpower of the Concord River; most of the area that was to become Lowell was farmland.

To build the mills, the Boston Associates needed to bring together money, machines, and workers. Many of the Boston Associates had earned their money in shipping and commerce. When the embargo on trade with England and then the War of 1812 interfered with trade, their money was available for new investments. Machines, and men with the skills to build machines, came mostly from England, some having stopped first at the mill in Waltham or at other mills in New England. Workers they drew from the New England countryside, farm girls who found the wages of factory work more attractive than the hard life of the farms of New Hampshire and Massachusetts.

The first investment the Boston Associates made at Lowell was in land and waterpower. They purchased both the waterpower of the falls and the land surrounding them. Next, they dug new canals, not to take ship traffic around the falls but to channel the water of the falls to the water-wheels that would power the mills of the new industrial city. Between the new canals and the river the Boston Associates had Irish laborers build their textile mills. The first mills were identical to the mill of the Boston Manufacturing Company at Waltham. They were red brick, four stories high, with a clerestory monitor to let in light to the top floor. Like the Waltham mill, these mills were fully integrated: cotton came in on the first floor and was processed as it went through the building, coming out as finished cloth. In 1835 there were twenty-two mills lining the canals of Lowell (fig. 11–11). In 1855 Lowell's fifty-two mills employed 8,800 women and 4,400 men and produced 2.25 million yards of cotton each week.

The Lowell mills were filled with machinery. Each machine represented the creativity of inventors, the skills of machine builders, and hour after hour and day after day in the lives of mill workers. In their complexities the machines caught in wood and steel the knowledge and abilities and labor of the largest industrial work force in America.

In the basement of each mill were the waterwheels that powered the machines. From them, shafting and belts ran to the machines above. Cotton bales came first to the picking machines, located outside the mill to minimize the risk of disastrous fire. From the pickers, which opened the bales, the cotton went to carding machines located on the first floor (fig. 11–12). Here carding took place, in several stages. When cotton

Fig. 11–11. A view of Lowell, 1840

Fig. 11–12. A carding machine and its operator

Textiles and the Styles of American Industrialization

had passed through these carding machines it was a loosely held to-gether strand of fibers called a sliver. The sliver was then fed into a drawing frame, which made it more uniform. Finally, the sliver was fed into a double speeder, which produced a coarse, slightly twisted strand of fibers called a roving, ready for spinning.

Spinning machines occupied the second floor. They drew out and twisted the roving, repeating in mechanism the action of the hand on the home spinning wheel. From these machines yarn went to the weaving room. Before that, though, the yarn to be used for the warp—the strands that ran the length of the cloth—had to be wound onto large spools, rewound onto a beam, and then sent to the dressing machines, which applied a starch paste to strengthen it. It was wound once again, this time onto a warping beam that would be placed onto the loom.

The looms were on the third floor (fig. 11–13). There the warping beams were mounted on the looms, and each piece of yarn drawn through the loom harnesses onto a front roller. Filling yarn, already spun onto bobbins, was mounted into shuttles and set in place on the loom. Finally the looms could be turned on: 100 times a minute hammers knocked the shuttle back and forth across the shed formed by the warp threads; the beams rotated to unwind the warp and wind the cloth; and a reed swept back and forth, "beating up" new strands of filling into cloth.

Fig. 11–13. A mill girl at her loom

ENGINES OF CHANGE

Most of the machines that filled the Lowell mills were built by the Lowell Machine Shop. They were designed to be operated by workers without a great deal of training. Looms at the mills, for example, had very few mechanisms that allowed adjustment; workers and overseers were not expected to know anything about mechanisms. Each mill produced a single type of standardized cloth, a practice that allowed relatively simple machines. Most of the machinery was equipped with "stop motions," devices that stopped them if a yarn broke, allowing one worker to attend several machines.

A mill was, in a way, one vast machine, connected by the complicated system of shafts and belts. If it was to work properly, all the spinners and weavers and carders and dressers had to be in place when it was started and work until it was stopped (fig. 11–14). The great cost of the machines meant that the mills had to be kept running, even when the market for their product was weak. That often meant cuts in the workers' pay. And most important, the machines' steady motion insisted on a machine-like pace for the workers. The managers set the speed of the machines, and the machines set the pace of work.

The mills of Lowell employed a new industrial work force. Not families, as in the mills of England and southern New England, but rather young women labored there. The 1820s were hard times for the farmers of New Hampshire and Massachusetts and Maine: the opening of the Erie Canal was bringing in cheaper goods from the West, and the West was luring their sons off the poor soil of the area. Their daughters, looking for work outside the home—some to earn money for their families, some to earn money for themselves—were attracted to Lowell (fig. 11–15).

When these young women arrived at Lowell, they found housing in the long rows of boardinghouses that surrounded the mills. Here respectable boardinghouse keepers, paid by the Lowell corporations, ensured the morality of the factory experience, reporting any misconduct to the agents of the corporations. Their guidance was supplemented by a code of moral rules in the mills themselves; girls were fired for offenses ranging from hysteria to insubordination and could be blacklisted and kept from working at other mills (fig. 11–16). Most mill girls stayed in Lowell only a few years before marrying or returning to their families' farms.

The mill girls of Lowell became famous for their attainments in literature and the arts. One group published *The Lowell Offering*, a literary magazine that was everywhere cited as an example of the elevated moral attainments of a truly American industrial work force.

Why did the proprietors of the Lowell mills spend the extra money to establish a paternalistic regime there? There is no easy answer. Some of

Fig. 11–14. Timetable of the Lowell mills

TIME TABLE OF THE LOWELL MILLS,
To take effect on and after Oct. 21st, 1851.

The Standard time being that of the meridian of Lowell, as shown by the regulator clock of JOSEPH RAYNES, 43 Central Street

	From 1st to 10th inclusive.				From 11th to 20th inclusive.				From 21st to last day of month.		
	1st Bell	2d Bell	3d Bell	Eve.Bell	1st Bell	2d Bell	3d Bell	Eve.Bell	1st Bell	2d Bell	3d Bell	Eve.Bell
January,	5.00	6.00	6.50	*7.30	5.00	6 00	6.50	*7.30	5.00	6.00	6.50	*7.30
February,	4.30	5.30	6.40	*7.30	4.30	5.30	6.25	*7.30	4.30	5.30	6.15	*7.30
March,	5.40	6.00		*7.30	5.20	5.40		*7.30	5.05	5.25		6.35
April,	4.45	5.05		6.45	4.30	4.50		6.55	4.30	4.50		7.00
May,	4 30	4.50		7·00	4.30	4.50		7.00	4.30	4.50		7 00
June,	"	"		"	"	"		"	"	"		"
July,	"	"		"	"	"		"	"	"		"
August,	"	"		"	"	"		"	"	"		"
September,	4.40	5.00		6.45	4.50	5.10		6.30	5.00	5.20		*7.30
October,	5.10	5.30		*7.30	5.20	5.40		*7.30	5.35	5.55		*7.30
November,	4.30	5.30	6.10	*7.30	4.30	5.30	6.20	*7.30	5.00	6.00	6.35	*7.30
December,	5.00	6.00	6.45	*7.30	5.00	6.00	6.50	*7.30	5.00	6·00	6.50	*7.30

* Excepting on Saturdays from Sept. 21st to March 20th inclusive, when it is rung at 20 minutes after sunset.

YARD GATES,
Will be opened at ringing of last morning bell, of meal bells, and of evening bells; and kept open Ten minutes.

MILL GATES.
Commence hoisting Mill Gates, Two minutes before commencing work.

WORK COMMENCES,
At Ten minutes after last morning bell, and at Ten minutes after bell which "rings in" from Meals.

BREAKFAST BELLS.
During March "Ring out"........at....7.30 a. m........."Ring in" at 8:05 a. m.
April 1st to Sept. 20th inclusive.....at....7 00 " " .... " " at 7.35 " "
Sept. 21st to Oct. 31st inclusive.....at....7.30 " " .... " " at 8.05 " "
Remainder of year work commences after Breakfast.

DINNER BELLS.
" Ring out" ....12.30 p. m........."Ring in".... 1.05 p. m.

In all cases, the *first* stroke of the bell is considered as marking the time.

Fig. 11–15. Mill girls

them took seriously the warnings about the evils of factory work. Some feared that they would not be able to attract workers to do the hard labor the mills required without the amenities they offered, or feared that the parents of the mill girls would not allow them to work at the mills otherwise. Some may have feared American reactions to Lowell if it adopted the English factory model, widely despised in this country.

Whatever the reasons, the paternalism of the Boston Associates, though widely admired, was not without its tarnish. The first strike of women factory workers in this country occurred at the Boston Manufacturing Company in 1821. When the company cut wages, a mechanic at the mill wrote in a letter, "The girls as one revolted, and the work

Fig. 11–16. Rules of work at Lowell

REGULATIONS

TO BE OBSERVED BY ALL PERSONS EMPLOYED BY THE

LAWRENCE MANUFACTURING COMPANY.

The Overseers are to be punctually in their rooms at the starting of the mill, and not to be absent unnecessarily during working hours.

They are to see that all those employed in their rooms are in their places in due season, and keep a correct account of their time and work.

They may grant leave of absence to those employed under them, when there are spare hands in the room to supply their places; otherwise they are not to grant leave of absence except in cases of absolute necessity.

All persons in the employ of the Lawrence Manufacturing Company, are required to observe the Regulations of the room where they are employed. They are not to be absent from their work without consent, except in case of sickness, and then they are to send the Overseer word of the cause of their absence.

They are to board in one of the boarding houses belonging to the Company, and to conform to the regulations of the house where they board.

The Company will not employ any one who is habitually absent from public worship on the Sabbath.

All persons entering into the employ of the Company are considered as engaged to work twelve months.

All persons intending to leave the employment of the Company, are to give two weeks' notice of their intention to their Overseer, and their engagement with the Company is not considered as fulfilled unless they comply with this regulation.

Payments will be made monthly, including board and wages, which will be made up to the second Saturday of every month, and paid in the course of the following week.

Any one who shall take from the mills or the yard, any yarn, cloth or other article belonging to the Company, will be considered guilty of stealing, and prosecuted accordingly.

These Regulations are considered a part of the contract with all persons entering into the employment of the Lawrence Manufacturing Company.

JOHN AIKEN, Agent.

stopped for two days in consequence."[3] At Lowell there were similar strikes when management cut pay or sped up the work. The mill girls appealed to American democratic ideals in their strikes. They struck for "liberty" against the "oppressing hand of avarice that doth enslave us."[4] They published labor newspapers and circulated petitions for shorter hours.

The 1820s and 1830s have been called Lowell's Golden Age: the time of New England mill girls, relatively unpressured working conditions, closely supervised boardinghouses, and *The Lowell Offering*. The 1840s saw a "speed up" and "stretch out" in the mills, with the machines run faster and each worker given more machines to tend, to make up for falling profits. The Yankee mill girls began to leave, replaced by Irish immigrants with no better options. The Civil War meant the end of Lowell as an industrial experiment, for the owners, thinking the war would last only months, mistakenly sold off their cotton to make a quick profit. When the mills reopened after the war, the "Lowell experiment" was over: the Yankee work force was gone, replaced with immigrant workers. Lower wages and sped-up machinery indicated a search only for profit, not for a moral workplace.

THE PHILADELPHIA STYLE

The mills of Lowell set the style for the textile industry of northern New England. In the rest of the country, that industry tended to be organized into smaller units. In southern New England, New York, and the Midwest, small mills in small towns were common. In Philadelphia, the textile industry was organized more along the lines of the English textile industry: many small mills and individual workers, with a great deal of commercial exchange between them. Where Lowell used low-skilled employees to produce standardized, coarse fabrics, the Philadelphia industry depended on skilled hand-loom weavers producing fancy and specialty goods beyond the capacity of power looms.

In 1820 only 3 percent of the power looms in the country were in Pennsylvania and Delaware; 60 percent were in New England. Philadelphia, though, had many more hand looms, some 4,500 in 1827. By 1850 more than 12,000 men and women worked in some 300 textile mills in Philadelphia. Two-thirds of these mills produced standard cotton or woolen goods, one-third specialty items: knits, carpets, silks, and so on.

Philadelphia mills were small. About one-third of the firms had fewer than 5 employees; only one-tenth had more than 100. They averaged 38, as compared with the Lowell firms, which averaged about 1,000 employees. Although small, most Philadelphia firms were sophisticated and highly specialized, making use of both power machinery and craft skills. Most were family-run partnerships. In addition to these firms, there were a large number of outworkers, employed by the shops but working at home with their own equipment. Finally, some 7,000 men worked on their own as hand-loom weavers in small backyard shops.

Jerome Kempton's mill in Manayunk was a typical Philadelphia textile mill, though larger than most. A family partnership, it employed 133 workers in 1850. It specialized (almost all Philadelphia mills specialized in something) in quickly meeting temporary demands for one type of cloth or another. If printed, finely woven fabrics were wanted, the looms at Kempton's mill could produce those. If cotton-wool blends were in demand, the skilled workers could make them. And, if the firm couldn't meet the demand, it was able to call on a vast network of smaller Philadelphia firms to help.

This flexible sort of manufacturing demanded a different sort of machinery than did Lowell's continuous production of coarse, plain goods. The machinery had to be flexible. Lowell looms were set to run one sort of cloth, and it was difficult to alter their output. The looms at Philadelphia mills, on the other hand, permitted easy changes in the size and type of yarn. Some looms could be run by either hand or waterpower. They had a variety of mechanisms that allowed operatives to change patterns easily. The style of machinery reflected the organization of the industry.

SOUTHERN MILLS

The Philadelphia textile industry existed side by side with the Lowell industry and the New England mill villages. All bought cotton from the South, processed it, and sold it throughout the country. Among the places buying northern cloth was the South—a state of affairs that could not help but displease southern merchants and planters, especially as tensions between the North and South increased before the Civil War.

Southerners, seeing their cotton shipped north, processed, and then shipped back at greatly increased prices, naturally enough wanted to capture the profits of manufacturing for themselves. Not only would it decrease their dependence on the North, but it would provide work for slaves and poor whites in areas where cotton had exhausted the soil.

What these southerners wanted was a second Industrial Revolution in America, a transfer of technology from the North to the South. But, just as some Americans had opposed the establishment of industry in the United States earlier, so there were some southerners who wanted to see industry kept north of the Mason-Dixon line. Others argued for it. The arguments and actions surrounding the development of the textile industry in the South recapitulate the rise of the northern textile industry a half-century earlier.

William Gregg, a South Carolina businessman and mechanic, was the foremost proponent of industry in the South. In an 1845 series of articles for the Charleston *Courier* and later in a pamphlet, he argued for a southern textile industry. Suggesting that the South and the North were soon to be hostile nations, he believed that the South needed to build factories so as to be independent of the North. He further argued that, with the depletion of the soil of the old South, new investments were needed to keep poor whites and southern capital from moving west. He took his own advice, establishing in Graniteville, South Carolina, in 1846 a mill modeled on those at Lowell. He imported machinery, managers, and overseers from the North.

While there was debate over the value of slaves as factory workers, and many mill owners, like Gregg, insisted on using only white labor, many of the workers in southern mills were slaves. Some of the slaves were hired from nearby plantations, and others were owned by the textile mill corporation itself.

Dozens of cotton mills were founded in the South in the 1840s. North Carolina alone saw thirty-two new mills in that decade, though only eleven in the 1850s when higher cotton prices encouraged investment in agriculture, not manufacturing. By 1860 the slave states produced almost 25 percent of the nation's cotton and woolen textiles. The mills of Lowell, by comparison, had as many spindles as the southern mills put together.

By 1860 the textile industry was well established throughout the eastern part of the country. In New England, 878 factories in mill towns like Webster (the new name for the manufacturing portions of Dudley and Oxford) and cities like Lowell produced some 940 million yards of cloth a year, the product of 105,000 workers. In the Middle Atlantic states, in small shops in cities like Philadelphia and small mills scattered in small towns, 816 factories employed 40,500 workers to produce 264 million yards of cloth, mostly intermediate and finer grades. And in the South, where almost all of the cotton was raised, 237 small mills employed 12,000 people and produced 58 million yards of cloth, mostly coarse cotton fabrics. The textile industry was beginning to find its way west; mills in Missouri and in Oregon were founded in the 1850s and 1860s. These western mills tended to be modeled on the small mills of New England and the Middle Atlantic states. In 1860, 328 mills—mostly woolen mills—in the western states employed 2,900 workers and produced 14 million yards of cloth.

By 1860 the textile industry was an important part of the economy of all parts of the country. Its effects were felt in the daily lives of almost every American—not only the factory workers who tended machines but also the consumer who no longer had to spin and weave her own cloth, and the millions to whom factory-made cloth meant cheaper clothes. With its large work force, many machines, and heavy use of water- and steam power, the textile industry seemed the exemplar of the Industrial Revolution. But not all industries adopted the same pattern. Many were located in shops too small to be called factories, or did not use machines, or continued to depend on hand power and skilled labor. The next chapter looks at some of these.

The Rise of the Factory

IN THE ERA OF THE AMERICAN INDUSTRIAL REVOLUTION, WORK MOVED increasingly from the home and the small shop to the factory. During the colonial period, most work was done in the household, both for the family and for outsiders as paid labor. Increasingly, work in the home was done for sale after completion, or to the specifications of a merchant and using his materials. In the first half of the nineteenth century work began to leave the home for the factory. The production of textiles, discussed in the previous chapter, is the classic example of that trend. But the transition from work in the home to the mechanized factory was not simple, and never complete. Some work remained in the household and small shop, some was done partially at home and partially in factories, and some moved to factories where machines were not used.

The determinants of the changes in work patterns were technological, economic, and managerial. Technology's role was sometimes foremost: industries that depended on powered machinery needed factories to provide the required space and power. Sometimes its role was secondary: new machines could fit into existing factories established for economic or managerial reasons. Factories were sometimes established in unmechanized industries to provide for rationalized production: division of labor and supervision were easier when work was gathered in one place.

One type of work remained in the home throughout this transition, and indeed is there to this day: housework. The eighteenth-century household was the site of a great variety of work. Both men and women worked to keep the "household factory" operating. Men were responsible for growing and processing grains, caring for and butchering animals, and producing or purchasing the various tools needed to keep the household working. Women were responsible for growing and preserving other foods, tending some animals, dairying, cooking, cleaning, spinning textiles, making beer, and a wide range of other tasks.

In the years between the Revolution and the Civil War, the Industrial Revolution began to affect the household, changing the nature of the work there. The increase of merchant mills for grinding grain meant less daily work about the house for men. Iron stoves meant that they needed to gather, cut, and split less wood. Factory-made boots and shoes meant less leather work for men at home. Factory-made pottery and tinware meant less demand for the utensils men made at home from wood.

Women's work, for the most part, did not leave the house: cooking, sewing, and laundering were still done at home (fig. 12–1). In fact, the complexity of demands upon women increased as new technologies raised expectations: the wood stove made cooking easier but allowed more complicated meals, finely ground wheat meant that yeast breads were possible, and factory-made textiles decreased spinning and weaving but increased the amount of clothing and home furnishings (and thus the amount of cleaning) most families thought necessary. The improving quality of life required that women do more varied work.

Although some women could take advantage of new opportunities for factory work, domestic service, and teaching outside the home, most had no choice but to stay home to care for their children. Housekeeping remained the most common occupation for women throughout the nineteenth and into the twentieth century.

Women's domestic work shaped the Industrial Revolution. It not only limited the industrial work force significantly but also established criteria for the work women did when they joined that work force. But perhaps most important, women's work in the home made possible an increased standard of living, which brought greater consumption and an enlarged market for the products of American industry. Consumption, the flip side of production, was equally essential to the American Industrial Revolution.

In addition to housework, other types of work remained in the home. Some of this work was done for sale, part of the traditional pattern of household production. Many farmers were artisans as well, manufacturing all sorts of products in addition to raising their crops: ceramics, woodwork, cloth, musical instruments, and tools, for example. The tradition of farmer-artisan continued throughout the Industrial Revolution, especially in frontier areas.

For farm families in New England and the Middle Atlantic states, this tradition began to change about the beginning of the nineteenth century. The household economy began to mesh with the beginnings of an economy based on exchange and factory production. In some cases, for example sawmilling and wool carding, the farmer increasingly took his goods to a nearby mill to have done that part of the job best accomplished by means of powered machinery. More and more, farmers and their families took in work, using their spare time to work on contract for merchants who provided the raw materials, gave instructions for the

work, and picked up finished products upon completion. The labor-intensive, unmechanized part of many kinds of work was done in the home by men and women.

Textiles, though one of the first factory-based industries in America, remained partly home-based for many years. Samuel Slater's mills, the first to use powered machinery, were only spinning mills; in the early decades of the century the yarn they produced was distributed to households throughout Rhode Island, Massachusetts, and southern New Hampshire for weaving into cloth. In Philadelphia, some 3,500 hand-loom spinners and weavers worked in their homes. In Connecticut, the making of parts for clocks was a common part-time craft. In many Massachusetts and New Hampshire households women spent time making straw hats, receiving Cuban straw plait from merchants and weaving it into hats and bonnets. The merchants picked up the hats, trimmed, pressed, and marketed them. Men, women, and children worked at many similar part-time occupations at home.

Fig. 12–1. Kitchen, c. 1790, recreated at the National Museum of American History

One of the most important of the outwork industries at which women labored was the manufacture of clothing. Sewing skills, necessary for women's own household chores, were also valuable commercially; women earned money by closing unfinished boot and shoe uppers, sewing together the legs and feet of stockings produced by knitting machines, covering buttons, and producing all sorts of clothing.

Like much of what became "women's work," the sewing of shirts and pants was originally done to meet the needs of the family. Some women specialized in this work and sold their products to neighbors or to merchants. Entrepreneurs soon discovered that by cutting the fabric, the part of the work with the highest risk of damage and the greatest capital requirements, and distributing the precut sections for assembly, they could greatly increase the output of finished goods.

In the years after 1830 most garment work moved from the farm to the city. In that year between 5,000 and 6,000 seamstresses were at work in Philadelphia, and many more in New York City. These women, most of them married or widowed and with children, worked at home. They received precut pieces, prepared at a central shop by tailors. The seamstresses sewed these sections together and returned them to the central shops. For their work, as many as 20,000 stitches per shirt, they received about 12½ cents. A seamstress could make between six and nine shirts a week, working six days of twelve to fourteen hours. An economist of the day estimated their actual average income at about $36.40 a year—at a time when a male worker might earn ten times that. This system of outside production, the lowest-paid work of the time, was called "sweating." It was widely regarded as one of the worst consequences of industrialization. Many magazines ran articles deploring the conditions of work in the garment industry (fig. 12–2).

Why was this industry set up as outwork? The most important reason was the low wages that could be paid to the seamstresses who, because they had to work at home to care for their families, had little choice but to accept whatever was offered. A second reason was the small capital available to the owners of the enterprises; by having the seamstresses work in their own homes, they transferred overhead costs to them.

Over the next thirty years, from 1830 to 1860, the garment industry underwent a series of technological revolutions: the invention of the sewing machine, the invention of standardized systems of measurement and standardized patterns, and the cheap cloth made available by the industrialization of the textile industry. These innovations intensified the labor of the outworkers but had a surprisingly small effect on the structure of the industry. In 1880, by which time the revolution in the

Fig. 12–2. *"Sweated" labor*

garment trade was complete and the sewing machine had become a common tool, there were still many thousand outwork garment makers in New York City.

The sewing machine was improved by a number of inventors over the years after 1830 (fig. 12–3). Many other patents followed those of Howe and Singer: 70 in the years 1842 to 1855, 843 between 1855 and 1867, and 2,144 between 1867 and 1877. These improvements made it possible to sew curved seams, to sew long seams, and to sew more quickly. The patents on these inventions were owned by a few companies that established the "Sewing Machine Combination" to create a monopoly. Sewing machine production just got under way before the Civil War— some 40,000 were produced in 1860, up from 1,600 in 1853.

Middle-class homes were one market for the new machines. Advertising campaigns convinced women that a sewing machine was highly desirable. Although some manufacturers aimed their sewing machines at the home market, they remained expensive. Only fairly well-to-do women bought sewing machines for their own use.

Garment factories provided a second market for the new technology. These factories, set up even before the sewing machine was introduced, employed up to several hundred women to produce women's outer clothing and hoopskirts (fig. 12–4). The women who went to work there were not the same ones who had previously sewed at home. Rather, they were young, unmarried women—a work force similar to that in textile mills or other factories. They were paid much better than women who

Fig. 12–3. *Sewing machine*

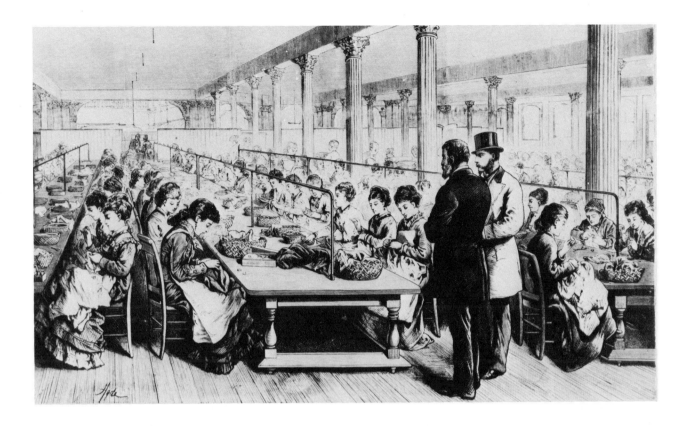

Fig. 12–4. A garment factory without sewing machines

worked at home—four to five times as much, the same rates as women who worked in other factories. The managers of these factories invested in the new technology of the sewing machine as soon as it was introduced (figs. 12–5, 12–6).

The cheapest grade of clothing was still made by women working by hand in their homes, for the cost of labor was very low and the cost of the machines relatively high. Some materials (heavy fabrics, for example) and some operations (buttonhole making and very short seams) still had to be done by hand. In the 1860s the cost of sewing machines came down to the point where the men who ran the shops could demand that women outworkers purchase their own machines for use in their homes. This lowered the price given for each piece produced to the point where a workday of fifteen to eighteen hours became necessary to earn a living wage. It brought about a subdivision of labor within the family household: men did much of the skilled work, assisted by their wives and children. Unrelated women and children often participated in this work—a new form of sweating. The home of the outworker became the third market for the sewing machine.

The newly invented sewing machine, then, fit into the industrial setting established by other constraints. Though it changed the details of the work, it did not make it easier, or any better paid. Garment workers

STRIVE TO EXCEL.

W.S.&C.H.THOMSON'S SKIRT MANUFACTORY.

remained among the lowest paid and hardest working of all laborers throughout the nineteenth century.

Fig. 12–5. A garment factory with sewing machines: the hoopskirt manufactory of W. S. and C. H. Thomson, New York City

THE BOOT AND SHOE MANUFACTURE

The boot and shoe industry, like the garment industry, started off in the homes of farm families and moved to the city. Unlike the garment industry, though, it moved into factories. In colonial times, most people wore shoes made at home by the man of the house, or bought them made to size from an itinerant cobbler. By the time of the American Revolution, the industry had begun to change. It became less "homespun" and more often done as outwork for entrepreneurs, not unlike the garment business.

As with garment making, cutting was the first part of the business to be centralized. Carriers delivered the material for several dozen shoes to each house, first to have the uppers stitched and bound, and then, often at another house, to be lasted and soled. Men—most of them part-time shoemakers and part-time farmers—worked in small shops called "ten-footers" located near their houses (fig. 12–7). They were paid piecework by merchants (called "bosses") who organized the industry and put up most of the capital required. Many a farmhouse in New Eng-

Fig. 12–6. Working in a clothes factory was one of the suitable "genteel" trades for unmarried women. Others, shown here in Harper's Bazaar in 1868, included paper collar cutters, hoopskirt makers, photograph mounters, candle makers, hat trimmers, and shoe fitters.

Fig. 12–7. Ten-footer, interior

land and the Middle Atlantic states had a ten-footer near by; many a family made a substantial part of its income from the stitching or lasting of shoes.

Early on, each man made a complete shoe, except for cutting the leather and the final binding. That began to change in the early part of the nineteenth century. Shoemakers hired apprentices and assistants to work with them. In the 1830s Gideon Howard, who lived in South Randolph, Massachusetts, "had a 'gang' over in his twelve-footer who fitted, made and finished: one lasted, one pegged and tacked on soles, one made fore edges, one put on heels and 'pared them up,' and in the case of handsewed shoes, two or three sewers were needed to keep the rest of the gang busy."[1] Only one of the men was a regularly trained shoemaker; the rest were less skilled, or skilled in only one part of the job, and paid by piece rate. The ten-footer became a workshop where not only shoes were made but an artisan culture evolved as well—a culture that was to affect the mechanization of the industry.

Women worked not in the ten-footers but in their kitchens, where they bound the shoes their husbands cut. They were not paid for their work separately from their husbands' pay, and because they were separated from one another, did not develop the same artisan spirit. That began to change in the 1830s, when women began to work directly for the shoe boss rather than for their husbands. Women shoe workers formed their own organizations. In 1837 some 15,000 Massachusetts women worked at the shoe industry.

The men and women working in their homes obtained materials and instructions from a "central shop" and sent back to the central shop the finished shoes. These shops, increasingly run by entrepreneurs who spent full time at it and less frequently by the merchants who had been responsible for the control of the industry earlier, took over a great part of the market.

The 1830s and 1840s saw a number of changes in the shoe industry, brought on by increasing competition, the Panic of 1837, an increasing market—shoes from New England were shipped to California and Australia—and a greater demand for more stylish, higher-quality shoes. One response was larger factories; a second, in the 1840s and 1850s, was increased mechanization and standardization.

The increase in the size of the factory allowed the shoe manufacturer to decrease transportation costs and to keep greater control of the quality of workmanship and the quantity of output. In factories foremen could more easily oversee the work. Greater division of labor and greater specialization meant faster production, less waste of time, money, and materials, greater uniformity, and often higher quality. The market began to demand shoes of set quality, at a given time; no longer could

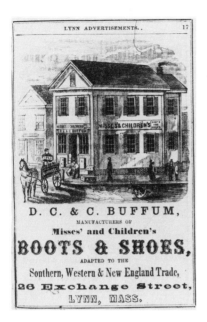

Fig. 12–8. A shoe factory in Lynn, Massachusetts

manufacturers depend on outworkers' working on their own schedules, making shoes when they had time between farm chores.

In 1850 the average shoe shop in New England employed nineteen men, the average shop in Massachusetts thirty-seven. (Outside of New England and the Middle Atlantic states the average shop employed two or three workers—typical of New England fifty years earlier.) Shoe shops became factories, called "manufactories" at the time. The towns where the shoe manufacture was centered became factory cities. Lynn, Massachusetts, famous as America's shoe city, produced about four million shoes in 1860 (fig. 12–8).

At first the work done in the factories was identical to the work done in the home—done by hand, using simple tools. The shoemaker's kit of tools in 1840 was unchanged from that used centuries earlier. His hammers, awls, stirrups for holding the shoe, nippers and needles, knives and scrapers would have been familiar to a shoemaker of medieval England. The American genius for mechanization began to change the daily work of the shoemaker: once the process was contained in a factory, larger, more expensive machines could be brought to bear on the process. Technological improvements included both new tools and techniques for cutting and sewing leather, which increased the uniformity of the product, and new patterns and styles of shoes. Tin patterns to guide the cutting of the sole meant greater accuracy. Closely related to new inventions that increased accuracy were marketing innovations that increased standardization, including a new system of sizing (not unlike that invented for clothing at about the same time), which allowed a better fit, and the invention of the "crooked shoe"—a different shoe for the right and left foot. (Another invention essential to the modern shoe industry—the shoe box—was also invented at about this time!)

In the late 1850s a variety of new shoemaking machines were invented. These machines—to make heels, to sew uppers, and, most important, the McKay sewing machine for "bottoming" or sewing together the inner and outer sole and the upper—were slowly introduced into the shoe manufactories. Women shoebinders, believing that the introduction of the machines would mean the end of their specialized domestic work, organized to oppose their introduction but with little success. The first steam-powered machines were introduced in 1858 and rapidly became common in the large factories of Lynn, their use speeded by demands for shoes by the northern army during the Civil War. The new machines produced many changes in work, but the most important part of industrialization, the factory system, arose in shoemaking before machines were introduced.

Though these new machines fit easily into the factories already in operation, they brought about some important changes in the work employees did. Women continued stitching even after machines were introduced, some in their homes, where a small amount of outwork continued, and some in factories, as machine operatives. In 1855 some 1,800 sewing machines were in use in the Lynn shoe manufacture, most of them run by young women. "Fancy stitchers," usually young single women, were among the best-paid female industrial workers in the late nineteenth century. Men's work too became more specialized, some men becoming unskilled machine tenders and others high-paid operatives. The tradition of apprenticeship died; no shoemaker learned his trade through a regular apprenticeship in Massachusetts after 1840.

The coming of the machines and factories to Lynn was accompanied by social strife. In 1860, just as the new system of production was becoming well established, there was a strike, the largest and one of the most important strikes in America before the Civil War (fig. 12–9). Precipitated by the hard times following the depression of 1857, the strike ripped the seams of the new system of production, revealing some of the discontent that was part of industrial America. Not only did the strike pit the workers against their employers, it also divided the strikers into those who supported the "family wage economy" of decentralized production—the outwork shoemakers who, with their wives working, could make a living—and the factory artisans who supported the factory system because of the increased wages it allowed.

The strikers, though divided on some of the goals of the strike, agreed on the need to stop the cut in wages. Their strike revealed some of the disagreements that accompanied the spread of factories and machinery, for it reflected the continuing presence of "preindustrial" values—values that affected the introduction of factories and machines. Large factories like those at Lynn meant the end of the master-apprentice relationship that had predominated in many industries before the Civil War. New relationships between owners and workers, mediated by a new class of managers, meant that wages and work conditions often were the only point of contact between the people who owned the factory and the people who worked in the factory. The coming of the factory meant the beginning of a new industrial age in America.

The new industrial age brought with it not only new kinds of work but also enormous increases in output. In 1860 the American shoe industry produced about 100 million pair of shoes. Lynn's factories turned out about 6 million pair, second only to Philadelphia. About 123,000 men and women were employed in making shoes, of whom 74,000 (52,000 men and 22,000 women) worked in New England. New England produced 60 percent of all the boots and shoes produced in the country—many of them in the new factories that characterized the industrialization of the United States.

Fig. 12–9. The Lynn strike, 1860

OTHER INDUSTRIES, OTHER FACTORIES

The rise of the factory was an important part of industrialization in many other areas as well. Of the ten largest industries only one, flour and grist milling, had fewer employees per firm in 1850 than in 1820. (Oliver Evans's inventions really did reduce the number of men needed to run a gristmill.) The average size of firms in other unmechanized industries increased from 11 percent (tanning) to 200 percent (hats and caps), taking advantage of the increased efficiency of the factory as compared with the artisan's shop. (Mechanized industries, by comparison, increased even more: the average size of a cotton textile mill increased more than 280 percent.) The following list shows the average size of factories in a variety of industries in the Northeast.

The role of mechanization in the rise of the new phenomenon of the factory varied widely from industry to industry. There is no simple way to describe its effects. The mechanization of some parts of housework freed men for work outside the home and raised standards for women's work within the home, increasing the consumption of industrial products. The coming of the sewing machine meant a new kind of factory labor for some women but very little change for the vast majority of outworkers, who simply substituted sewing machines for needle and thread in their homes—the same sort of work for similarly little pay. Shoes were factory-made, in part, even before machinery entered the industry; machines speeded up the transition to factories.

In some industries, the transition from craft shop to factory and from handwork to machine production was accompanied by enormous technological advance. The next chapter examines two industries that took mechanization to its antebellum limits: clockmaking and gunmaking.

Average Number of Employees at Factories in the Northeast		
Industry	*1820*	*1850*
Boots/shoes	19.1	33.6
Cotton textiles	34.6	97.5
Flour and grist milling	2.4	1.8
Glass	56.9	64.6
Hats and caps	8.4	17.0
Iron and iron products	19.6	24.2
Liquors	2.7	5.0
Paper	14.3	22.4
Tanning	3.8	4.2
Wool and mixed textiles	10.6	24.5

Clocks and Guns: The "American System" of Production

LARGE-SCALE PRODUCTION WAS CENTRAL TO THE INDUSTRIAL REVOLUtion. In eighteenth-century America, many things were made one at a time, either in craft shops or in the home. In the nineteenth century production moved increasingly to the factory. Inventors devised new machines, and businessmen devised new ways to organize and control machines and workers for mass production. The most celebrated method of large-scale production developed during the American Industrial Revolution was the "uniformity system." The uniformity system, which came to be known as "the American system," depended on interchangeable parts; the component parts of any one object were interchangeable with the component parts of other identical objects. To make economical the additional setup expenses that such a system demanded, a large market was necessary.

Two markets in early nineteenth-century America were large enough to justify the costs of setting up a uniformity system. One was the military market: the army needed a vast number of similar weapons for its troops. Weapons with interchangeable parts were of great importance, for generals wanted guns to be easily and quickly fixed on the battlefield. The military favored interchangeability for ideological reasons as well. The system of arms production by interchangeable parts was developed by and for the federal government.

The second market was for timekeeping devices: with the coming of cities and factories, many people needed to know the time and would buy clocks if they were cheap enough. Clockmakers discovered that the use of interchangeable parts made clocks cheaper to produce.

Clockmakers could take advantage of new techniques of mass production because of the presence of the large market for cheap clocks. They used interchangeable parts because it made production cheaper. Arms makers found in interchangeable parts not cheapness—guns made to the military's principles of uniformity were more expensive than those made one at a time, by hand—but rather ease of replacement of spare parts. Both clockmakers and arms makers found that they could combine the new technologies of mass production with new techniques of managerial hierarchy to keep close control over workers and products.

CLOCKS FOR THE MASSES

Clocks were made in America long before entrepreneurs began to produce them in large numbers in factories. From the early eighteenth century skilled craftsmen, many of them immigrants from England, made tall clocks. Clockmakers used many tools, among them hand-powered wheelcutting engines to cut gear wheels from imported cast brass. Cabinetmakers applied their skill to clock cases. Clockmakers, working in small shops, produced small numbers of timepieces; their clocks were works of art (fig. 13–1). They were expensive, usually more than fifty dollars without a case. Like many products of the craft shop, clocks were usually the work of more than one set of hands. American clockmakers bought parts from one another and imported parts, and sometimes whole movements, from Europe to take advantage of the benefits of the division of labor.

The cost and scarcity of brass encouraged the production of wood-movement clocks. By 1800 wood clocks accounted for the majority of American clock production. Many of the same techniques used in making brass clocks were modified and used for producing wood clocks. Their gears were cut on hand engines, their parts turned on foot-powered lathes. Their form, too, imitated brass clocks; most were tall clocks. Clocks with wooden gears cost less than half the price of clocks with brass gears. Like them, they were made one at a time, by hand.

Making clocks this way was a slow process. Daniel Burnap, one of the best-known makers, produced an average of only four clock movements per year from 1787 to 1805. (He and his journeymen and apprentices also made other products of brass, including surveyors instruments and jewelry.) Clocks, though of standardized construction, were still made one at a time.

In the eighteenth century timepieces were expensive and few in number. One historian has calculated that there were about 42,500 clocks in the United States in 1800, and about 64,000 watches. Approximately one white American adult in fifty had a clock, one in thirty-two a watch. The vast majority of the population depended on other means of telling the time. City dwellers could use the mechanisms of "public time": tower clocks, church bells, and town criers. In the countryside, sundials, "noon marks," and almanacs were common. One writer claimed in 1786 that almanacs were used

Fig. 13–1. Reconstruction of the clock shop of George Bond of Boston, who produced the first chronometer made in the United States, as it may have looked in the mid-nineteenth century

by nine-tenths of mankind and in fair weather are far more sure and regular than the best timepiece. . . . Twenty gentlemen in company will hardly be able, by the help of their thirty-guinea watches, to guess within two hours of the true time of night, . . . whilst the poor peasant, who never saw a watch will tell the time to a fraction by the rising and setting of the moon and some particular stars, which he learns from his almanack.[1]

Merchants, professionals, innkeepers, and shopkeepers were the eighteenth-century Americans most likely to own timepieces—over half of the members of these groups had a watch or clock. Artisans were twice as likely as farmers to have the means of telling time. City dwellers were much more likely to own clocks or watches than were men who lived in the country. Almost half of the men who lived in major cities had a timepiece of some kind. Many people, though, did not need to know "clock" time. Farmers kept the rhythms of nature, not the rhythms of the clock. Craft shops, too, followed seasonal and daily rhythms, not clock rhythms.

The groups that felt they needed watches and clocks were the groups that grew with the coming of the Industrial Revolution. Economic rhythms, beat by the pendulum of the clock, began to overpower the rhythms of nature in the early nineteenth century. More people began to participate in market economies. Farmers began to sell more produce to city dwellers. Industry expanded. People went to work in factories. With increasing wealth, industrialization, and urbanization, more people needed to or wanted to know the time.

The industry responded to the demand with both new technology and new techniques of investment and marketing. Large-scale production, along with new techniques of marketing, were first applied to clockmaking by Eli Terry, of Plymouth, Connecticut, in 1802. Terry had served apprenticeships to Daniel Burnap and Benjamin Cheney, among the foremost clockmakers in the country. Terry made traditional wooden and brass clocks for awhile, in the traditional small numbers, but was hampered by his small capital and the small market (fig. 13–2). "The demand for clocks was limited as well as the means for making them," his son wrote many years later. "Only three or four could be safely commenced at one undertaking, and most of these when completed were to be delivered to purchasers, who had previously engaged them."[2]

Terry found a way to avoid marketing his clocks himself by concentrating on production. In 1802 he built a factory that used waterpower to increase the speed of production. He started making clocks in larger quantities, as many as 200 at a time, and consigned them to peddlers to sell. Five years later, Levi and Edward Porter, merchants from Waterbury, Connecticut, contracted with Terry to sell 4,000 wooden clock movements in three years.

The Porters provided Terry with money he needed, tying up their capital for several years. Terry used the money to build new machinery and to buy materials. Yankee peddlers sold these clocks throughout the United States. They often allowed families to keep the clock for a few months, hoping that when they returned to collect the clock or the money to pay for it, few families would give up a luxury that had become, it seemed, a necessity.

The gamble that Terry and the Porters took, like the gamble the clock peddlers took, paid off. Terry and the Porters caught the rising tide of demand for clocks. Moreover, with Terry's new factory methods of production, costs went down, and with decreasing costs, more people could afford to buy clocks. A larger market meant cheaper clocks, which meant a larger market.

Terry's early clocks were traditional, not too much different from the

Fig. 13–2. Terry tallcase clock movement

handmade clocks he had earlier produced. They cost about ten dollars without a case. At that price, many people could afford them. Terry produced—and the Porters sold—about 3,000 clocks in 1809. The next year Terry's contract with the Porters expired and he retired, selling his factory to two of his employees for $6,000.

He did not stay retired for long. He reentered the business only four years later, joining many others in a rush to mechanize further the production of wooden clocks. One reason for his return to the business was his invention of a new kind of clock, a clock designed for machine production. His earlier clocks were similar to the tall clocks craftsmen had long made. The new clock was both a stylistic and a technological innovation. A thirty-hour shelf clock of simplified construction, it could be manufactured by unskilled workers and required less fitting to assemble (fig. 13–3). Terry licensed this clock to Seth Thomas to manufacture and continued to innovate, developing by 1822 a new style of clock—called the "pillar and scroll" clock from the design of its case (fig. 13–4). This clock became the standard of the industry for the next fifteen years.

Fig. 13–3. Terry thirty-hour clock

To his innovations in technology, marketing, and clock design, Terry added a legal innovation. He protected his inventions with patents, becoming one of the first inventors who tried to use the patent system to secure his place in industry. Only the heavily capitalized Boston textile industry filed more claims for patent protection on the design and construction of its machines than did Terry.

Terry's attempt to protect his invention failed. The patent system did not provide the protection he sought, and many manufacturers, most of them located in a few small towns in central Connecticut, began to manufacture clocks based on Terry's design for distribution throughout the country. The 1820 census of manufactures listed six clock factories in the towns of Litchfield and Plymouth, Connecticut, together employing sixty-six men and thirteen women. In that year they produced 8,450 clocks. The factory system of clock production brought the average price down to less than $7.50.

The factories that produced wooden clocks were small, with little equipment. An entrepreneur needed only about $2,000 worth of machinery to enter the trade. By means of specialization (many parts were

Fig. 13–4. Seth Thomas pillar and scroll clock

subcontracted to other shops), the division of labor (each worker specialized in making a single part), mechanization, and the use of water-power, a handful of workers at each factory could produce more clocks in a month than a craftsman working alone could make in a lifetime.

The manufacture of wooden clocks depended on automatic powered machinery, specialized tools, and, most important, a rationalized system of manufacture. Water-powered machinery was used to turn pinions and cut gears. Templates—pieces of sheet metal with the outline of the gears cut into them—were used to ensure that each gear or pinion was the proper size. These templates were used along with drop gauges—an indicator attached to a lathe that signals when a workpiece is cut to the proper diameter—and other pattern pieces to ensure that parts for a clock would fit together the first time they were assembled, removing the risk, and some of the skill, from the process of clockmaking. The wooden clock industry was among the earliest industries to make use of specialized tools to allow mass production. Though most of the work was handwork, it was continually informed by the information contained in the patterns and gauges. The work was repetitive but not unskilled; machines were still, to some extent, under the control of the workmen. Simple machines and templates were used to take the uncertainty out of the work.

The machinery was only half of the triumph of mechanization that the wooden-works clock industry represented. Interchangeability and specialization were just as important. Clock parts made by one manufacturer were interchangeable with parts made by many other manufacturers. This allowed specialization in production and, with it, increased mechanization.

In 1836, the year the industry hit its peak, workers at Connecticut factories produced more than 80,000 wooden clocks. They were made in shops not too much larger than those the census enumerator had found sixteen years earlier, using many of the same techniques. The next year a depression hit the country. Wood clock makers, the prices of their products already at rock bottom because of competition and many of them expanding too quickly with too little capital, were hard hit. In the course of a few years, the first American clock industry almost disappeared.

Fig. 13–5. Brass clock, New Haven Clock Company, c. 1860

The second American clock industry produced brass-works clocks. Brass rolling, established in this country about 1830, provided for the first time cheap, good-quality brass suitable for clock gears. Some of the techniques of the wooden-works clock industry were carried over into the new industry. Mass production techniques proved even more amenable to this new material.

Brass gears were stamped and punched from sheets of brass. The presses and dies brought with them their own intrinsic uniformity—gauges were not needed to ensure that parts would fit together. With the newly cheap rolled brass and easy stamping, the problem brass clock manufacturers had to overcome was the slowness of assembly. Brass pieces were first riveted together and later made in one piece (fig. 13–5). By 1845 one man could assemble seventy-five movements a day.

Brass clocks were made in enormous quantities, in large factories (fig. 13–6). The cost of entering the brass clock industry was much

Fig. 13–6. Seth Hoadley factory workers

higher than the wood clock industry. About $25,000 worth of machinery was needed. In 1853 a British visitor to one of the largest brass clock factories found 250 men employed, making 600 clocks each day. Specialization and division of labor reached new heights: each clock passed through the hands of about sixty people. A more typical brass clock factory, the Jerome Manufacturing Company of Derby, Connecticut, employed 100 men to make 130,000 clocks a year. Machinery worth $80,000 turned 1.25 million feet of pine boards and 625,000 feet of brass—the materials cost about $64,000—into $275,000 worth of clocks. Each one sold for only $2.00.

The $2.00 clock, and within a few years, the $1.50 clock, were affordable to almost everyone. Hundreds of thousands were sold in this country each year, and many more exported. Chauncey Jerome bragged that he sold "millions" of his clocks. Mass production using interchangeable parts made the clock a standard feature of every American household.

THE ARMORY SYSTEM OF MASS PRODUCTION

Like clock manufacturers, arms makers wanted to produce large quantities of complex mechanical goods. And like the clockmakers, they found that to do this, they needed to make use of new techniques of management and machinery. Guns, like clocks, were assembled from a number of precision-made small parts. Guns, though, required much greater precision than did clocks. Wooden clock gears can be made to plus or minus one-tenth inch accuracy; gun parts need to be accurate to one-hundredth of an inch or less.

The difference in required tolerances made for differences in production techniques. Even larger differences in production techniques, though, came from the differences in intent between the clock manufacturers and arms makers. Clockmakers merely wanted to produce large numbers, cheaply; they applied the principle of interchangeability as a means to that end. The military had interchangeability as a goal from the beginning. They wanted to be able to repair guns on the battlefield merely by substituting new parts, just as they "repaired" a tattered battalion on the battlefield by sending in new men to take the place of those who fell. They also wanted close control over those who made the guns, both the managers of the factories to whom they gave contracts and the workmen at those factories and at the government-run armories.

The government was willing to pay for the ability to interchange parts. It invested in special-purpose machinery and techniques to make the parts of rifles identical, and to close tolerances. The result was rifles that did indeed have interchangeable parts, at least after 1827, but that were not as cheap as rifles made without interchangeable parts. Cost was not the primary consideration in the government's purchases of weapons.

It was not easy for the government to establish its system of mass production by interchangeable parts. The first contract for guns made in this new way was given in 1798 to Eli Whitney, the most vocal advocate of interchangeability and famous as the inventor of the cotton gin. Whitney was to produce 10,000 muskets in two years (fig. 13–7).

Fig. 13–7. Whitney musket

Whitney was neither an experienced factory manager nor a skilled arms maker; in fact, he had lost a great deal of money in his earlier attempt to manufacture cotton gins. He wanted the contract at least in part because he needed the advance payments from the government to bail him out of his financial difficulties. It took Whitney nine years to complete the rifles he had promised to produce in two. They were not assembled from interchangeable parts, though he had promised that they would be.

The first successful steps toward the new pattern of arms production that came to be called the "American system" of production took place at the Springfield, Massachusetts, armory (fig. 13–8). In the 1790s the Springfield Armory was not too much different from a large craft shop. Many skilled workmen worked together to make guns. There was specialization and division of labor, but only to a small degree: one man would make the entire stock, barrel, or lock. Starting about 1800 the managers of the armory increased the number of men working on each gun. In 1815 there were 36 different operational specialties; in 1825, 100. By 1855 there were more than 400 separate operations involved in making a gun, each with its own wage.

Along with the division of labor, machinery was introduced to allow unskilled workers to do some of the work previously done by skilled craftsmen. This special-purpose machinery allowed guns to be made faster and with the accuracy necessary for interchangeability. Thomas Blanchard, a mechanic, invented a gunstock-turning lathe in 1819 (fig. 13–9). His lathe copied a pattern piece to allow the rapid production of irregular wooden objects. By 1825 Blanchard had invented a series of fourteen machines that largely mechanized gunstock production. Except for the remaining handwork, these machines allowed workers to produce a gunstock in only twenty-two minutes. They were constantly improved. By 1855 armories had a large complement of automatic, special-purpose wood- and metal-working machines.

Fig. 13–8. Springfield Armory

Fig. 13–9. Blanchard lathe

Blanchard's machines required less skilled labor. An inside contractor at the armory, he was able to hire his own workers. He hired, the superintendent wrote, "men and boys at very low wages, that know little or nothing of the business, & is often changing hands."[3] This displeased the skilled workers and made the superintendent's job "rather unpleasant." Despite this opposition, the managerial, economic, and technological advantages of the new machines were too great to ignore, and eventually the new machines were adopted at the national armories.

New machines to speed up the metal-cutting part of the work were another part of the new system of arms manufacture. The milling machine, invented and put in service at Simeon North's arms factory in Connecticut about 1816 and improved at John Hall's Rifle Works at the Harpers Ferry Armory in the 1820s, brought a new accuracy to the cutting of metal parts. Earlier, hand filing was necessary to shape parts. Now a powered hardened steel cutter revolving at great speed did the work—though some filing was still called for. Hall redesigned the rifle to allow the machinery to be put to its full use (fig. 13–10).

Even more important than new machinery to do old jobs faster were new manufacturing techniques to allow greater control of output. The armories led the way in the development of the "uniformity principle," the use of gauges to make the parts of guns interchangeable.

The theory behind interchangeable parts was simple; the difficulties came in developing techniques to implement it. How could workers and inspectors be sure that each part was of identical dimensions as the ones before it and the ones after it? How could armories widely distributed across the country make parts identical to one another? How could managers keep track of the work of each employee, making sure that they were producing parts that matched those being made by others?

The development of a complex system of jigs and fixtures and pattern pieces and gauges solved these problems. For each rifle or pistol (or, later, each piece of artillery or ammunition), a pattern piece was made. The pattern piece was an exemplar of the type, a model finished to great accuracy and precision. Then for every piece of the firearm, a system of

Fig. 13–10. Detail, Hall rifle

jigs and fixtures was designed. These devices, which held each part as it was being worked on, ensured that holes were drilled and edges and surfaces cut in exactly the same location on each piece. Finally, a set of gauges was made. These gauges, called "go or no-go" gauges, allowed an inspector to tell quickly and with certainty whether an element of the firearm was correctly sized and finished. Either the component fit correctly into the gauge, or it did not; either the holes lined up, or they did not. The system of gauges was the solution that ensured interchangeability (fig. 13–11).

Jigs, fixtures, and gauges were the mechanical part of the solution.

Fig. 13–12. Thornton's cartouche, "WAT," stamped in a gun stock.

Their necessary accompaniment was managerial: a system of inspectors who used the gauges, and who had the power and authority to punish the workmen whose parts were badly made. Each armory or contractor had a group of inspectors who checked each piece made there, stamping it with their cartouche to show that it had passed the test of the gauges and was of proper dimensions and finish. These inspectors were in turn checked by a corps of inspectors established by the ordnance department, whose members went from armory to armory, contractor to contractor, checking to see that the products matched one another—that arms were interchangeable no matter where they were made.

William A. Thornton, an 1825 graduate of West Point who worked his way through the ranks of ordnance duty to become a captain and inspector of contract arms in 1840, was one of these inspectors. As inspector, Thornton was to certify that the quality and workmanship of arms bought by the government were up to the standard of the contract. Arms he approved carried his "WAT" cartouche stamped into the stock (fig. 13–12). Thornton was at the top of a long line of "quality control" specialists. If at any point defective work was discovered, the workman responsible for the mistake was charged the entire cost of lost labor and materials—often several days' pay.

The system of inspectors was part of a new, more tightly controlled system of labor at the armories. Workmen at the Harpers Ferry Armory, in particular, were used to "preindustrial" habits of independent work. They insisted on retaining control of their work, setting their own hours, taking frequent holidays, and drinking whiskey on the job. Not until a "Yankee" superintendent from Springfield was put in charge of Harpers Ferry in the late 1820s did that armory install labor-saving machinery and implement new methods of work. And even then, there were continuing protests: a superintendent who tried to enforce the new work rules was shot, and petitions were sent to the Secretary of War and the President objecting to the new controls of time and work.

The managers of the armories introduced new work rules and new management techniques along with the new machines. Time and materials were carefully acounted for; each workman was held responsible for his work. The following excerpts from the regulations imposed at Springfield Armory in 1816 make clear the importance of managerial control to the new system of arms manufacture:

1ˢᵗ   *All Materials for the manufacture of arms and tools and implements for carrying on the work will be put in charge of the Master Armorer who will be made Debtor therefor, and will be held accountable for the same.*

2ⁿᵈ   *He will deliver to the Foremen Assistants & others on the order of the Supᵗ such articles as may be missing for the various parts of the work in their respective branches, they making returns therefor.*

4th   *The foremen & assistants will severally be responsible for all articles re-*
ceived by them. They will keep accurate accounts with the individual
workmen under their charges who will be held strictly accountable for
any article of public property delivered them.

The regulations went beyond merely accounting for supplies and labor. Managers at the armories, like those at other factories, believed
that careful regulation of the work force would instill values conducive
to the moral well-being of the country. The regulations continued:

13th *Fighting among the workmen will not be tolerated, nor any indecent*
or unnecessary noise allowed in or about the shops.

14th *It is enjoined upon every workmen in this est. not to begin, excite or*
join in any Mutinous, riotous or Seditious Conduct against the Reg-
ulations of the Armory, nor oppose the officer when in the execution of
their Duty, nor willfully refuse to observe the lawfull direction of the
officers of the Armory, nor enter into any combination against them.

15th *Gambling of every description, and the drinking of Rum, Gin, Brandy,*
Whiskey or any kind of ardent spirits is prohibited in or about the pub-
lic workshop.

21st *Due attention is to be paid to the Sabbath and no Labor, Business,*
amusement, play, recreation, . . . or any proceding incompatible with
the Sacred Duties of the day will be allowed.[4]

Factory discipline had a cultural purpose larger than mere control of the
factory work force.

The technological, managerial, and social principles of the American
system, first experimented with in clock factories and armories, soon
found their way into other industries as well. Metal-working industries
of all kinds were amenable to the new machinery, new techniques of
interchangeable parts, and new work discipline that, together, came to
be called "armory practice."

The watch industry was one of these. Men trained at Springfield
Armory helped to set up the American Watch Company at Waltham,
Massachusetts, just up the river from the Boston Manufacturing Company's textile mills, in 1859. They added to the techniques a new one.
They made watch parts in large numbers, as close to tolerance as they
could, and then selected parts that would fit well together. The Civil War
brought on an unprecedented demand for watches and ensured the success of the American Watch Company (fig. 13–13). In 1865 it produced
about 70,000 watches.

Some makers of sewing machines, too, adopted the principles of armory practice. In 1856 the Wheeler and Wilson Manufacturing Company hired as its factory superintendent William H. Perry, who had been
trained as a machinist at Samuel Colt's Hartford Armory. Perry, along
with men trained at other armories, brought to the job the new tech-

niques: sewing machine parts were drop-forged and then machined by specialized tools to tolerances measured by a system of gauges. By 1863 Wheeler and Wilson's $500,000 investment produced 30,000 sewing machines a year. A decade later the factory was turning out almost 175,000 machines a year. Other sewing machine companies, too, adopted armory techniques; a notable exception was the Singer Manufacturing Company, which competed successfully using techniques much like European machine makers (fig. 13–14). Its factories were full of vises to hold parts while workers filed them to fit. It invested its capital in advertising and marketing, not the many machines and tools needed for a system of manufacture based on armory practice.

The success of the Singer Company, which did not adopt the "best" or most modern manufacturing techniques of the day, helps cast light on the development of factory production in the antebellum era. The techniques adopted at the armories and at the clock factories were useful for those factories. The armories, using the new techniques of uniformity or interchangeable parts, produced firearms that could be quickly and easily repaired in the field and, not unimportant, could be made in factories where workmen were kept under close supervision. The techniques employed in clock factories allowed production of extremely large quantities at extremely low prices. These techniques were chosen

Fig. 13–13. Watch made by the American Watch Company, Waltham, Massachusetts, 1868

Fig. 13–14. Singer Company factory, 1854

and were continually modified for a mixture of economic and cultural reasons. They reflect the changing technologies of the Industrial Revolution.

Those technologies, applied to a wide range of mass-production industries, helped produce the consumer society of the second half of the nineteenth century. Clocks, watches, furniture, sewing machines— there seemed no end to the cornucopia of products that the machines of the American Industrial Revolution could turn out. The increasing population, many of them earning wages by tending the machines, could buy the products the factories produced. The American industrial economy grew strong selling the goods it made to the men and women who made them.

Clocks and Guns

XIV

Communitarian Experiments and the Problems of Industrialization

CHANGE, ESPECIALLY TECHNOLOGICAL CHANGE AND THE ORGANIZA-
tional changes associated with industrialization, produced multiplying
problems. The benefits anticipated by those who pushed change often
were realized, but for the whole population the benefits were uneven;
some were injured and everyone experienced unexpected results. No
national or state social planning related to mechanization was ever attempted. On a small scale, however, isolated communities did try to co-
ordinate technological change with social change.

Utopian communities flourished in the United States during the first
half of the nineteenth century. Not a few were begun by immigrants anxious to make the most of American freedom to build new and hap-
pier lives. In some degree, the emphasis on community represented a
counter effort to one of the most characteristic of American qualities—
individualism. Religious reform was usually an objective, and some
form of socialist organization was almost universal. The effects of industrialization were paramount to only a few of these communities, but all
of them had to face the role of technology. Some promoted an agrarian
life, and those that favored technological improvement were divided between improved craft production and reformed industrialization.

Nearly all were failures, lasting only a few years. Frequently, a single
charismatic figure carried a community through its beginning, but his or
her death was followed by the collapse of the community. The most successful organization, in terms of growth and influence, was the Mor-
mons, or the Church of Jesus Christ of Latter-day Saints, although it is
viewed more as a religion than as a community. It was founded in New
York by Joseph Smith in 1830 and today boasts a membership of nearly
five million. The Shakers, too, survive to the present, although they are
now on the verge of extinction. A few, such as Oneida and Amana, are
known because their names have been perpetuated in manufacturing
corporations that continue, although the communities themselves have
ceased to exist.

NEW HARMONY

One community effort that was directly related to industrialization was Robert Owen's New Harmony, established in Indiana in 1825. Owen was a successful English industrialist who had become disenchanted with the social results of his success. As a good business manager, he had applied the new technologies to textile production at the New Lanark mills in England. He involved himself both in conventional matters of production and in the problems of the workers and their community. He came to the conclusion that reform of the sort he believed essential to improve education and aid labor could never be carried through at New Lanark.

He concluded that mechanization had increased Britain's productivity fifteen or twenty times during the twenty-five years before 1817. This offered an enormous power that had not been realized. As he put it, "Mechanism, which may be made the greatest of blessings to humanity, is under the existing arrangements, its greatest curse." He developed plans and programs for a community in which profits would be shared by all. Labor in particular would benefit.

His objective was to encourage invention and improvement, including the mechanization of household activities, which had hardly begun, but only under circumstances that would help the worker, rather than put more difficult burdens and more uncertainties upon him. "Mechanism and science," he asserted, "will be extensively introduced to execute all the work that is over-laborious, disagreeable, or injurious to human nature." Mechanism and science would become "the only slaves or servants of men."[1] Owen agreed with critics that the rigid schedules and demanding work that had come with the machine had just the opposite effect. They made slaves of the workers.

He projected a socialist community, no larger than 2,500 in size, in which all would share the benefits of mechanization (fig. 14–1). All would also work for the common good and decide critical questions together. His ideal community would be small enough to avoid the problems of urbanization. It would combine agriculture with industrial production in a manner he had been unable to achieve at New Lanark.

Owen came to the United States to establish a community based on these ideas. Here he found some Americans already familiar with and favorable to his writings. Even more happily, he found an existing community, Harmonie, on the Wabash River in Indiana, that he was able to purchase. This had been founded by Father George Rapp and his Harmony Society of German emigrants. It was a religious community that had tried to combine agriculture with industry in something of the social pattern that Owen projected. Owen's effort, indeed, differed most

Fig. 14–1. Owen community design

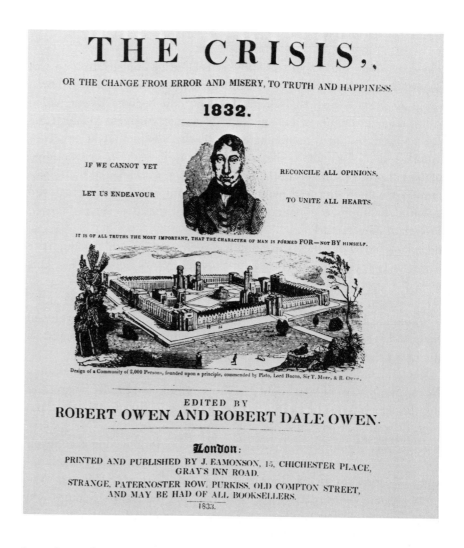

THE CRISIS,

OR THE CHANGE FROM ERROR AND MISERY, TO TRUTH AND HAPPINESS.

1832.

IF WE CANNOT YET

LET US ENDEAVOUR

RECONCILE ALL OPINIONS,

TO UNITE ALL HEARTS.

IT IS OF ALL TRUTHS THE MOST IMPORTANT, THAT THE CHARACTER OF MAN IS FORMED FOR—NOT BY HIMSELF.

Design of a Community of 2,000 Persons, founded upon a principle, commended by Plato, Lord Bacon, Sir T. More, & R. Owen.

EDITED BY
ROBERT OWEN AND ROBERT DALE OWEN.

London:
PRINTED AND PUBLISHED BY J. EAMONSON, 15, CHICHESTER PLACE,
GRAY'S INN ROAD.
STRANGE, PATERNOSTER ROW. PURKISS, OLD COMPTON STREET,
AND MAY BE HAD OF ALL BOOKSELLERS.
1833.

from the earlier American communities in its wholly secular approach.

He called his community New Harmony and lived in it himself for a year and a half. It did not work. Industrial and agricultural production both failed to reach satisfactory levels, and the organization and supervisory arrangements never functioned happily. Owen expended most of his fortune in launching and subsidizing the community before he gave up in 1827. New Harmony continued, but not as the same sort of experimental community. His influence continued there as well as in other Owenite communities that arose. The idea of designing a more just and happy society on a rural town scale was widespread, and as late as 1850 many were still underway. They were scattered throughout the country, except in the southern states, but were most numerous in the Midwest. By 1860 they were nearly all gone; only a handful survived of nearly 150 separate communities.

THE SHAKERS

The several villages established by the Shakers provide a striking contrast to Owen and the Owenite communities. Both groups actively encouraged invention and made technology a central part of their life. The contrast is that the Shakers were not opposed to mechanization but applied it to the improvement of handcraft technologies, not to factory production. They offered an alternative to industrialization—rather than a different way of organizing it. In addition, the Shakers differed from the Owenites in their religious commitment, which dominated their everyday life.

The first Shaker village was begun in 1774 by Mother Ann Lee, a one-time English Quaker who had worked as a Manchester mill girl before coming to America. Community ownership of property and celibacy were the two primary precepts she established, typical of utopian communities where socialism of some sort was usual, and, not infrequently, some reform of conventional sexual mores was endorsed. Beginning in New York, Shaker villages were established in New England and later in the Midwest.

Shaker architecture, furniture, and tools all reflected a deep concern for simplicity. The Shaker style was elegant in that simplicity and, at the same time, functionally well designed. Shakers became known for their fine woodwork. Although they encouraged invention, they discouraged patents, because the patent system celebrated the inventor and rested upon the profit motive. As a result, most Shaker inventions were not patented and are hard to trace.

The bulk of their inventions were labor-saving devices intended to make work more pleasant and easier. One of the most famous is the flat broom, which came into general use (fig. 14–2). There were many farming devices, too, such as improved horse collars and wagons—but also threshers and butter churns. Most of their machinery extended traditional technologies: turbines, circular saws, planing machines, and propellers. Less attention was given to the new technologies such as mechanized textile production, although a silk reeling machine and a machine to cut and bend teeth for a carding machine were invented.

Inventions and designs characteristic of the Shakers include both famous and little-known devices. Less known, for example, than the conventional wooden clothespin, is the four-legged tilt chair that was accomplished by pivoting a small portion of the back legs (fig. 14–3). This permitted anyone sitting in the chair to lean backward, pushing the two front legs up without slipping or putting as much strain on the chair.

Technology, in both its development and its use, was important to the Shakers, although they remained committed to individual craft or do-

Fig. 14–2. Shaker flat brooms

Fig. 14–3. Shaker tilt chair

mestic activities. A little later, the Shaker washing machine became a successful product. In isolated communities, the Shakers managed technology well, but their approach was not applicable to the rising high technology of the day and it did not help much to solve the problems of industrialization that motivated Robert Owen.

ENGINEERS' UTOPIAS

One of the most fascinating communal stories is also one of the least known. It is the saga of two German engineers, John A. Roebling and John A. Etzler, who came to the United States on the same ship in 1831 with a number of their fellow citizens. Their objective was to found two separate communities, in each of which the leaders intended that technology play an important role.

Etzler's community was established in Ohio after a number of other possibilities were discarded. It failed quickly and left behind almost nothing in the way of records. Roebling felt that the failure was a function of Etzler's leadership, pointing out that the least-educated and most-impoverished immigrants in the group were the ones who followed him. Etzler concluded that part of the reason for his failure was the harsh winter weather his people had to endure. His solution was to launch a second community in Venezuela, with English settlers and financial support. That, too, failed quickly.

Nothing of significance was achieved in his communitarian movement, but Etzler left behind designs and ideas that are significant, even though they have received no attention and were not influential. As an engineer in the middle of the American Industrial Revolution, he reached toward technology for answers to all the human and social problems he found. In this he differed from most communitarians who looked to social reform as the solution to their needs.

As Etzler thought through the human needs of his community, he dreamed out technological solutions. They cannot be called engineering solutions, because he did not work out his ideas specifically enough to dignify them by that term. His concepts remained in the realm of science fiction; he reached beyond his own world to new systems of production and transportation that put together components, some of which had never been tested, in combinations, none of which had been tried. He had noble ideas, but they were always too far removed from the real world to be useful.

In 1833 Etzler published a book that was the fruit of ideas he developed while trying to make his community go. It was entitled *Paradise within the Reach of All Men, Without Labor, by Powers of Nature and Machinery*. In it, Etzler described a mechanized agricultural system based on the conversion of wind power to waterpower and then to mechanical motion. He went on to describe means for similarly mechanizing manufacturing and commerce. In the age of the steam engine, he used only natural forces, including tidal and solar power. He asserted that his ideas would, in importance, supersede steam power.

Etzler is known today almost solely through the review of his book written by Henry David Thoreau, the influential writer and critic. Thoreau was fascinated by Etzler's ideas but ultimately repelled by a world in which most of man's work would be done for him. He decided that little more would be needed in Etzler's world than a "short turn of some crank." Thoreau found two faults. First, Etzler sought "the greatest degree of gross comfort merely." Second, and with remarkable accuracy, Thoreau wrote, "Mr. Etzler is not one of the enlightened practical men, the pioneers of the actual. . . . He has more of the practical than usually belongs to so bold a schemer, so resolute a dreamer. Yet his success is in theory and not in practice. . . ."[2]

Etzler's farming system used a windmill to pump water into a reservoir that then powered a water mill, which moved what he called a satellite, a mobile cart that rotated in concentric circles around a central pivot point and to which plows, harrows, seeders, and reapers could be attached for preparing the soil, planting, harvesting, and processing crops (fig. 14–4). He also devised methods to use it to cut down trees, to excavate land, and to move earth. He was convinced that anything that had to be done could be mechanized. His view was that machinery was nothing but "tools more or less combined."[3] Unfortunately, he did not bother to work out the specific design of either the components or the modes of connecting them. When a small version of his satellite was built and tried, it failed (fig. 14–5).

John Roebling had an education and experience remarkably similar to Etzler's, but his success with technology was "in practice" (fig. 14–6). In contrast with Etzler's grandiose, science fiction patents, Roebling's patents were limited in scope and much more specific. During his life-

Fig. 14–4. Etzler's "satellite"

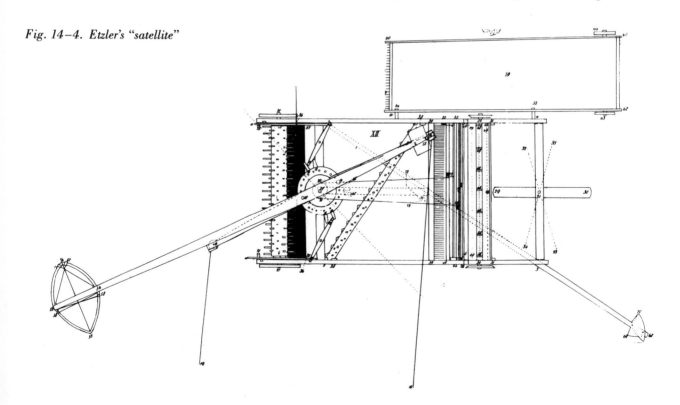

ENGINES OF CHANGE

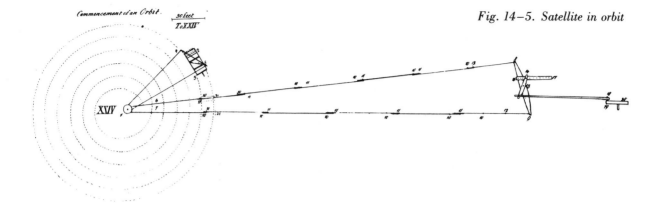

Fig. 14–5. Satellite in orbit

time he was awarded nine patents, all of them relating to work he was doing at the time. Most were detailed improvements related to bridge construction. Perhaps his most important patent was a device for laying suspension bridge cables on site (fig. 14–7). That method as well as his cable-wrapping machine and his method for anchoring bridge cables were improved techniques—not new bridge designs (fig. 14–8). These critical, engineering solutions were precisely what was lacking in everything that Etzler did.

Roebling's leadership in the community he founded also differed from Etzler's. He kept in view the large objective of a community established on good land that would prosper because of the hard work of the members. Initially all efforts were put into farming, but his intention was that manufacturing and industrial enterprises should become a part of his Saxonburg community, located near Pittsburgh. Roebling threw himself into the enterprise, building farm structures and engaging in farming. For six years, he stuck to the project and had much to do with carrying it through to success. The community never flourished, but it survived and continued.

Roebling seems to have devoted this period of his life to building and farming because he had to, not because he liked it. He continued to dream of industry and technological design, but, unlike Etzler, he planned no grand systems. Instead, he designed a steam plow, which never came to fruition, and a machine for making twisted wire cable, which he did patent. While in Saxonburg, he began the manufacture of twisted wire, both from his own internal motivation and in the hope of developing manufacturing within the community. The project prospered and indeed became the foundation for his later success. At the same time, he undertook canal engineering, using his twisted wire cable to pull canal boats up a ramp. While at Saxonburg, he also built his first

Fig. 14–6. John A. Roebling

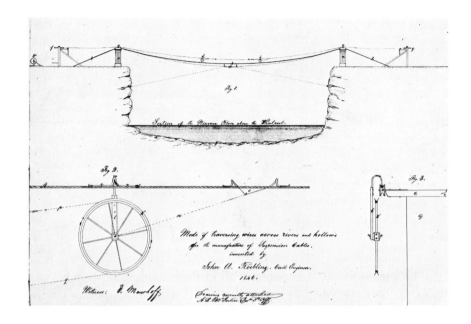

Fig. 14–7. Roebling cable-laying device, patent drawing

Fig. 14–8. Roebling cable-wrapping machine

ENGINES OF CHANGE

suspension bridge, the Allegheny suspension aqueduct—as well as his second, a true bridge over the Monongahela.

As he began to see broader and broader horizons, he concluded that he must move to an industrial center where he could carry through more of what he was capable of doing. In 1848, he moved his family to Trenton and, remarkably, never visited Saxonburg again. The manufacture of wire rope became a reliable source of income for Roebling's Trenton company, but his major attention turned to bridge building. He became the leading builder of suspension bridges in the United States, his Niagara Railroad bridge being completed in 1853 (fig. 14–9).

The communities were merely interludes in the lives of both Etzler and Roebling, but their dreams and accomplishments were closely related to them. Their differences showed in the fate of their communities and, very specifically, in one experience they shared. They both were deeply influenced by the ship on which they crossed the Atlantic, the *August Edward*. Each applied what he learned in another demonstration of science fiction versus disciplined engineering thought.

Etzler took off in an unrestrained flight of fancy, deciding that sailing vessels had to be totally redesigned and mechanized. Both in the United States and in Britain, he patented what he called "The Naval Automaton" (fig. 14–10). He substituted, for two or three masts and many sails, a single mast and a single, semicircular sail. The sail could be opened and closed, like a Japanese fan, and it could be rotated on the mast. The "pull of two ropes only" would "expand" the sail to any degree, while two more ropes would furl it and another two would rotate it on the mast. In place of the crew required to man existing sailing ships, a small windmill on the stern of the vessel would do the work required. A single helmsman could control the entire operation.[4]

This solved all the needs for handling a sailing vessel, but Etzler saw further possibilities for mechanization by applying other forces. To power paddle wheels, he designed a mechanism to harness the motion of the waves. A platform suspended beneath the ship would move up and down relative to the ship as the drag of the platform held it from following the up-and-down motion of the ship caused by its own bouyancy. A system of ratchets and gearing on the deck converted this irregular motion into usable power. Again, a small version of Etzler's design was tried. Again, it failed totally. The drag of the platform pulled the vessel under, and it sank.

Roebling had an entirely different reaction to the ship he and Etzler sailed on. He was fascinated by the sails and the standing rigging, by the stays that were able to hold the masts in place even against the heaviest gale winds. He studied them minutely and talked at length with the first mate about the whole system. He examined and made notes on

*Fig. 14–9. Roebling's Niagara
bridge, 1855*

*Fig. 14–10. Etzler's naval
automaton patent drawing*

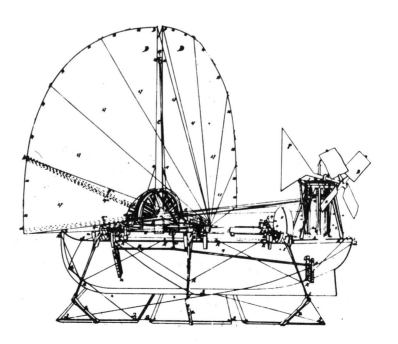

ENGINES OF CHANGE

the ropes, the deadeyes, and the chainplates to which the stays were fixed. He sketched out the standing rigging, and the system became a part of his thinking (fig. 14–11).

Years later, this understanding of ship stays became an integral part of his suspension bridge design. He was highly sensitive to the suspension bridges that had failed because of inadequate stiffening, and although he used weight, trusses, and girders, he relied heavily on diagonal stays. He saw them as "the most economical and most efficient means for stiffening the floor."[5] Diagonal or inclined stays were not a new idea but became almost his trademark, a means by which a Roebling bridge could be identified.

Every community, whatever its religious or social objective, had to decide how it would handle technology and production. Most of them, being small in size, concentrated on farming, but nearly all combined farming with some form of craft or, occasionally, industrial production. The Shakers mechanized aspects of craft production and developed it as an art, a new style. It is not without meaning that the founder of the Shakers had worked in a Manchester textile mill. Shakers focused on using technology to benefit the individual. Robert Owen and the Owen-

Fig. 14–11. Roebling's sketch of ship's mast and stays

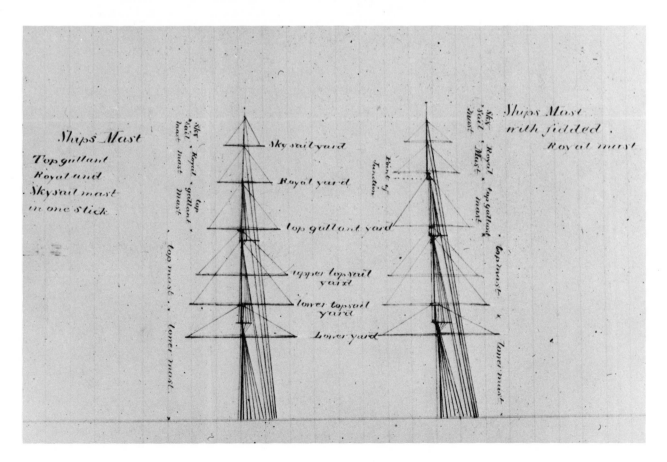

ites represented a sustained effort to reorganize society and to use industrialization to the advantage of humanity, eliminating the growing evils it was producing. The communities of the two German engineers, Etzler and Roebling, were less significant in themselves, but their leaders offer even more insight on the promise of technology. Roebling's resounding success as a bridge builder seems to cast Etzler in a deep shadow. Yet, in an extreme way, Etzler expressed the prevailing, almost unbridled hopes for the improvement of the human condition through technology. Roebling, too, believed that he was working toward that end, but in the real world without flights of fancy.

XV

The London Crystal Palace Exhibition and the Recognition of American Technology

JUST AS AMERICAN COMMUNITARIAN EXPERIMENTS COMBINED UTOPIAN insights with innovative technology, so, too, did the Crystal Palace Exhibition, the first great world's fair. The exhibition, held in London in 1851, was an enormous international trade show, a gathering of the best art and machinery from nations throughout the world, an expression of hope for the future focused on technology and the industrial arts. An American newspaperman spoke of the exhibition in utopian terms: it was to be a "great pacific Congress of Nations . . . the first ecumenical council of the new civilization."[1]

The British sponsors and organizers of the exhibition had several goals in mind. They wanted to promote peace through the encouragement of the "useful arts." They hoped to encourage improved industrial design. Not least important, they hoped to show the benefits of the British policy of free trade, and to make money by selling British products. To accomplish these goals, they brought together as eclectic a collection of goods as had ever been seen in one place. Tennyson's *Ode* for the opening of an exhibition a decade later applied equally to the 1851 Crystal Palace Exhibition:

> *. . . lo! the giant aisles*
> *Rich in model and design;*
> *Harvest-tool and husbandry,*
> *Loom and wheel and enginery,*
> *Secrets of the sullen mine,*
> *Steel and gold, and coal and wine,*
> *Fabric rough or fairy-fine . . .*
> *And shapes and hues of Art divine!*
> *All of beauty, all of use,*
> *That one fair planet can produce.*[2]

Everyone, Briton and foreigner alike, thought the exhibition would have great and lasting effects on the world of art, trade, and industry. An

American visitor to the exhibition, reflecting on what he had seen, thought it impossible to "anticipate all the beneficial results" that would flow from it:

That it is to have a most important and salutary influence upon the industrial progress of the world, appears to me most manifest. Its bearing upon the social condition of the world, cannot, I think, be otherwise than gratifying to every well wisher to the progress of the race.[3]

Technological progress especially was touted as an objective of the exhibition. Americans, more than any other people, believed that their future was tied to the new technology. It was fitting, therefore, that American exhibitors did especially well at the Crystal Palace. Americans won more prizes, proportionately, than any other country.

Ironically, the American exhibits were initially the laughing stock of the exhibition. The United States committee had asked for more space than it had entries to fill, and it took a while for all the entries to arrive in London. Further, the American entries, utilitarian and not stylishly designed, seemed unexciting compared with the elegant and ornamented products submitted by other countries—until the judges had a chance to test them. Then, the exhibits from the United States became the most praised of the fair. American ingenuity took the day; many American entries won awards. The British public was enthusiastic, and the American section of the fair became one of the most popular. The products of American industry exhibited at the Crystal Palace so impressed the British government that it appointed a commission to visit the United States and report on the "American system" of production. The Crystal Palace marked the beginning of the ascendancy of American industry and technology.

The Crystal Palace was an enormous popular success, both in England and, through reports in books, periodicals, and newspapers, in the United States. Americans were fascinated by the exhibition, enough so that they planned one of their own, for New York City, only two years later. The Crystal Palace appealed to American interests and, by providing an international showplace, met the commercial and patriotic needs of the rapidly industrializing country.

American reactions to the fair were overwhelmingly positive. George Bond, an American whose system of astronomical observations won a gold medal, wrote in his diary: "The art of man can go no farther than it has done in the contents of the Crystal Palace. . . . The Arabian Nights are thrown far into the shade by the realities of the Crystal Palace."[4]

Americans especially praised the American prizewinners. One enterprising American author published a book entitled *American Superiority at the World's Fair* and had a chromolithograph printed to go with it. Nathaniel Currier produced a lithograph that bragged about American success and poked fun at British defeats (fig. 15–1). P. T. Barnum made and displayed a "Monster Panorama" showing the highlights of the exhibition and published a book to accompany it. (Not one to miss a chance to make money, he sold advertisements in the book to the exhibitors of products he mentioned!) Several states published descriptions of the exhibition, emphasizing the successes of their native sons. Americans who visited the Crystal Palace published descriptions, adding to the vast outpouring of official catalogs and unofficial travel guides.

William A. Drew, Maine's commissioner for the exhibition, was responsible for one of these descriptive guides. His *Glimpses and Gatherings, during a Voyage and Visit to London and the Great Exhibition, in the Summer of 1851* combined a naïve fascination for things British with a strong nationalistic fervor for American ways and the American exhibits. Drew, guiding his reader through the exhibition, wrote proudly of the American products on display and of the success of American exhibitors:

> *We find ourselves, first of all, in the American Department, amongst the matters and things brought here by our countrymen. An immense organ stands at the head of the first gallery, that has the American Eagle perched upon it, with golden wings spread in the act of rising, like our own rising*

Fig. 15–1. Currier lithograph of the Exhibition

states, bearing the Republican crest in his beak, a quiver of arrows in his talons, and half enfolded in the American Flag. . . .

There is another fact in connection with this matter that is highly encouraging. The United States will take more Premiums than any other nation, *according to the number of articles exhibited. It is the* useful *that takes the Premiums, and therefore it is that America will lead all the others.*[5]

The Crystal Palace Exhibition was organized by the British Royal Society of Arts, under the direction of Prince Albert. The Society of Arts had been holding smaller fairs, limited to British entrants, for many years, and industrial exhibitions were familiar throughout Europe and the United States. Until this time, however, there had been no international fair. The French first conceived the idea of an international exposition, but when their government declined to offer financial support, the British decided to have one. Queen Victoria established a Royal Commission to plan an exhibition to open at Hyde Park on May 1, 1851.

The Royal Commission proceeded to raise money and opened a competition for the design of the building to house the exhibition. Almost 250 plans were submitted, all of which were turned down in favor of the commission's own plan. After the deadline, however, the commission changed course and accepted a proposal from Joseph Paxton for a strikingly modern building of glass and iron modeled on the greenhouses for which he was famous. The design caused *Punch* to coin the name by which the exhibition of the world's industry became known: the Crystal Palace.

Paxton, designer of greenhouses for the Duke of Devonshire, was a respected builder and engineer. His design was more engineering than architecture. The Crystal Palace was the world's first large, freestanding iron-frame building. Perhaps as striking as its size was the speed of its erection. Unlike any other building of its day, it was put together with mass-produced components. Every element was standardized and modular; the building was assembled rather than built. The Crystal Palace provided almost a million square feet of exhibit space (fig. 15–2).

The building underway, the Royal Commission needed submissions with which to fill it. British entries for the exhibition were no problem. But this was to be an international fair, and so the commission asked the British government to invite officially other governments to appoint their own national committees to select their country's entries. The British ambassador in Washington wrote to the State Department, which passed the letter on to the National Institute for the Promotion of Science and declared that body the "central authority or commission" with responsibility for picking the entrants.

The National Institute was a Washington organization, established in 1840 to "promote Science and the Useful Arts, and to establish a National Museum of Natural History, &c., &c." Formed with the intent of receiving James Smithson's bequest to establish an institution for the "increase and diffusion of knowledge" in the United States (which instead went to fund the Smithsonian Institution), the National Institute was semigovernmental, chartered by the Congress, with many government officials on its board.

To oversee the American effort at the Crystal Palace the National Institute appointed a central committee made up of distinguished scientists and men of affairs: Joseph Henry and Walter Johnson, of the Smithsonian Institution; Charles Wilkes, the naval officer who led the Wilkes exploring expedition; Peter Force, a Washington publisher; and Joseph C. G. Kennedy, Superintendent of the Census. Congress gave its moral support to the exhibition but declined to appropriate any money.

The first task of the committee was to send letters to state governors requesting that they name state committees. Twenty-eight of the thirty-two states organized committees, which then advertised the exhibition,

Fig. 15–2. The Crystal Palace

decided the best among the articles they were offered, and forwarded them to the central committee for final decisions.

The state committees advertised in local newspapers, published pamphlets, and did their best to make the exhibition known. In October and November 1850, notices like this one from Massachusetts appeared in newspapers across the country:

In conformity with the request of the "Central Authority" at Washington, the undersigned would respectfully solicit contributions from the Agriculturist, the Manufacturer, the Mechanic, and from all the industrial classes in every department of human labor throughout the Commonwealth, so that the citizens of Massachusetts, known for their inventive genius and productive skill, may be fully and honorably represented at this assemblage of the industry of the world.[6]

It seemed as though everything was sought, and that was not far from the truth. The exact nature of the submissions was never made quite clear, perhaps because those in charge of the Crystal Palace Exhibition aimed so widely. Official regulations called for nothing less than showing "the points which human industry and ingenuity have reached in the arts of civilized life."[7]

Americans debated what should be sent to London. Their debates reflected the American political scene; some argued that only manufactured objects should be submitted, while others wanted to play up America's vast wealth of raw materials. The *New York Herald* wanted to use the exhibition to show off American advances in technology:

This is the first opportunity we have had of fairly laying before the world our productions of art and it should not be passed lightly by. It is of more importance to us politically and commercially, than to any other nation. We are as yet unknown in the market of Europe except as the producers of raw material. Now we can show them that we not only produce cotton, iron, coal, copper and gold in greater abundances than any other nation, but that we can work them up into manufactures often equally, sometimes surpassing the oldest nations in a perfection and with a facility unknown to them.[8]

Others suggested that America's greatest strength lay in its agricultural production, and that this area should lead the American exhibits at the Crystal Palace. This debate mirrored a much larger political debate in the United States between agricultural interests, centered in the South and West, and manufacturing interests, located largely in the Northeast.

American entries to the exhibition numbered 599 (fig. 15–3). The range of entries was as broad as officials of the fair or the American committee could have wanted, perhaps broader. Every aspect of American productive industry was represented, from "A model of a floating church for seaman at the Port of Philadelphia" to "A machine for manufacturing ice," from "A book-mark, made by a little Choctaw girl" to "A gold-headed walking stick."

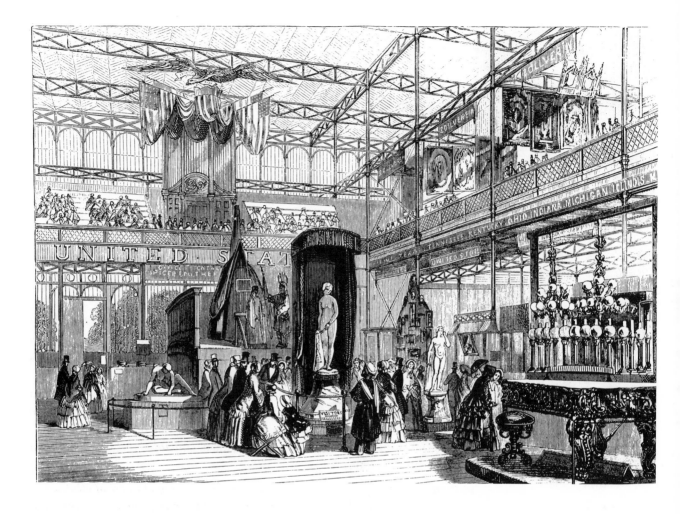

The American exhibits, reflecting the strengths of the American economy and the character of American society, were heavily weighted toward agricultural items and mass-produced goods.

Best represented at the Crystal Palace was American agriculture. The *Official Descriptive and Illustrated Catalogue* mentioned this and found it appropriate:

The Industry of the United States . . . is, in a very large proportion, devoted to the pursuit of agriculture. . . . The natural effect of this has been to give prominence in the exhibition of industrial results to raw materials and articles of food rather than to manufactured goods.[9]

Though some exhibitors simply showed samples of their crops or produce, many showed the application of science or technology to agriculture. Among the examples of scientific agriculture were new varieties of crops; among the technological improvements in agriculture were many new plows, reapers, scythes, and churns. Most common of the agriculture exhibits, though, were examples of processed crops and foodstuffs,

Fig. 15–3. The American displays at the Crystal Palace

Fig. 15–4. The Greek Slave displayed at the Crystal Palace was carved from marble using this plaster model as a form. The marks on the plaster cast were used, in conjunction with a copying machine, to make many copies of the sculpture.

everything from ginned cotton and lard oil to maple syrup, smoked hams, and wine. Other natural resources were popular as well. Many exhibitors showed examples of ore from American mines and wood from its forests.

Manufactured objects filled a large part of the American exhibit. These products were representative of American industry. They, too, attracted comment from the English press, for they seemed different from the manufactured goods the English were used to seeing at industrial fairs. They were plain and simple, for the most part, with only the minimum of decoration.

A glance at almost any object at the exhibition could betray the country of its manufacture. American objects tended to be utilitarian, their design functional and plain. The style of the European exhibits, on the other hand, tended to be elaborate and ornate, characterized by what one art historian has called "a universal replacement of the straight line by the curve," a "delight in abundant protuberances" and "swollen corpulence." Many an object was decorated to the point where the object lost its usefulness, not to mention its shape: clocks more decoration than timepiece, curtain hooks all leaves and flowers, chairs with small sculptures of dogs for arms. A Spanish pistol was inscribed with floral detailing from butt to barrel, a British one decorated with finely inscribed lines; an American pistol was not only relatively unmarked, but also squared off, so that it could be easily made by machine.

The British authors of the Crystal Palace *Official Catalogue* explained the difference this way:

The absence in the United States of those vast accumulations of wealth . . . and the general distribution of the means of procuring the more substantial conveniences of life, impart to the productions of American industry a character distinct from that of many other countries. The expenditure of months or years of labour upon a single article, not to increase its intrinsic value, but solely to augment its cost . . . is not common in the United States. On the contrary, both manual and mechanical labour are applied with direct reference to increasing the number or quantity of articles suited to the wants of a whole people.[10]

The products of American industry reflected the mercantile democracy of American society. Industry in this country produced relatively cheap goods, for a mass market. English and European goods tended to be fancier, more decorated, and more expensive.

The fine arts were excluded from the fair, except for "Sculpture, Plastic Art, Mosaics, Enamels, etc." Exhibits were limited to "those departments of art which are, in a degree, connected with mechanical processes which are applicable to the arts." In the nineteenth century, sculpture was considered, in some ways, a mechanical product as well as an artistic one, for it was seldom executed by the artist. He made a model for his assistants to reproduce in stone, mechanically. It was sometimes hard to tell sculpture from industrial art, for not only was it often reproduced mechanically, but furniture and tableware often looked like sculpture.

Sculpture was a popular part of the fair. The doggerel of the day had it:

> *There's statues bright*
> *Of marble white,*
> *Of silver and of copper,*
> *And some of zinc,*
> *And some I think*
> *That isn't overproper.*[11]

The last line was a reference to Hiram Powers's *The Greek Slave*, the centerpiece of the American exhibit and one of the great hits of the fair (fig. 15–4). Powers meant the statue to represent a Greek girl captured by the Turks and sold in the slave market of Constantinople. The sculpture was enormously popular; copies touring throughout the United States and England were seen by great crowds, up to 50,000 a day in some cities. Its popularity came not only from the artistic skill and the uncommon nudity presented, but from the meanings that the Victorian public read into it. The public found in this statue great piety and religious feeling, chastity and spirituality: the spirit of "true womanhood." Some went further and interpreted the statue as a protest against black slavery in America (fig. 15–5).

Though Britons at first mocked the American exhibits, after the prize committees judged the entrants not by appearance but by their functional excellence, the British changed their opinion. American success in three well-publicized contests brought about the more respectful attitude: the yacht *America* beat the British in an international yacht race; Alfred Hobbs, an American lock maker, picked the "unpickable" Chubbs and Bramah locks; and the McCormick reaper won the reaping competition. *Punch* poked fun at the British reaction to the American successes, to the tune of "Yankee Doodle":

> *Yankee Doodle sent to town*
> *His Goods for exhibition;*
> *Every body ran him down*
> *And laughed at his position;*
> *They thought him all the world behind*
> *A goney, muff, or noodle.*
> *Laugh on, good people—never mind—*
> *Says quiet Yankee Doodle.*[12]

THE VIRGINIAN SLAVE.
INTENDED AS A COMPANION TO POWER'S "GREEK SLAVE."

Fig. 15–5. Punch's abolitionist comment on The Greek Slave

Fig. 15–6. Dick's antifriction press

For the number of exhibits entered, the Americans fared well in prizes. They did not win prizes in all categories but excelled in certain fields. In the "Raw material" category they won 64 prizes; 37 in "Machinery, Implements, &c."; and 15 in "Miscellaneous Manufactures." In all, Americans won 159 of the 5,084 total prizes; about one of every four American entrants received an award.

The categories in which Americans excelled gave an excellent indication of the future course of American industry. They reflected not so much the state of the American economy in 1851 as the areas in which American industry was developing strength. Americans did best with machinery, especially woodworking tools and agricultural implements, and machines for firearm production.

They won 5 of the 170 Council Awards, the highest award given at the exhibition. The judges honored Gail Borden's meat biscuit: "a more simple, economical, and efficient form of concentrating food has never before been brought before the public."[13] David Dick's mechanical presses were recognized for their clever arrangement of levers that allowed them to exert a constant force (fig. 15–6). William Bond and Sons, famous for both their marine chronometers and their ingeniously designed precision clocks, displayed an astronomical apparatus that allowed an observer to record electrically the exact time of astronomical observations—a method that became known to British astronomers as the "American method" of astronomical observation (fig. 15–7). Charles Goodyear, the American inventor of rubber, received the Council Award for his display of items made of "India rubber," among them knife handles, musical instruments, a rubber-surfaced desk, waterproof fabrics, and a lifeboat and pontoon (fig. 15–8).

Cyrus McCormick's reaper not only won a Council Award but was widely celebrated in the English press. Two other American entries also won wide acclaim, helping to build public opinion about American technological prowess, though neither won a Council prize. Alfred Hobbs, the owner of a small Louisiana lock factory, came to London in 1851 both to display his locks at the Crystal Palace and to gain fame by picking the "unpickable" locks on display in London. The Chubbs lock, at the State Papers office, took him twenty-five minutes. The Bramah lock, unpicked for sixty years, took him longer, over a month—and the whole time, Hobbs was getting unsurpassed publicity. While Hobbs was traveling around England picking locks, his own lock stood up to the best effort of the keenest locksmiths in England. It did not win a prize at the fair—Hobbs had missed the deadline for entries—but was a great popular success, winning praise for American ingenuity. And it did help him sell his locks—including several to the Bank of England.

An entry that received even more attention was the great yacht race.

Fig. 15–7. Bond astronomical timekeeper

Yachts were representative of traditional wood shipbuilding, an area where Americans excelled. The *America*'s victory was overwhelming (fig. 15–9). *Punch* offered another "Yankee Doodle" verse:

Yankee Doodle had a craft,
  A rather tidy clipper,
And she challenged while they laughed,
  The Britishers to whip her.
Their whole yacht squadron she outsped,
  And that on their own water,
Of all the lot she went ahead,
  And they came nowhere after.[14]

The products of mechanized American factories were among the entries that won recognition. Six American pianos received awards. Pianos were extremely popular in the United States, produced in factories in large numbers (fig. 15–10). Firearms were another product of American factories that received wide attention and several awards. Samuel Colt's

Fig. 15–8. Goodyear lifeboat

Fig. 15–9. The America

Fig. 15–10. Chickering square piano

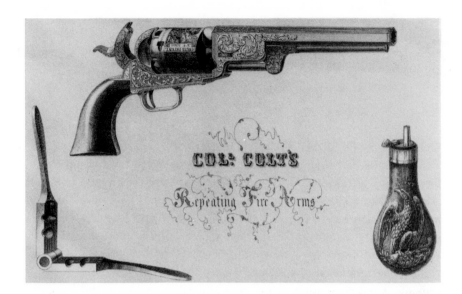

Fig. 15–11. Colt revolver

revolver was patented in 1836, but its use in the Mexican War brought it attention that was still rising at this time (fig. 15–11). The first practical repeating pistol based on the revolving principle, the Colt revolver was produced by the "American system" of manufactures: interchangeable parts, division of labor, and special-purpose machine tools. Colt's exhibit at the Crystal Palace was "hands-on"—visitors were encouraged to fire the revolver. The recognition given Colt at the Crystal Palace led to his establishment of a pistol factory in England where the American system of manufactures was used.

The Robbins and Lawrence military rifle was manufactured by a Vermont firm that also used the American system of manufactures (fig. 15–12). It was one of the influences that led the British to send a commission to examine American manufacturing plants following the Crystal Palace Exhibition. This visit was followed by an order to Robbins and Lawrence for the required machinery to equip the Enfield Armory to produce arms in this manner.

Textile machinery was still another field of industry in which America excelled, and American exhibitors won several medals for textiles and textile machinery. The Hayden drawing regulator, a device that compensates for irregularities in spinning cotton yarn, won a prize medal, as did cloth made by the Amoskeag Manufacturing Company and several other mills and machine card clothing (used for preparing cotton or wool for spinning) manufactured by the T. K. Earle Company. Sewing machine manufacture was just getting underway; several American inventors and manufacturers contributed to the development of a practical sewing machine. One of the commercial sewing machines produced on a design patented by Sherman C. Blodgett and John A. Lerow in 1849

Fig. 15–12. Robbins and Lawrence
military rifle

received a medal at the Crystal Palace (fig. 15–13).

Americans entered their products or inventions in the Crystal Palace for a variety of reasons. William Austin Burt used the Crystal Palace to advertise his 1836 solar compass, useful for surveying areas of large magnetic disturbance (fig. 15–14). Because it took the full fourteen-year life of the patent to develop the solar compass into a workable instrument and convince surveyors to use it, Burt petitioned the United States government for a monetary reward for his invention and began to promote it—among other ways, by exhibiting it at the Crystal Palace.

Like many companies that won awards at the Crystal Palace, the makers of Herring safes made good use of this distinction in their advertisements (fig. 15–15). So did J. A. Fay & Co. Their advertising broadside reproduced the medal the company won, hoping that the approbation of the judges would encourage customers to buy (fig. 15–16). The

Fig. 15–13. Blodgett and Lerow
sewing machine

Fig. 15–14. Burt solar compass

Fig. 15–15. Herring's patent safe advertisement

New York Iron Bridge Company did the same thing. They advertised the success of their bridge—the largest object displayed in the American section of the Crystal Palace—to set it apart from the hundreds of other iron truss bridges patented in the United States in the nineteenth century (fig. 15–17).

This advertising did not always work. The nautical compass was one of many inventions of John Ransom St. John, a Buffalo jack-of-many-trades who worked as a printer, surveyor, and engineer. He patented it in 1852 and moved to New York City to manufacture it (fig. 15–18). St.

Fig. 15–16. J. A. Fay & Co.
advertisement

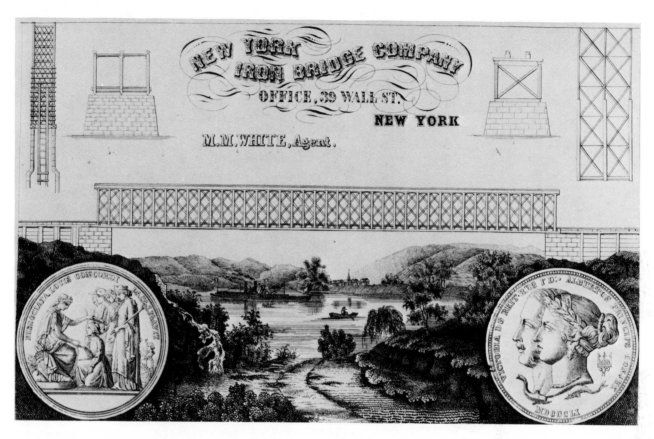

Fig. 15–17. New York Iron Bridge
Company advertisement

Fig. 15–18. St. John nautical
compass

Fig. 15–19. B. F. Palmer's
artificial leg advertisement

PALMER'S PATENT LEG,

As Exhibited at the WORLD'S EXHIBITION, LONDON, 1851, and NEW
YORK, 1853, with the Gold and Silver Medals awarded.

The Cut represents Mr. J. M. SANFORD, of West Medford, (near Boston, Mass.,) as he appeared in the CRYSTAL PALACE, walking *without the
aid of a cane,* even, upon TWO OF PALMER'S PATENT LEGS, one applying ABOVE THE KNEE.
Mr. S. appears so perfect, both in form and motion, as to *entirely conceal the nature of his misfortune.*

"Palmer's Patent," differs radically from all other artificial limbs, both in its mechanism and external appearance. The articula-
tions of knee, ankle, and toes, are united upon a new principle, and in such improved manner as to present the most natural and
symmetrical shapes and proportions.
The exterior is covered with a strong material, indissolubly fastened, which prevents the possibility of splitting. This covering
is fitted without perceptible seam, and then coated with a cement impervious to water, which gives an enameled surface, and color
so natural that the most delicately wrought hose and slipper are sufficient to conceal the work of art.
It is adapted to every form of amputation, and successfully applied to the shortest and tenderest stumps. The peculiar characteristics of this limb, are *life-like elasticity and flexibilty, excessive lightness, durability, adaptability, and perfection of exterior
appearance.*
"I have examined carefully the artificial Leg invented by Mr. B. Frank. Palmer, of this country. Its construction is simple, and
its execution is beautiful ; and what is most important, those who have the misfortune to require a substitute for the natural limb, and
the good fortune to possess it, all concur in bearing practical testimony to its superiority in comfort and utility."
NEW YORK, JANUARY 29, 1851   VALENT NE MOTT.
                                                        Professor of Surgery in the New York University.
"I have seen several of the Artificial Legs manufactured by Mr. B. F. Palmer in use, and consider them superior to any with
which I am acquainted."   WILLARD PARKER, M. D.
    New York, January, 29, 1854.   *Professor of Surgery in the College of Physicians and Surgeons, New York.*
                                                        PHILADELPH A, MARCH 28, 1851.
"I have examined, with great care, the Artificial Leg invented by Mr. B. F. Palmer and do not hesitate to recommend it in the
strongest terms,   THOS. D. MUTTER, M. D.
                                                        Professor of Surgery in the Jefferson College, Philadelphia

Thirty GOLD and SILVER MEDALS, (or First Premiums) have been awarded the Inventor ; among
which are the great PRIZE MEDALS of the WORLD'S EXHIBITIONS in LONDON and NEW YORK.

376 Chestnut St., Philadelphia, ⎱ Manufactories, ⎰ Burt's Block, Springfield Mass.
378 Broadway, New York,   ⎰   ⎱ 24 Savile Row, London.
All applications from the Middle, Southern and Western States should be directed to Philadelphia.

PALMER & CO.

Fig. 15–20. The New York Crystal Palace

John's compass, designed to find magnetic north on a ship heavy with iron, was ingenious but basically impractical. Even though it won a prize medal at the Crystal Palace and a gold medal from the American Institute in New York, the compass never achieved commercial success.

Among the more curious American prizewinners was a sample artificial leg manufactured by Dr. B. Frank Palmer (fig. 15–19). This prosthesis attracted great attention. The London *Times* called it "so remarkably characteristic of the country from whence it comes . . . the patentee lost his leg, and having tried the best substitutes hitherto devised for such a case, like a true American, he set himself to think whether he could not improve on them." [15] That comment perhaps best sums up the reputation for mechanical ingenuity that Americans were beginning to obtain in England. It was a reputation gained, in good part, at the Crystal Palace.

The Crystal Palace Exhibition marked a turning point for American technology. Part of the change was psychological; American success in London was a coming of age for American inventors and industrialists. The "American system of manufactures" was recognized as a new style of industrial production. The United States, a mere seventy-five years after independence, had shown that it could compete with the established nations of Europe. The practical effects were equally important; the renown Americans gained opened European markets to American industry. The second half of the century saw American products sold in increasing numbers in England and on the Continent.

Americans were pleased with their success, so much so that they decided to hold their own international exhibition in New York only two years later (fig. 15–20). The New York Crystal Palace Exhibition of 1853 was modeled directly on the London Crystal Palace, both in its goals and in the architecture of the building that housed it. American farmers, inventors, manufacturers, and industrialists looked forward to a chance to show off their products on their home ground. The New York exhibition, though, was not as successful as its London predecessor. Much smaller, it was neither as well organized nor as well financed, and few foreign exhibitors entered their products. Not until 1876, at Philadelphia's Centennial Exposition, did Americans organize a truly successful world's fair.

Still, the success of the American exhibits at the London Crystal Palace prompted interest in American technology, and when the New York Crystal Palace was scheduled, the British government sent a team of engineers and manufacturers to the United States to visit it. Because New York's fair did not open on schedule, the British visitors took advantage of their presence in this country to visit factories and shops. They reported favorably and placed orders for machines believed to be superior to those made in England—a final seal of approval. The United States had begun to surpass its mentor.

XVI   *Epilogue: The Role of Technology, Past and Present*

THE UNITED STATES SUDDENLY ASSUMED A NEW GUISE IN THE MINDS OF many who witnessed the Crystal Palace Exhibition of 1851. Less than a century earlier, the American colonies had exported nothing much but raw materials. American presentations at the London world's fair catapulted the country into recognition as an industrial power, actually ahead of the rest of the world at certain points. How had this happened? What were the secrets of this success?

That interval between the Revolution and the Civil War brought the nation into a new and somewhat strange world. Technological change had been proceeding at a rising rate since before the dawn of civilization, but an important acceleration occurred during the Industrial Revolution. It was then that the process of invention was invented and then that humanity moved toward a capability for effecting planned technological and associated social change that has now become awesome. This was first a European, then a Western, and finally a world story. What happened in this country during those years is particularly important. From those beginnings, the nation moved into our present century so rapidly that Gertrude Stein commented, "The United States is just now the oldest country in the world . . . the mother of the twentieth century civilization."[1]

The new world that began to be perceived in the early nineteenth century had many facets, but perhaps the most important was humanity's increasing control over nature. Previously, most people, wherever they lived, walked in order to get from one place to another. Only the well-to-do or those in special situations could use horses regularly. Only the wealthy could afford continuing ocean travel—and they were subject to wind, tide, current, and other hazards totally beyond their control. Farming, carpentry, and most craft production depended on processes and tools that had changed but little since the Roman era. Spinning and weaving were, similarly, still recognizable. Power sources had not moved beyond human, animal, wind, and water. Residential and commercial building was not functionally very different. Medicine's ability to treat disease and injury had improved but slightly, and most of that improvement proceeded from the fortuitous discovery of specifics—such as cinchona bark for malaria—rather than from improved understanding. But by the nineteenth century, all that was beginning to change in a dramatic fashion.

Now it became possible to transcend one after another of the limitations of nature through a variety of processes, to apply power sources such as steam that were but little limited by natural conditions, and increasingly to mechanize and automate both production and transportation. One result was greater freedom of choice and fewer constrictions from time, weather, season, and location. Another was the increased quantity and variety of both farm and manufactured products, lower costs, and wider distribution and marketing. Also transportation and communication improved, and their costs came sharply down.

These advances did not come free, although the full costs were initially hard to specify. Both benefits and costs were unevenly distributed. Some entrepreneurs benefited enormously, but many more failed, indeed some failed many times. The well-to-do often became still richer. Some workers benefited from more regular and higher wages for low-skilled work. Others found their skills dropping in value, and all workers suffered from inadequate security. Farmers had larger markets and were able to specialize more successfully; they benefited from improved transportation, better storage, and better implements. They, however, found themselves increasingly subject to decisions beyond their control on transportation, milling costs and availability, and the prices of implements and fertilizers.

Indeed, dependence upon other individuals grew as mechanization advanced and industrialization increased. Producers of all sorts, as well as those who supplied such services as transportation and communication, were less and less subject to the vagaries of nature. Increasingly, however, it became clear that individual independence had been gained at the cost of dependence upon other individuals. For most people, the quality of life was improving but the accompanying dependence on suppliers, transportation, finances, and market conditions increased. The meaning of this change did not become clear until much later.

It meant that the new power, the new freedom, the rising affluence, and the exciting changes all came with unexpected responsibility. Throughout all preceding time, humanity had had very limited responsibility for its condition. The distribution of a small pie produced almost automatic injustices; some individuals were severely injured, while others received unreasonably high returns. The large catastrophes of fire, flood, famine, and plague were hardly more beyond human control than the small disasters of droughts, soil exhaustion, losses at sea, and endemic poverty. Now, market forces affected more people. As the pie grew in size and men and women increasingly took responsibility for aspects of its production, everyone's responsibility for everyone else became increasingly inescapable.

Today it has become so frightening that a few have almost given up hope. Now the greatest conceivable disasters, as well as the continuing inequities in even so favored a country as the United States, are not in the hands of nature but in the unsteady hands of humankind.

Today's technology and its social causes and effects can be better understood by considering the continuities that connect them with the formative period of the American Industrial Revolution. In order to know where we are, it is essential to know from whence we have come. Much of the essence of technology remains the same, and the look of some technologies continues to reflect characteristics acquired in earlier development. But the simpler technology of the past is easier to comprehend than the more complex, black box technology of the present. Even more difficult to untangle are the increasingly multifaceted relationships between technology and economics, society, and government. Knowledge of continuities highlights the real differences between past and present and offers help in understanding the present, as well as in looking toward the future.

THE TRANSFER OF TECHNOLOGY

Significant interest in the transfer of technology arose not from historians studying the past but from those who sought to transfer current technology to the undeveloped nations of the Third World. After the Second World War, major efforts were made in that direction, with confusing results. Third World leaders almost universally sought high technology, but that proved to be difficult to manage because of their lack of the supporting infrastructure. As a consequence, some proposed instead to transfer small, intermediate, or "appropriate" technology—that is, to use technologies developed in the West some time back and no longer at the forefront of use. One special student of waterwheels, gristmills, and other pre-industrial technology, Jean Gimple, is even now trying to improve old-time machines, make models of them, and introduce them to undeveloped parts of the Third World.

The need for transferring technology today made the transfer of technology a familiar term and led historians to investigate transfers of the past. Their results have been important, revealing that while there are many similarities between technology transferring before 1860 and today there are also significant differences.

The differences relate to changes both in technology and in society.

One of the more important is the increased interrelationship between science and technology and the consequent need for a higher level of scientific knowledge on the part of receiving countries. Now that most invention and technological change have been integrated within well-supported research and development programs, the same process extends to transfer. Adapting any technology to a new setting requires continuing alteration, and that is best done in much the same manner as the original development process.

Similarities that continue grow out of the characteristics of technology itself. Working with technology always demands good visual or spatial thinking, whether or not science is a major component of the process. For designers and inventors as well as for operatives, technology requires an ability to think in three dimensions and to manipulate possible changes and actions in the mind. Because this ability lies at the core of technological change, it remains a requirement of receivers of technology transfer.

Of course, this center of technology, mechanization, and ultimately of industrialism is not meaningful in isolation. It is only effective in relationship with the economic and social circumstances surrounding it. These circumstances have changed enormously since the early nineteenth century, and the scene in one line of development is different from that in another. Nevertheless, the processes that governed development in the early period are recognizable in today's world.

England was taken aback at the Crystal Palace Exhibition of 1851 when she finally recognized American technological and industrial success. Realizing that the United States had forged ahead in critical areas, the English sent a commission to this country to study what was going on. Even after that, however, Americans continued to be more sensitive to new developments in Britain than the British were to ours. Still, a substantial interchange between the two countries arose, and it did run in both directions.

That was a distinctly different sort of transfer from today's transfers from the United States and other developed countries to the Third World. The problem with that interchange is that undeveloped countries of the present lack the practice and the capability in working recent technologies as well as the economic and social circumstances that are required to sustain the new technologies. They cannot support a single high-tech system in isolation. They must introduce a maintenance and support infrastructure, and they must adapt their own society to this alien mechanical form. Because that does not usually work well, lower or intermediate technologies often come to seem more appropriate. India, most African nations, and many in Latin America are simply not in a position to transfer the high technology of the present in the same manner that the United States received the best technology of the day during the early period.

On the other hand, the example of Japan today is much more comparable. By the time of the Second World War, Japan had imported and made her own the technological systems of the Western world. Surprised at losing the War, she decided that the cause had been American superiority in: (1) mass production and (2) the development of new technologies. The Japanese set out to rectify their disadvantages in those areas—with active American cooperation that far exceeded British help to the United States in the nineteenth century. They rapidly solved the needs and soon began, in selected areas, to surpass the United States in production and marketing and in the development of new technologies. When Americans became aware of this, they felt much the same shock that Britain had experienced in 1851.

Japan focused on the technology of industrialism. The support she gave science was relatively slim; just as the United States did over a century earlier, she depended upon other nations for most new scientific discoveries. Japan's object was to improve the mass production of key products, and she paid special attention to production that seemed to be at the heart of American industrial power—steel and automobiles. The country concentrated on further mechanizing and improving these processes in ways that would reduce costs and improve the product. Her business leaders studied American business practice but insisted on closer management ties to the actual technology than has become common in the United States. They were at home with three-dimensional processes. Aided by lower wage levels that kept rising but never came close to American rates, their achievements in low-cost, high-quality volume output were remarkable. Japanese steel production, based on highly mechanized facilities that were much superior to the American, nearly passed that of the United States. Automobile production took over an increasing share of the American and the world markets. This too was based on superior processes and more effective attention to quality output.

Unlike the Americans in the early nineteenth century, the Japanese had sufficient capital to carry through these efforts and they also enjoyed much higher levels of government support. By the twentieth century, American government action was largely limited to regulation, maintaining competition, and correcting injustice—rather than improving output and profit. The Japanese entry into the rapidly rising electronics market, which burgeoned only after the war, was begun by firms that entered the field because capital needs there were relatively low. Soon capital became plentiful, and Japanese electronics sales came to dominate the American market even more than automobiles did. The Americans in the early nineteenth century had succeeded by making products as cheaply as possible—through the use of mechanized processes and improved organization—but also by reaching for the mass, low-price market. The Japanese did the same thing. Also, like the early Americans, they paid little attention to luxury and ornamentation but emphasized a product that did its basic job as well as possible.

The Japanese encouraged inventiveness by laborers as well as engineers and managers, with good results. But to date, their major inventions have not been numerous. They could produce technologically superior products without much scientific research and development in their smokestack industries, or for their optical products and cameras, which took over a large share of the world market. In electronics, however, and computer technology, they have now moved at points to the cutting edge of new development. Not until after its technological success did the United States move toward leadership in science; Japan is following this pattern, too, three Japanese having received Nobel prizes in physics and one in chemistry since World War II.

Another totally different form of transfer contrasts with a preindustrial American pattern that faded away in the nineteenth century. The underdeveloped American colonies produced components or materials used in industrial production by developed countries. Specifically, America exported pig and bar iron, tall trees for masts, sawed timber, and potash in this pattern. With independence and American industrialization, that process decreased abruptly. Recently, technologically underdeveloped countries such as Korea, Hong Kong, Taiwan, Mexico, and Brazil are exporting high-tech components in electronics and optics production, depending not on processing raw materials but on cheap labor. Very recently this sort of component supply has begun to come from Japan as well. Its future is not clear, but the increasing role of multinational corporations will certainly extend it.

Despite the difference in time and in the nature of the technologies involved, the comparison of Japan today with the early American experience is fascinating. In both cases, a broad market, quantity production, and simplified design were emphasized. Both nations began with less capital than their primary competitors, and both achieved superiority in chosen lines of industrial production. Perhaps the biggest difference is the American emphasis on individualism and adversarial competition versus the Japanese hierarchical, group commitment. American individualism was a major factor in encouraging invention. Japan has already achieved a frightening superiority in much industrial production—without proportionate creative invention. It remains to be seen whether that will develop in the future. It also remains to be seen whether the United States can recover the sectors of industrial leadership it has lost to the Japanese.

GOVERNMENT SUPPORT
FOR TECHNOLOGICAL DEVELOPMENT

Support, primarily financial support, has always been critical in technological change. The process of industrialization requires a great deal. Both in the early period and today, social attitudes as well as economic conditions have been fundamental in providing or denying support. However, the sharpest and most clearly recorded support has always been that received from the government. In the early period, the federal government as well as state governments were called upon to help in various ways along the route toward industrialization. Some of the help given was indirect, as were patents, tariffs responding to specific production interests, and state tax advantages. The federal government and the states helped in both direct and indirect ways to improve transportation through roads, canals, steamboats, river improvement, and railroads. But the largest and most effective government support for stimulating technological change was in military development. This is still true today.

The military support that led to the most significant technological change during the early period was the development of the uniformity system, or manufacture by interchangeable parts. From this success, which had real military importance, the development of the American system of manufactures followed—by applying armory practice to other industries. This did not come, as it might have, from the similar approaches that were developing in clockmaking, but from gunmaking.

Government support, civil and military, has continued since the Civil War. Transcontinental railroads were made possible by federal grants, mostly land grants, and river and harbor improvement became a government responsibility—carried out by the army. State and local governments played large roles in supporting some forms of transportation, notably canals. The United States, which had lagged in oceangoing steamship development, was given a jump forward by the new steel navy of the 1880s, and a parallel improvement of specialized steel production. Varied manufactures continued to be aided by tariffs. In the recent past, techniques such as mail contracts were used to subsidize railroads and airlines.

From the late nineteenth century on, however, the most direct federal attention to industrial development has been given to regulation of transportation and, mostly on an interstate basis, manufacturing. In the name of competition, monopolies were broken up, while unfair practices were attacked. Since the 1930s, increasing attention has been given to social justice and to mitigating the worst inequities. These developments have made government more visible as a regulator of industrial process than as a supporter. On the other hand, since the Second World

War, federal military support has grown enormously, and that support continues the long tradition of aid through the military for technological change.

Today, nearly half of all research and development money spent by the federal government goes to the military, and almost none of the rest goes to industry. There are no engineering, technology, or business support systems similar to the National Science Foundation or the National Endowment for the Arts. Much of today's advanced technology has come out of wartime and postwar government support. United States leadership in commercial aircraft production grew out of military aircraft building. Electronics were pushed into major importance by radar, the proximity fuse, and wartime communications. The maser and laser grew out of war research, and space rocketry and communications satellites were a consequence of military efforts, later continued by the National Aeronautics and Space Administration (NASA).

The most dramatic military technologies that have changed the world are the digital computer and the atom bomb. Though the computer had deeper roots, its true beginning was during the War when ENIAC was funded by the Army Ordance Department and Project Whirlwind was funded initially by the Navy. From those beginnings, the still spreading extension of microprocessing developed. The Manhattan Project produced the atom bomb, later efforts the hydrogen bomb, and continuing government support led to nuclear-powered ships and commercial nuclear power.

On the other hand, it has been charged that the successful Japanese competition with American technology and production is related to that country's very limited military research expenditures compared with its large government monetary and policy support of industrial production. Direct American government support of industrial production is almost accidental. Government policy, resting upon what it believes to be the support of free enterprise, declines actions for the purpose of aiding production. That, of course, represents a continuation of the limited support by government of early nineteenth-century industrial development, which, however, was based much upon a lack of available moneys. At the present, government support of military research is far beyond earlier centuries. Support for science, by comparison, is not large—but in the early nineteenth century, there was none at all. Science is well supported today, and this has brought American leadership in many fields of science; there is no comparable support for nonmilitary technological research.

Government support for new technologies gave new vigor to some industries and launched others. It remains as fundamentally important today as it was in the nineteenth century, but by any quantitative measure it is vastly larger now. Exciting developments of the present have proceeded from government support, most of them from military activity, just as the American system of manufactures came out of armory production of guns. Compared with Japan, the prime American deficiency is the almost total lack of nonmilitary support for industry.

THE EXHILARATION OF INVENTION

The exhilaration of early inventors and entrepreneurs, driven by the excitement of their achievements and their hopes, is clear. They were also propelled by the anticipation of personal financial profit and further encouraged by the conviction that their work would be beneficial to their country. John Fitch and Oliver Evans clearly expressed this belief, and others accepted it as a useful line, whether they believed it or not. Few participated in technological development without expecting personal profit, and few who were successful escaped capture by the enthusiasm of creating new solutions to technological and industrial problems.

Similarly, enthusiasm is a vibrant part of Japanese industrial production. Government support is important, but it goes along with a driving force that independently impels most groups. The new technologies, even though they still originate elsewhere, spark great interest. Individualism is less a part of the scene than in America, and therefore, wholly new ways of doing things may not arise as frequently. However, team effort is an essential part of industrial development, technological research, and even scientific research everywhere. That is more intrinsic to the Japanese than to the Americans, as is the comfortable acceptance of a hierarchical society.

For a time, the enthusiasm that grows out of new technologies was suppressed in the United States by disenchantment with the threats and disorder that accompanied them. That reaction seems to have peaked in the late 1960s and the 1970s, but the questions remain. Some are skeptical if not antagonistic. How have engineers, mechanics, and business managers fared in this doubting world?

The question cannot be answered with full satisfaction. Early operatives or laborers in factories were often negative about technologies and the new systems of production. On the other hand, some were enthusiastic, particularly those who built them or who found new jobs. That scene may not be entirely different today. Some workers are still enthusiastic, but many are conscious of, and occasionally driven to action because of, perceived injustices in their employment. Enthusiasm has always been most evident on the part of those who invented or built new technologies; today, such people have their enthusiasm restrained.

Engineers, as a group, experience resentment from those who blame technology for poverty, unemployment, and the war threat. Even more blamed are entrepreneurs and corporations, for not exercising the social responsibility required to prevent the worst results of technological change. Technological creativity is encouraged in specific directions by corporations and by the government—but the inventor encounters varied resistance and decreasing enthusiasm.

Nevertheless, the internal excitement of conceiving, designing, and testing new technological concepts is so great that it bubbles up within all those inventors and designers who continue to work toward change. It is not very evident in the areas of nineteenth-century development, such as textile mills, steam engines, and railroads, since they have become stable, old technologies. The most visible current excitement is in such fields as microprocessing, computers, word processing, CAD-CAM programs, microchips, and telecommunications. Here, rapid growth has highlighted individual inventor-entrepreneurs who have performed in much the same fashion as their counterparts did in the earlier period. Whole new patterns of development have been opened, and computers have become big business. Individuals have won fortunes for themselves. Aspects of the economy and of society have been abruptly changed—again with little or no general planning or effective technology assessment. As the "state of the art" reached a point where new electronics systems became possible, such systems emerged as soon as economic and social patterns permitted.

In a measure, they are correct who argue that technology is a social product. New technologies can become effective only within social patterns and needs. But the great internal force remains the exhilaration that conceiving and carrying through new technologies and new industrial systems produces. Individual creativity is as much at the center of new technologies as it ever was.

THE IMPACT OF TECHNOLOGY UPON WORKERS AND CONSUMERS

Every technological advance has come at a price—but the full price is seldom known until long after the achievement. By 1860, the price of industrialization was known only in part. The advantages of factory life were initially more celebrated and publicized than the disadvantages, although some of the negatives were understood from the beginning. The effects of wage labor: the loss of skills, rigid discipline, and the loss of employment in bad times, became clear after only a little time. But there are so many factors involved in major social change that, even from a long-time perspective, it is difficult to assess the specific contribution of a technological change or one particular work plan.

In the nineteenth century, the prices of farm products dropped and the quantity increased. The same thing happened in the production of textiles, steam engines, and locomotives. Food price and quantity owed less to machines than did the availability of manufactured products. For the consumer, however, the result was beneficial regardless of the cause, although at the same time other changes occurred, not all of which were beneficial. Products were more accessible, transportation and communication were better, and individual options kept increasing. But there was a growing disparity between the very rich and the very poor. Economic decline and job loss could strike the most innocent without warning and without redress.

This pattern has continued to the present with both benefits and costs multiplying. Nearly all citizens live far better lives in material terms than early Americans, and a large but uncertain part of this improvement is the result of technological change and development. On the other side of the coin, the tensions and strain of society have increased and pollution and toxic wastes keep rising. The sense of injustice becomes more evident among disadvantaged groups, and the threat of nuclear war hangs over everyone.

The need to assess costs and benefits of major technological change has become inescapable. Increasing mechanization often decreases the labor component or converts it to service rather than manufacturing operations. The consumer lives better; the quality of life has risen. But the costs, at worst the cost of the nuclear threat, have sometimes been so high that they may invalidate the benefits. Costs can never be eliminated, but benefits are enormous, and the best that can be hoped is to push forward the highest benefits at the lowest cost. Fortunately, technology has improved the tools for dealing with problems at the same time that it has created many of those problems.

The technology of industrialization has moved us into an increasingly complex world. Human power has been greatly increased, but whenever exercised, the new power brings ills as well as good. Humankind has reached a point where it must work consistently to exercise its new power over technology and social organization.

Quotation Sources

CHAPTER II

1. Quoted by Charles M. Andrews, *The Colonial Period of American History* (New Haven, 1934) vol. 1, 58.
2. Thomas Paine, *Common Sense* (Philadelphia, 1776; reprint Danbury, CT, 1976), 34.
3. Thomas Jefferson, *The Declaration of Independence* (1776).
4. *Constitution of the United States*, Amendments, Article I (1791).
5. Tench Coxe, *An Address to an Assembly of Friends of American Manufactures, Convened for the Purpose of establishing a Society for the Encouragement of Manufactures and the Useful Arts* Philadelphia, 1787; reprinted, Michael Brewster Folsom and Steven D. Lubar, eds., *The Philosophy of Manufactures: Early Debates over Industrialization in the United States*, (Cambridge, MA, 1982), 44.
6. Quoted in Edgar F. Smith, *Priestley in America, 1794–1804* (Philadelphia, 1920), 50.

CHAPTER III

1. Johann David Schöpf, *Travels in the Confederation, 1783–1784*, trans. by Alfred J. Morrison (Philadelphia, 1911), I, 30.
2. Quoted in Brooke Hindle, *The Pursuit of Science in Revolutionary America* (Chapel Hill, NC, 1956), 255.
3. Alexander Hamilton, "Report on the Subject of Manufactures," *The Papers of Alexander Hamilton*, ed. by Harold C. Syrett and Jacob E. Cooke (New York, 1966), X, 251.
4. Tench Coxe, "An Address," Folsom and Lubar, eds., *Philosophy of Manufactures*, 38.
5. John Adams, *A Defense of the Constitutions of Government of the United States of America* (London, 1787).
6. George Washington, *The Washington Papers*, ed. by Saul K. Padover (New York, 1955), 267–68.
7. George Logan, "Five Letters Addressed to the Yeomanry of the United States" (1792), Folsom and Lubar, eds., *Philosophy of Manufactures*, 110.
8. John Morgan, "Whether it be most beneficial to the United States to promote agriculture, or to encourage the mechanic arts and manufactures" (1789), ibid., 74.
9. Thomas Jefferson, *Notes on the State of Virginia* (1st ed. 1785; reprint New York, 1964), 157–58.
10. Thomas Jefferson to Thomas Digges, June 19, 1788, *The Papers of Thomas Jefferson*, ed. by Julian Boyd (Princeton, 1955), XIII, 260.

CHAPTER IV

1. "Letters of Phineas Bond," *American Historical Association Annual Report*, I (1889), 552.

CHAPTER V

1. Robert Fulton quoted in Alice Crary Sutcliffe, *Robert Fulton and the Clermont* (New York, 1909), 60.
2. *Constitution of the United States*, Article I, Section 8.
3. "Patent Act, 1790," Henry L. Ellsworth, *Digest of Patents Issued by the United States, 1790 to January 1, 1839* (Washington, 1840).
4. *Constitution of the United States*, Article I, Section 8.
5. Thomas Ewbank, *A Description and Historical Account of Hydraulic and Other Machines for Raising Water* (New York, 1842), vi.
6. Munn & Co., *The United States Patent Law: Instructions How to Obtain Letters Patent for New Inventions* (New York, 1866), [109].
7. Quoted in John F. Kasson, *Civilizing the Machine: Technology and Republican Values in America: 1776–1900* (New York, 1976), 44.
8. Ibid., 82.
9. Jabez Hollingworth in *The Hollingworth Letters: Technical Change in the Textile Industries, 1826–1837*, ed. by Thomas W. Leavitt (Cambridge, MA, 1969), 93.
10. Thomas Mann, *Picture of a Factory Village* (Providence, 1833), 1.
11. William E. Channing, *Works* (Boston, 1884), 39.
12. Quoted in Kasson, *Civilizing the Machine*, 130–31.

CHAPTER VII

1. John Fitch, quoted in Brooke Hindle, *Emulation and Invention* (New York, 1981), 28. 1981), 28.

CHAPTER VIII

1. Quoted in Leo Marx, *The Machine in the Garden: Technology and the Pastoral Ideal* (New York, 1964), 13.
2. John H. White, Jr., *The John Bull: 150 Years a Locomotive* (Washington, 1981), 24.
3. Petition to the Legislative Council and General Assembly of the State of New Jersey, Nov. 12, 1827, and Petition of the "Inhabitants of the Township of Greenwich" to the Legislative Council and General Assembly of the State of New Jersey, no date; Division of Archives and Records Management, New Jersey.
4. *Address of the Directors of the Camden and Amboy Railroad to the People of New Jersey* (Trenton, 1846), 9.
5. *First Annual Report of the President and Directors of the Camden and Amboy Railroad and Transportation Company* (Trenton, 1831), 14.
6. Ibid.
7. Nicholas Wood, *A Practical Treatise on Railroads* (Philadelphia, 1832), xiv–xv, quoted in Carlson, *The Liverpool and Manchester Railway* (New York, 1969), 13.
8. Warren, *A Century of Locomotive Building*, 90.
9. Trenton *Emporium and True American*, November 12, 1831, 3.
10. Quoted in White, *The John Bull*, 24.

11. *First Annual Report*, 17.

12. *Memoir of the Delaware and Raritan Canal and Camden and Amboy Railroad* (n.p., 1834), 7.

13. *Harper's Weekly*, 1865.

14. "A Burlingtonian," *The Late Camden and Amboy Railroad Accident: A Review of the Camden and Amboy Company's Report on the Accident of the 29th of August 1855* (Burlington, NJ, 1855).

15. Philadelphia *Ledger and Transcript*, October 15, 1855.

CHAPTER IX

1. Samuel Colt's testimony is quoted in David A. Hounshell, *From the American System to Mass Production, 1800–1932: The Development of Manufacturing Technology in the United States* (Baltimore, 1984), 19.

2. Daniel Webster, "Lecture before the Society for the Diffusion of Useful Knowledge" (1836), reprinted in Folsom and Lubar, *The Philosophy of Manufactures*, 397.

3. Asa Briggs, *Iron Bridge to Crystal Palace: Impact and Images of the Industrial Revolution* (London, 1979), 37–38.

4. Philadelphia *Public Ledger*, January 30 and February 1, 1841, reprinted in John R. Commons, et al., eds., *Documentary History of American Industrial Society* (Cleveland, 1910–11) VII, 102–4.

5. Ibid.

6. Alexis de Tocqueville, *Democracy in America* (1835, reprint New York, 1960), II, 46.

7. *Preliminary Report on the Eighth Census, 1860* (Washington, 1863), 60.

8. West Chester *Village Record*, November 13, 1849.

9. Andrew Ure, *Philosophy of Manufactures, or An Exposition of the Scientific, Moral, and Commercial Economy of the Factory System of Great Britain* (3d ed., 1861; reprint New York, 1969), 15.

10. De Tocqueville, *Democracy in America*, II, 168–71.

11. Quoted in Thomas Dublin, *Women at Work: The Transformation of Work and Culture in Lowell, Massachusetts, 1826–1860* (New York, 1979), 86.

12. Seth Luther, *Address to the Workingmen of New England* (Boston, 1833).

CHAPTER X

1. Quoted in Caroline F. Ware, *The Early New England Cotton Manufacture: A Study in Industrial Beginnings* (Boston, 1931), 20.

2. Quoted in John H. White, Jr., "Once the Greatest of Builders: The Norris Locomotive Works," *Railroad History*, 150 (1984), 31.

3. Quoted in *Gazetteer and Business Directory for Addison County [Vermont], 1881–82*.

CHAPTER XI

1. Thomas Jefferson to Thaddeus Kosciusko, June 28, 1812, quoted in Folsom and Lubar, *Philosophy of Manufactures*, 28.

2. Quoted in Barbara Tucker, *Samuel Slater and the Origins of the American Textile Industry, 1790–1869* (Ithaca, NY, 1984), 89.

3. Isaac Markham to David Markham, May 30, 1821, Markham Collection, Sheldon Museum, Middlebury, VT.

4. Quoted in Dublin, *Women at Work*, 86.

CHAPTER XII

1. Blanche Evans Hazard, *The Organization of the Boot and Shoe Industry in Massachusetts before 1875* (Cambridge, MA, 1921; reprint New York, 1969), 85–86.

CHAPTER XIII

1. Quoted in Milton Drake, comp., *Almanacs of the United States* (New York, 1962), I, ix.

2. Henry Terry, *American Clock Making, Its Early History*, in *Illustrated Catalogue of Clocks Manufactured by the Terry Clock Company* (Pittsfield, MA, 1885), 4.

3. Quoted in Merritt Roe Smith, *Harpers Ferry Armory and the New Technology: The Challenge of Change* (Ithaca, NY, 1977), 136.

4. Record Group 156, Letters Received, Springfield Armory, 1816, Entry 1362, National Archives.

CHAPTER XIV

1. Quoted in Arthur E. Bestor, Jr., *Backwoods Utopias: The Sectarian Origins and the Owenite Phase of Communitarian Socialism in America, 1663–1829* (Philadelphia, 1950), 75.

2. Henry David Thoreau, "Paradise (to be) Regained," reprinted Folsom and Lubar, *Philosophy of Manufactures*, 423, 415, 417.

3. John A. Etzler, *The Paradise within Reach of all Men, without Labor, by Powers of Nature and Machinery* (Pittsburgh, 1833), 48.

4. John A. Etzler, "Description of the Naval Automaton," reprinted John Nydahl, ed., *The Collected Works of John Adolphus Etzler* (Delmar, NY, 1977), 3.

5. John A. Roebling, *Report . . . to . . . the Covington and Cincinnati Bridge Company* (Trenton, 1867), 50.

CHAPTER XV

1. *New York Tribune*, February 16, 1850, quoted in Robert F. Dalzell, Jr., *American Participation at the Great Exhibition of 1851* (Amherst, MA, 1960), 27.

2. Quoted in Nikolaus Pevsner, *High Victorian Design: A Study of the Exhibits of 1851* (London, 1951), 12.

3. Benjamin P. Johnson, *Great Exhibition of the Industry of all Nations* (Albany, NY, 1852), 154.

4. Edward Singleton Holden, *Memorials of W. C. Bond and G. P. Bond* (San Francisco, 1897), 87–88.

5. William A. Drew, *Glimpses and Gatherings, during a Voyage and Visit to London and the Great Exhibition, in the Summer of 1851* (Augusta, ME, 1852), 318, 326.

6. *Springfield Republican*, November 13, 1850, quoted in Dalzell, *American Participation*, 21.

7. Central Committee for the United States, *On the Exhibition of Industry of all Nations, to be Held in London, 1851* (Washington, 1850), 17.

8. *New York Herald*, August 1, 1850, quoted in Dalzell, *American Participation*, 27.

9. *Official Descriptive and Illustrated Catalogue of the Great Exhibition 1851* (London, 1851), 1431.

10. Ibid.

11. Quoted in Pevsner, *High Victorian Design*, 119–21.

12. Quoted in Nathan Rosenberg, *The American System of Manufactures: The Report of the Committee on the Machinery of the United States 1855 and the Special Reports of George Wallis and Joseph Whitworth 1854* (Edinburgh, 1969), 18.

13. *Reports of the Juries*, 65.

14. Quoted in Rosenberg, *The American System*, 18–19.

15. London *Times*, September 19, 1851, quoted in C. T. Rogers, *American Superiority at the World's Fair* (Philadelphia, 1852), 123.

CHAPTER XVI

1. Gertrude Stein quoted in Gilbert A. Harrison, *Gertrude Stein's America* (Washington, 1965), 67.

Suggested Readings

The American Industrial Revolution

Books on the American Industrial Revolution have appeared with increasing frequency. No major syntheses have yet emerged, but works based upon specific studies with broadening insights are rapidly improving our understanding of the technological, economic, and social dimensions of this period.

A brief general overview of early developments is Thomas C. Cochran, *Frontiers of Change: Early Industrialism in America* (New York, 1981). David A. Hounshell, *From the American System to Mass Production, 1800–1932: The Development of Manufacturing Technology in the United States* (Baltimore, 1984), applies wide historical concerns to selected technologies. Joseph and Frances Gies, *The Ingenious Yankees* (New York, 1976), covers a range of important questions in a popular presentation. Michael Brewster Folsom and Steven D. Lubar, eds., *The Philosophy of Manufactures: Early Debates over Industrialization in the United States* (Cambridge, MA, 1982), reprints critical contemporary viewpoints on industrialization.

The approach of economic historians has been very fruitful. A survey of exactly this period is Douglas C. North, *Economic Growth of the United States, 1790–1860* (New York, 1961). Nathan Rosenberg, most accessibly in *Technology and American Economic Growth* (New York, 1972), brings the understanding of an economist within the context of history. More typical of the questions asked by economic historians is Peter Temin, *Causal Factors in American Economic Growth in the Nineteenth Century* (New York, 1975). Herbert G. Gutman, *Work, Culture, and Society in Industrializing America, 1815–1920* (New York, 1976), represents the increasing concern for labor history.

American civilization studies, especially literary histories, are few in number, but some are significant. John F. Kasson, *Civilizing the Machine: Technology and Republican Values in America, 1776–1900* (New York, 1976), brings a literary history approach to the examination of technology. Leo Marx, *The Machine in the Garden: Technology and the Pastoral Idea* (New York, 1964), has had continuing influence on interpretations.

The new social history and recent interest in women's history have not dealt in surveys and have led to only a few books touching the Industrial Revolution. Related chapters are a part of Martha Moore Trescott, ed., *Dynamos and Virgins Revisited* (Metuchen, NJ, 1979), and of James B. Gardner and George Rollie Adams, *Ordinary People and Everyday Life: Perspectives on the New Social History* (Nashville, 1983). Richard D. Brown, *Modernization: The Transformation of American Life, 1600–1865* (New York, 1976), applies a social science concept to this period.

The following supplementary readings relate to the sequence of the text in each chapter. The major locations of associated artifacts are also suggested. Quotation sources are separately identified.

CHAPTER I

The Industrial Revolution and Technological Change

Technology had been growing and its economic and social relationships expanding since antiquity, but the most specific forecast of the mechanization associated with the Industrial Revolution was pictured in the theaters of machines that began to appear in the sixteenth century. Most of them, such as Jacques Besson, *Theatre des Instrumens Mathematiques* (Lyons, 1579), and Giovanni Branca, *Le Machine* (Rome, 1629), are available only in their original languages. One of the best, Agostino Ramelli, *Le diverse et artificiose machine* (Paris, 1588), initially published with both Italian and French texts, has been translated into English by E. S. Ferguson and M. T. Gnudi under the title *The Various and Ingenious Machines* (Baltimore, 1976).

Although England was the primary center of the classical Industrial Revolution of the eighteenth and early nineteenth centuries, it produced no theaters of machines. The closest English parallels were cheaper and cruder works such as Joseph Moxon, *Mechanick Exercises or the Doctrine of Handy-Works* (London, 1683), which initially appeared as a succession of pamphlets at six pence each. The third (1703) edition is available in a 1979 reprint by the Early American Industries Association.

The term "industrial revolution" was coined in England and continues to be used most often by British scholars. Arnold Toynbee generally is credited with introducing the term in lectures published posthumously in 1884; a reprint of the lectures is entitled *The Industrial Revolution* (Boston, 1962). Asa Briggs, *Iron Bridge to Crystal Palace: Impact and Images of the Industrial Revolution* (London, 1979), is a popular tour with good emphasis on pictorial dimensions.

From the beginning, attention was given to the long chronology and the wide diffusion of English advances. John U. Nef, *The Conquest of the Material World* (Chicago, 1964), makes a strong case for the critical change having taken place in the move to a coal-based technology in the sixteenth and seventeenth centuries. David S. Landes, *The Unbound Prometheus: Technological Change and Industrial Development in Western Europe from 1750 to the Present* (Cambridge, UK, 1969), begins with the English Industrial Revolution and follows its diffusion and chronological extension. Siegfried Giedion, *Mechanization Takes Command: A Contribution to Anonymous History* (Oxford, 1948) follows a similar course, focusing on American as well as British and French experiences.

Much has been written on the topical aspects of the English Industrial Revolution. Effective examples are: Richard L. Hills, *Power in the Industrial Revolution* (Manchester, UK, 1970); Jennifer Tann, *The Development of the Factory* (London, 1970); and Theodore A. Wertime, *The Coming of the Age of Steel* (Chicago, 1962), which is broader in scope, beginning about 1400. Giving primary attention to steam engine development, Frances M. Honour, *The State of the Industrial Revolution in 1776* (New York, 1977), examines the English Industrial Revolution at the time the American Revolution began.

A number of sites of important activity during the English Industrial Revolution have been identified and restored. One of the most important is the Ironbridge Gorge Museum at Ironbridge, UK. It embraces the original iron bridge, Abraham Darby's iron furnace, operating steam engines, and important collections. The broadest collections are housed in the Science Museum, South Kensington, London.

CHAPTER II

The New United States: Land of Opportunities

Many historical writings give some attention to the great opportunities the United States offered individuals, but few deal centrally with them. Louis B. Wright, *The Dream of Pros-*

perity in Colonial America (New York, 1965), considers anticipations of material wealth from the beginning. Bernard Bailyn, *Ideological Origins of the American Revolution* (Cambridge, MA, 1967), covers the reception and development of libertarian views. Fred Somkin, *Unquiet Eagle: Memory and Desire in the Idea of American Freedom* (Ithaca, 1967), examines the use and misuse of the concept of freedom.

The gift of land and natural resources is assumed by most historians. Ralph H. Brown, *Mirror for Americans* (New York, 1943), remains a helpful geographer's view of the early land. Effects of the plenty of wood is presented in Brooke Hindle, ed., *America's Wooden Age: Aspects of its Early Technology* (Tarrytown, NY, 1975). The best overview of iron is Arthur C. Bining, *British Regulation of the Colonial Iron Industry* (Philadelphia, 1933). Margaret Hindle Hazen and Robert M. Hazen, eds., *Wealth Inexhaustible: A History of America's Mineral Industries to 1850* (New York, 1985), provides a survey of early mineral exploitation.

A good picture of the population at the beginning of the country is presented by Robert V. Wells, *The Population of the British Colonies in America* (Princeton, 1975). David Brion Davis, *The Problem of Slavery in the Age of Revolution, 1770–1823* (Ithaca, 1975), presents an influential view of the role of the slave. Gary B. Nash, *Red, White, and Black: The Peoples of Early America* (Englewood Cliffs, NJ, 1974), is a social survey.

CHAPTER III

The Promise of Technology

Most traditional technology was well represented in America before independence, its success always depending on individual skills. Carl Bridenbaugh, *The Colonial Craftsman* (New York, 1950), approaches the question through the artisans, Charles F. Montgomery, *America's Arts and Skills* (New York, 1957), through the artifacts, and Silvio A. Bedini, *Thinkers and Tinkers* (New York, 1975), through both. Brooke Hindle, *The Pursuit of Science in Revolutionary America, 1735–1787* (Chapel Hill, NC, 1956), views this technology in a larger context.

The long history of water milling is presented in Terry S. Reynolds, *Stronger than a Hundred Men: A History of the Vertical Water Wheel* (Baltimore, 1983). A good view of the mill in America is Charles Howell and Alan Keller, *The Mill at Philipsburg Manor, Upper Mills and a Brief History of Milling* (Tarrytown, 1977).

A number of wood technologies are reviewed in Brooke Hindle, ed., *Material Culture of the Wooden Age* (Tarrytown, 1981). More focused studies are Charles F. Hummel, *With Hammer in Hand: The Dominy Craftsmen of East Hampton* (Charlottesville, VA, 1968); Carl W. Condit, *American Building: Materials and Techniques from the First Colonial Settlements to the Present* (Chicago, 1968); C. A. Weslager, *The Log Cabin in America from Pioneer Days to the Present* (New Brunswick, 1969); John Fitchen, *The New World Dutch Barn: A Study of Its Characteristics, Its Structural System, and Its Probable Erectional Procedures* (Syracuse, 1968); and Joseph A. Goldenberg, *Shipbuilding in Colonial America* (Charlottesville, VA, 1976). James A. Mulholland, *A History of Metals in Colonial America* (Birmingham, 1981), examines the story of metals, which was less important than wood at that time but grew more rapidly when the Industrial Revolution began.

Both work in traditional technologies and such advances as Americans made tended to be anonymous. Henry J. Kauffman in *The Pennsylvania-Kentucky Rifle* (New York, 1960) follows one of the more important of these developments. The usual nonverbal demeanor of the artisan is reversed in *The Autobiography of John Fitch*, ed. by Frank D. Prager (Philadelphia, 1976). John Worrell, "Ceramic Production in the Exchange Network," in Sarah Peabody Turnbaugh, ed., *Domestic Pottery in the Northeast United States* (San Diego, 1985), 153–69, discusses a specific farmer-artisan who made pottery. Brooke Hindle, *David Rittenhouse* (Princeton, 1964), tells the story of the most celebrated American artisan, who worked entirely within traditional technologies.

The Smithsonian Institution's National Museum of American History holds craft collections, instruments, Pennsylvania rifles, ship models, and even a sawmill. Surviving craft products often fall into the category of decorative arts; these are well represented in the Henry Francis du Pont Winterthur Museum, Winterthur, Delaware. Many gristmills have been restored to working condition, a good example being at Philipsburg Manor, Upper Mills, North Tarrytown, New York.

CHAPTER IV

The Transfer of Technology

The transfer of technology came under serious scrutiny in the 1950s and 1960s. The process began with the first settlements, but the Industrial Revolution transfers reached a developed technological society. Brooke Hindle, *Technology in Early America* (Chapel Hill, NC, 1966), places transfer in context and offers bibliographical leads. Rowland T. Berthoff, *British Immigrants in Industrial America, 1790–1950* (Cambridge, MA, 1953), examines the most important mechanism of transfer: the immigration of informed artisans and mechanics.

Perhaps the most visible transfer, begun by immigrant mechanics, was that of the new textile technologies. David J. Jeremy, *Transatlantic Industrial Revolution: The Diffusion of Textile Technologies between Britain and America, 1790–1830s* (Cambridge, MA, 1981), covers just this process, plus the reverse transfer from the United States that began early. Still useful on the outstanding transfer is George S. White, *Memoir of Samuel Slater* (1st ed., Philadelphia, 1836; reprint New York, 1967); more current is Barbara M. Tucker, *Samuel Slater and the Origins of the American Textile Industry, 1790–1860* (Ithaca, 1984). The wool transfer is covered by Arthur H. Cole, *The American Wool Manufacture* (1st ed., Cambridge, MA, 1926; reprint New York, 1969). Anthony F. C. Wallace, *Rockdale: The Growth of an American Village in the Early Industrial Revolution* (New York, 1972), includes transfer questions within a community study.

Of the same order of importance to the Industrial Revolution as textile machinery was the steam engine, but it was transferred to America in a somewhat disorderly fashion. The effort to introduce the Newcomen engine failed. The English background of this is well covered by L. T. C. Rolt, *Thomas Newcomen* (Dawlish, Devon, 1963), but the Hornblower transfer is offered only in the ancient and journalistic William Nelson, *Josiah Hornblower and the First Steam Engine in America* (Newark, 1883).

The successful introduction of the steam engine was associated with the rise of the steamboat, which is presented in chapter 7. It was soon paralleled by the use of stationary steam engines, reviewed in Carroll W. Pursell, Jr., *Early Stationary Steam Engines in America: A Study in Migration of a Technology* (Washington, 1969), with a major emphasis on the transfer process. Louis C. Hunter, *A History of Industrial Power in the United States, 1780–1930*, Volume II, *Steam Power* (Charlottesville, VA, 1985), examines in detail the contribution of steam power to manufacturing and industrialization.

Although late, the effective initial railroads in the United States reverted to the importation of the key machines, English-built locomotives. Other methods had been projected earlier by John Stevens; these are at least noted in Archibald Douglas Turnbull, *John Stevens: An American Record* (New York, 1928).

The long delay in putting new ironmaking techniques to use was economically understandable but has received little attention. Something of the picture emerges in James M. Swank, *History of the Manufacture of Iron in all Ages and Particularly in the United States from Colonial Times to 1891* (2d ed., Philadelphia, 1892). Paul F. Paskof, *Industrial Evolution: Organization, Structure, and Growth of the Pennsylvania Iron Industry, 1750–1860* (Baltimore, 1983), confronts the delayed development, although his explanations have been criticized.

The largest collection of artifacts considered critical in the transfer of technology is held by the National Museum of American History. These include a cylinder from the Newcomen engine first erected in 1753, two of Slater's machines, Stevens's 1804 steamboat engine and boiler, Fitch's 1793 French patent, the *John Bull*, and parts of other locomotives.

CHAPTER V

Invention and Technological Change

Contemporary writings express best the early feelings about invention. Two such publications are T. G. Fessenden, *The Register of Arts, or a Compendious View of the Most Useful Modern Discoveries and Inventions* (Philadelphia, 1808), and J. Leander Bishop, *A History of American Manufactures from 1608 to 1860: Exhibiting the Origin and Growth of the Principal Mechanic Arts and Manufactures . . . With a Notice of the Important Inventions, Tariffs, and the Results of Each Decennial Census* (Philadelphia, 1861). Particularly graphic are the presentations by Munn & Co., the leading patent company and publisher of *Scientific American*, headed "How to Invent" and "Mechanical Movements," in *The United States Patent Law: Instructions How to Obtain Letters Patent for New Inventions* (New York, 1866), 3–4, 83–95. A relatively recent review is L. Sprague de Camp, *The Heroic Age of American Invention* (Garden City, NY, 1961).

Brooke Hindle, *Emulation and Invention* (New York, 1981), examines the process of invention and inventive thinking in this period, using the steamboat and the telegraph as case studies. Eugene S. Ferguson, "The Mind's Eye: Nonverbal Thought in Technology," *Science*, 197 (1977), 827–36, stresses nonverbal or spatial thinking. Cyril S. Smith, *From Art to Science: Seventy-two Objects Illustrating the Nature of Discovery* (Cambridge, MA, 1980), presents the viewpoint that art, science, and technology all involve the same sort of spatial thinking.

A controversial study of labor saving as a motivation for invention is H. J. Habakkuk, *American and British Technology in the Nineteenth Century: The Search for Labour-Saving Inventions* (Cambridge, UK, 1962). W. Paul Strassman, *Risk and Technological Innovation: American Manufacturing Methods during the Nineteenth Century* (Ithaca, 1959), approaches invention and innovation from the economic viewpoint.

The patent system has not been adequately studied, but many helpful approaches have been made, among them P. J. Federico, "Outline of the History of the United States Patent Office," *Journal of the Patent Office Society*, 18 (1936), 1–251, and Stacy V. Jones, *The Patent Office* (New York, 1971).

Most celebrated inventors have been studied by a number of historians. Approaches to John Fitch, Robert Fulton, and Samuel F. B. Morse are offered in Hindle, *Emulation and Invention*. Oliver Evans and Cyrus McCormick are included in chapter 6 notes below. Preston W. Barker, *Charles Goodyear: Connecticut Yankee and Rubber Pioneer* (Boston, 1941), is a biography. Elias Howe and Isaac Singer are covered in Grace Rogers Cooper, *The Sewing Machine: Its Invention and Development* (Washington, 1976).

The relationships of government to technology have not been written in those terms. The standard review of the tariff is Frank W. Taussig, *The Tariff History of the United States* (8th ed., New York, 1931). Clay's "American system" can be approached through biography, Clement Eaton, *Henry Clay and the Art of American Politics* (Boston, 1957).

The role of a major voluntary organization and of the relation of science to technology is considered in Bruce Sinclair, *Philadelphia's Philosopher Mechanics: A History of the Franklin Institute, 1824–1865* (Baltimore, 1974). Robert C. Post, *Physics, Patents, and Politics: A Biography of Charles Grafton Page* (New York, 1976), relates science, technology, and government in a specific case study.

The best collection of patent models is held by the National Museum of American History, some of which, as in the case of sewing machines, are full-scale working machines. In addition, the museum holds early versions of many inventions, such as revolvers, muskets, and improved lathes and other power machines. Some replicas and models are also valuable. The Hagley Museum, Wilmington, Delaware, holds important patent models as well as collections related to early powder manufacture and an excellent, operating machine shop.

CHAPTER VI

Farming and Raw Materials Processing: Causes and Effects of Mechanization

A general overview of farming with a sensitivity to technology appears in John T. Schlebecker, *Whereby We Thrive: A History of American Farming, 1607–1972* (Ames, IA, 1975). Aspects of the early story are presented in Darwin P. Kelsey, ed., *Farming in the New Nation: Interpreting American Agriculture, 1790–1840* (Washington, 1972), and the northern developments in Clarence H. Danhof, *Change in Agriculture: The Northern United States, 1820–1870* (Cambridge, MA, 1969).

The history of implements is reviewed in R. Douglas Hurt, *American Farm Tools: From Hand Power to Steam Power* (Manhattan, KS, 1982). More detailed examinations are R. L. Ardrey, *American Agricultural Implements* (1st ed., Chicago, 1894; reprint New York, 1972); Leo Rogin, *The Introduction of Farm Machinery in Relation to the Productivity of Agriculture in the United States during the Nineteenth Century* (Berkeley, CA, 1931); and Reynold M. Wik, *Steam Power on the American Farm* (Philadelphia, 1953). The reaper story is fully covered in William T. Hutchinson, *Cyrus Hall McCormick* (New York, 1930, 2 vols.).

The relation of science to farming is introduced in Margaret W. Rossiter, *The Emergence of Agricultural Science: Justus Liebig and the Americans, 1840–1880* (New Haven, 1975).

The large picture of milling is presented in John Storck and Walter Dorwin Teague, *Flour for Man's Bread: A History of Milling* (Minneapolis, MN, 1952). The most current interpretation of Oliver Evans is Eugene S. Ferguson, *Oliver Evans: Inventive Genius of the American Industrial Revolution* (Greenville, DE, 1980); more detailed is Greville and Dorothy Bathe, *Oliver Evans: A Chronicle of American Engineering* (1st ed., Philadelphia, 1935; reprint New York, 1972). The primary source is Oliver Evans, *The Young Mill-Wright and Miller's Guide* (1st ed., Philadelphia, 1795; reprint New York, 1972).

A brief overview of American iron is W. David Lewis, *Iron and Steel in America* (Greenville, DE, 1976). Peter Temin, *Iron and Steel in Nineteenth Century America* (Cambridge, MA, 1964), is an economic analysis. Specific studies are Joseph E. Walker, *Hopewell Village: A Social and Economic History of an Iron-Making Community* (Philadelphia, 1966), and James D. Norris, *Frontier Iron: The Maramec Iron Works, 1826–1876* (Madison, WI, 1964).

The introduction of new ironmaking methods was directly dependent on coal availability, which is explained in Alfred D. Chandler, "Anthracite Coal in the Beginnings of the Industrial Revolution in the United States," *Business History Review*, 46 (1972), 147–81. A more extended examination is Frederick Moore Binder, *Coal Age Empire: Pennsylvania Coal and Its Utilization to 1860* (Harrisburg, PA, 1974).

Many agricultural museums display useful artifacts and implements, but the most attractive are the living historical farms that reproduce farming patterns of specific regions and periods. Among the more successful are Old Sturbridge Village, Sturbridge, Massachusetts; the Farmer's Museum, Cooperstown, New York; and the Pennsylvania Farm and Museum of Landis Valley, Lancaster, Pennsylvania. Western farms tend to be late, but the Living History Farms of Des Moines, Iowa, reach back to this period. Among surviving iron furnaces, Hopewell Village, Elverson, Pennsylvania, offers a well-restored view of production through most of this period.

CHAPTER VII

Transportation and the Need for Invention

The state of roads and road transportation at the beginning of this period is well described in Christopher Colles, *A Survey of the Roads of the United States of America, 1789* (1st ed., New York, 1789; reprint with introduction, Cambridge, MA, 1961). The continuing bad state of roads is documented in W. M. Gillespie, *A Manual of the Principles and Practice of Road-Making* (New York, 1847). The use of roads is chronicled in Oliver W. Holmes and Peter T. Rohrbach, *Stagecoach East: Stagecoach Days in the East from the Colonial Period to the Civil War* (Washington, 1983).

The best canal histories deal with individual canals, but a popular overview is Madeline Sadler Waggoner, *The Long Haul West: The Great Canal Era, 1817–1850* (New York, 1958). Carter Goodrich, Julius Rubin, H. Jerome Cranmer, and Harvey H. Segal examine the economic side with limited interest in technology in *Canals and American Economic Development* (New York, 1961). The greatest canal is studied in Ronald E. Shaw, *Erie Water West: A History of the Erie Canal, 1792–1854* (Lexington, KY, 1966); the Chesapeake and Delaware in Ralph D. Gray, *The National Waterway: A History of the Chesapeake and Delaware Canal, 1769–1965* (Urbana, IL, 1967); and the Pennsylvania scene in William H. Shank, *The Amazing Pennsylvania Canals* (York, PA, 1973).

Still the best overall history of steamboats is James Thomas Flexner, *Steamboats Come True: American Inventors in Action* (New York, 1944). Several previously mentioned works are important here, too: Hindle, *Emulation and Invention*; Fitch, *Autobiography*; Turnbull, *John Stevens*; and Pursell, *Stationary Steam Engines*. Among Fulton biographies, John S. Morgan, *Robert Fulton* (New York, 1977), may be mentioned. Although ancient, Robert MacFarlane, *History of Propellors and Steam Navigation* (New York, 1851), is pertinent. Louis C. Hunter effectively combines economic history and the history of technology in *Steamboats on the Western Rivers* (New York, 1949).

Remnants of early roads are found throughout the country, the most evident being covered bridges; the longest covered bridge is at Windsor, New Hampshire. Segments of many canals survive, for example, the Erie Canal in New York and the Chesapeake and Ohio in Maryland. Few early steamboats survive, the most helpful components being preserved at the National Museum of American History.

CHAPTER VIII

The John Bull *and the Rise of American Railroading*

Aspects of early railroading are covered in many books. Good general sources are John F. Stover, *American Railroads* (Chicago, 1961), and George Rogers Taylor, *The Transportation Revolution* (New York, 1951). The railroad as symbol of American progress is considered in Marx, *Machine in the Garden*. The history of the locomotive is exhaustively covered in John H. White, Jr., *American Locomotives, An Engineering History, 1830–1880* (Baltimore, 1968), and "Railroads: Wood to Burn," in Hindle, *Material Culture of the Wooden Age*. The management of railroads is emphasized in Alfred D. Chandler, Jr., *The Visible Hand: The Managerial Revolution in American Business* (Cambridge, MA, 1977); the nature of work on the railroads is covered by Walter Licht, *Working for the Railroad: The Organization of Work in the Nineteenth Century* (Princeton, 1983).

On the occasion of the *John Bull*'s 150th anniversary, the locomotive was put back into working order and run. At that time John H. White, Jr., wrote *The John Bull: 150 Years a Locomotive* (Washington, 1981). The place of the *John Bull* in the history of American locomotives is presented in White's *American Locomotives*, which includes reproductions of the detailed working drawings prepared in 1939 to produce a working replica of the locomotive.

The *John Bull* and a movie taken when it was operated in 1981 are on display at the National Museum of American History. The replica can be seen at the Pennsylvania Railway Museum in Strasburg, Pennsylvania.

The history of the Camden and Amboy Railroad can be found in a number of sources, among them Wheaton J. Lane, *Indian Trail to Iron Horse: A History of Transportation in New Jersey* (Princeton, 1939), which also covers earlier transportation on the New York–Philadelphia route; J. Elfreth Watkins's "Historical Address" in *Ceremonies upon the Completion of the Monument . . . to Mark the First Piece of Track* (Washington, 1891); and Roger Avery Barton, "The Camden and Amboy Railroad Monopoly," *Proceedings of the New Jersey Historical Society* (October 1927), 405–18.

For the history of the Liverpool and Manchester, on which the Camden and Amboy and so many other early railroads were modeled, see Robert E. Carlson, *The Liverpool and Manchester Railway Project 1821–1831* (New York, 1969). The story of the Robert Stephenson and Company shops, which made the locomotives for both railroads, is well told in J. G. H. Warren, *A Century of Locomotive Building by Robert Stephenson and Company, 1823–1923* (Newcastle, UK, 1923).

CHAPTER IX

The Business of Production

American business history is the subject of many general works, including Chandler, *The Visible Hand*; Thomas C. Cochran and William Miller, *The Age of Enterprise: A Social History of Industrial America* (New York, 1942); Keith L. Bryant, Jr., and Henry C. Dethloff, *A History of American Business* (Englewood Cliffs, NJ, 1983); and Elisha P. Douglass, *The Coming of Age of American Business: Three Centuries of Enterprise 1600–1900* (Chapel Hill, NC, 1971). On the history of the corporation, Joseph Stancliffe Davis's *Essays in the Earlier History of American Corporations* (Cambridge, MA, 1917) remains valuable.

Many historians have examined, on the community level, the social and commercial systems that allowed the rapid development of American business. See, for example, Michael B. Katz, *The Social Organization of Early Industrial Capitalism* (Cambridge, MA, 1982); Paul G. Faler, *Mechanics and Manufacturers in the Early Industrial Revolution: Lynn, Massachusetts, 1780–1860* (Albany, NY, 1981); Philip Scranton, *Proprietary Capitalism: The Textile Manufacture at Philadelphia, 1800–1885* (Cambridge, UK, 1983); Howard M. Gitelman, *Workingmen of Waltham: Mobility in American Urban Industrial Development 1850–1890* (Baltimore, 1974); and Susan E. Hirsch, *Roots of the American Working Class: The Industrialization of Crafts in Newark, 1800–1860* (Philadelphia, 1978).

The most complete history of industrial power in the United States is Hunter, *History of Industrial Power Vol. I: Waterpower* and *Vol. II: Steam Power* (Charlottesville, VA, 1985). On steam power, see Pursell, *Early Stationary Steam Engines* and the *Letter from the Secretary of the Treasury, Transmitting . . . Information in Relation to Steam Engines, &c.* (Washington, 1838). Surviving steam engines can be found in many museums; the best collections are at the National Museum of American History and at the Henry Ford Museum, Dearborn, Michigan. Slater Mill Historic Site, Pawtucket, Rhode Island, has reconstructed a breast wheel of 1826; part of the canal system of Lowell, Massachusetts, is interpreted as part of the Lowell National Historic Park.

The development of labor organizations and other responses to the new industrial order is the subject of many books. See, for example, Alan Dawley, *Class and Community: The Industrial Revolution in Lynn* (Cambridge, MA, 1976); Sean Wilentz, *Chants Democratic: New York City and the Rise of the American Working Class, 1788–1850* (New York, 1984); Gutman, *Work, Culture and Society in Industrializing America*; and David Montgomery, *Worker's Control in America: Studies in the History of Work, Technology, and Labor Struggles* (Cambridge, UK, 1979).

The statistical story of the rise of the factory can be found in a number of publications. Most useful are the United States Treasury Department's *Documents Relating to the Manufactures in the United States* (Washington, 1833), better known as the McLane Report, and the United States Censuses of 1810–1860. Some of this material is summarized in *Historical Statistics of the United States, Colonial Times to 1957* (Washington, 1960). Extensive, detailed information on many individual productive enterprises is available in two multivolume works: Victor S. Clark, *History of Manufactures in the United States* (New York, 1929), and John Leander Bishop, *A History of American Manufactures from 1808 to 1860* (3d ed., Philadelphia, 1868).

CHAPTER X

Machine Shops: Machines to Make Machines

Illustrations and a description of the shops of the Norris Locomotive Works are available in "A Visit to the Norris Locomotive Works," *United States Magazine* (October 1855), reprinted in John H. White, Jr., "Once the Greatest of Builders: The Norris Locomotive Works," *Railroad History*, 150 (1984). A model of the shops is on display at the National Museum of American History. There are few contemporary descriptions of antebellum machine shops. One can be found in *Early Engineering Reminiscences (1815–40) of George Escol Sellers*, edited by Eugene S. Ferguson (Washington, 1965).

The technical history of machine tools is described in Robert S. Woodbury, *Studies in the History of Machine Tools* (Cambridge, MA, 1972). Many more studies cover the use of machine tools in manufacturing establishments. Joseph Wickham Roe, *English and American Tool Builders* (New York, 1926), looks at the shops that made machine tools. Merritt Roe Smith, *Harpers Ferry Armory and the New Technology: The Challenge of Change* (Ithaca, 1977), and Felicia Johnson Deyrup, *Arms Makers of the Connecticut Valley: A Regional Study of the Economic Development of the Small Arms Industry, 1798–1870* (Northampton, MA, 1948), examine the development of machine tools in the arms industry. George Sweet Gibb, *The Saco-Lowell Shops: Textile Machinery Building in New England, 1813–1949* (Cambridge, MA, 1950), and Thomas R. Navin, *The Whitin Machine Works since 1831: A Textile Machinery Company in an Industrial Village* (Cambridge, MA, 1950), are business histories of textile machine builders. The role of machine shops in technological change is considered in several case studies in Hounshell, *From the American System to Mass Production*, and, more generally, in Rosenberg, *Perspectives on Technology*.

Several museums have recreated period machine shops. The National Museum of American History has recreated a machine shop of about 1855. Later period shops are at Slater Mill Historic Site, Pawtucket, Rhode Island (c. 1890); The Hagley Museum, Wilmington, Delaware (c. 1880); and the Henry Ford Museum, Dearborn, Michigan (c. 1900). The American Precision Museum, Windsor, Vermont, has an extensive display of the development of machine tools.

CHAPTER XI

Textiles and the Styles of American Industrialization

The American textile industry has been intensively studied, for historians have identified it as the leading edge of American industrialization. The New England branches of the industry are the best covered by historians. An important early work is Caroline F. Ware, *The Early New England Cotton Manufacture: A Study in Industrial Beginnings* (Boston, 1931; reprint New York, 1966).

The small villages of southern New England, and especially Samuel Slater's role in their founding and operation, are the subject of two recent books: Barbara Tucker, *Samuel Slater and the Origins of the American Textile Industry, 1790–1860* (Ithaca, NY, 1984), and Jonathan Prude, *The Coming of Industrial Order: Town and Factory Life in Rural Massachusetts, 1810–1860* (Cambridge, UK, 1983). Many important and illuminating documents about these mill villages are reproduced in Gary Kulik, Roger Parks, and Theodore Penn, eds., *The New England Mill Village, 1790–1860*, Volume 2, in *Documents in American Industrial History* (Cambridge and North Andover, MA, 1982). Perhaps the best book for conveying the "feel" of the mill village, its people, buildings, and machines, is David Macauley's *Mill* (Boston, 1983), an imaginative, historically accurate set of drawings showing the growth of a typical (though nonexistent) New England mill town. Slater's original mill and the area around it is now a museum: Slater Mill Historic Site, Pawtucket, Rhode Island.

Just as the city of Lowell attracted much attention in the nineteenth century, it has caught the attention of historians today. The ideology of the founders of Lowell has been the subject of several books, among them Kasson, *Civilizing the Machine*, and Thomas Bender, *Toward an Urban Vision: Ideas and Institutions in Nineteenth-Century America* (Lexington, KY, 1975). The work at the mills, the central part of the Lowell experience, is best discussed in Thomas Dublin, *Women at Work: The Transformation of Work and Community in Lowell, Massachusetts, 1826–1860* (New York, 1979). A personal view of work from the inside is found in the mill girls' letters compiled in Thomas Dublin, ed., *Farm to Factory: Women's Letters, 1830–1860* (New York, 1981). Lowell's architecture is covered in John Coolidge, *Mill and Mansion: A Study of Architecture and Society in Lowell, Massachusetts, 1820–1865* (New York, 1942). Finally, the economics of the mills is discussed in Paul F. McGouldrick, *New England Textiles in the Nineteenth Century: Profits and Investment* (Cambridge, MA, 1969). Today, a part of the Boston Manufacturing Company's original mill is a museum (The Charles River Museum of Industry, Waltham, Massachusetts), and the city of Lowell is a National Historic Park, where exhibits, films, tours, and demonstrations make the history of the city and the textile industry come alive.

Philadelphia's textile industry has not been so well covered by historians. One small mill village on Philadelphia's outskirts is described intensively in Wallace, *Rockdale*. The city's textile industry more generally is the subject of Scranton's *Proprietary Capitalism*.

The early southern textile industry is the subject of a few articles and books, among them Ernest McPherson Lander, Jr., *The Textile Industry in Antebellum South Carolina* (Baton Rouge, LA, 1969), and Broadus Mitchell, *William Gregg, Factory Master of the Old South* (Chapel Hill, NC, 1928; reprint New York, 1966). Gregg's *Essays on Domestic Industry* has also been reprinted (Charleston, SC, 1845; reprint Graniteville, SC, 1941).

An important overall study of the technology of the industry is Jeremy, *Transatlantic Industrial Revolution*. Some of the machines studied in that book can be seen at the several museums that have exhibits on the textile industry, among them the Museum of American Textile History, North Andover, Massachusetts; Old Slater Mill, Pawtucket, Rhode Island; and the National Museum of American History.

CHAPTER XII

The Rise of the Factory

The transition from household economy to a market economy is a classic subject in American history: see Rolla Tyrone, *Household Manufactures in the United States, 1640–1860* (Chicago, 1917; reprint New York, 1966). An early attempt at factory labor as employment for the poor is discussed in Gary B. Nash, "The Failure of Female Factory Labor in Colonial Boston," *Labor History*, 20 (1979), 165–88.

The history of housework has just begun to receive the attention it deserves. Two recent books are Susan Strasser, *Never Done: A History of American Housework* (New York, 1982), and Ruth Schwartz Cowan, *More Work for Mother: The Ironies of Household Technology from the Open Hearth to the Microwave* (New York, 1983).

The garment trades have recently been the subject of several studies. Christine Stansell, "The Origins of the Sweatshop: Women and Early Industrialization in New York City," in Michael H. Frisch and Daniel J. Walkowitz, eds., *Working-Class America: Essays on Labor, Community, and American Society* (Urbana, IL, 1983), and Ava Baron and Susan E. Klepp, "'If I Didn't Have my Sewing Machine . . .': Women and Sewing-MachineTechnology," in Joan M. Jensen and Sue Davidson, *A Needle, A Bobbin, A Strike: Women Needleworkers in America* (Philadelphia, 1984), pay special attention to the women who worked in the industry. Raymond Allen Mohl, Jr., *Poverty in New York, 1783–1825* (New York, 1971), and Wilentz, *Chants Democratic*, look more generally at the laboring classes in New York City.

Blanche Evans Hazard, *The Organization of the Boot and Shoe Industry in Massachusetts before 1875* (Cambridge, MA, 1921; reprint New York, 1969), is an excellent pioneering study of that important industry. More recently, several historians have examined Lynn, Massachusetts: Faler, *Mechanics and Manufacturers*; Keith Melder, *Life and Times in Shoe City: The Shoe Workers of Lynn* (Salem, MA, 1979); Dawley, *Class and Community*; William H. Mulligan, "Mechanization and Work in the American Shoe Industry, Lynn, Massachusetts, 1852–1883," *Journal of Economic History*, 41 (1981), 59–63; and Mary H. Blewitt, "Work, Gender and the Artisan Tradition in New England Shoe Making, 1780–1860," *Journal of Social History*, 17 (1983), 221–48.

CHAPTER XIII

Clocks and Guns: The "American System" of Production

The production of goods by means of interchangeable parts, and the various approaches made to that ideal, have been a central subject in the study of the history of American technology. Giedion, in *Mechanization Takes Command*, made a broad survey of the field. More detailed, and centered on the American scene, are Hounshell, *From the American System to Mass Production*, and Otto Mayr and Robert C. Post, *Yankee Enterprise: The Rise of the American System of Manufactures* (Washington, DC, 1982).

Clocks and time consciousness generally are the subject of David Landes, *Revolution in Time: Clocks and the Making of the Modern World* (Cambridge, MA, 1983). On the American clock industry, in addition to the general books mentioned above, see Kenneth Roberts, *Eli Terry and the Connecticut Shelf Clock* (Bristol, CT, 1973); John Joseph Murphy, "Entrepreneurship in the Establishment of the American Clock Industry," *Journal of Economic History*, 24 (1966), 169–86; and Chris Bailey, *Two Hundred Years of American Clocks and Watches* (Englewood Cliffs, NJ, 1975). Collections of American clocks and watches are displayed at many museums; among the best collections are those at the American Clock and Watch Museum, Bristol, Connecticut; the National Association of Watch and Clock Collectors Museum, Columbia, Pennsylvania; the Time Museum, Rockford, Illinois; and the National Museum of American History.

The American arms industry has been the traditional focus of research into the nineteenth-century origins of mass production. The best analysis of the production of arms is Smith, *Harpers Ferry Armory and the New Technology*. Other studies include Edwin Battison, *From Muskets to Mass Production: The Men and the Times that Shaped American Manufacturing* (Windsor, VT, 1976); Deyrup, *Arms Makers of the Connecticut Valley*; and Robert A. Howard, "Interchangeable Parts Reexamined: The Private Sector of the American Arms Industry on the Eve of the Civil War," *Technology and Culture*, 19 (1979), 633–49.

The extension of the American system of manufactures beyond clocks and guns is the subject of Hounshell, *American System*. Detailed studies on specific industries include Cooper, *The Sewing Machine*.

A contemporary view of the American system at work is found in the parliamentary reports on the American system inspired by the impressive American showing at the London Crystal Palace. Nathan Rosenberg has edited these: *The American System of Manufactures: The Report of the Committee on the Machinery of the United States 1855 and the Special Reports of George Wallis and Joseph Whitworth 1854* (Edinburgh, 1969). An excellent early technical survey of the field is Charles Fitch, "Report on the Manufacture of Interchangeable Mechanisms," *Report on the Manufactures of the United States at the Tenth Census*, Vol. 2 (Washington, 1880).

CHAPTER XIV

Communitarian Experiments and the Problems of Industrialization

The story of Robert Owen within a somewhat larger setting is presented in Arthur E. Bestor, Jr., *Backwoods Utopias: The Sectarian Origins and the Owenite Phase of Communitarian Socialism in America, 1663–1829* (Philadelphia, 1950). A more limited study is J. F. C. Harrison, *Quest for the New Moral World: Robert Owen and the Owenites in Britain and America* (London, 1969). Better attention has been given to Shaker technology, notably in Marian Klamkin, *Shaker Folk Art and Industries* (New York, 1972), and June Sprigg, *By Shaker Hands: The Art and the World of the Shakers, the Furniture and Artifacts, and the Spirit and Precepts Embodied in their Simplicity, Beauty, and Functional Practicality* (New York, 1975).

The comparison between John A. Etzler and John A. Roebling has been sketched in Brooke Hindle, "Spatial Thinking in the Bridge Era: John Augustus Roebling versus John Adolphus Etzler," *Bridge to the Future*, Margaret Latimer, Brooke Hindle, and Melvin Kranzberg, eds. (New York, 1984), 131–47. Henry David Thoreau's "Paradise (to be) Regained" is reprinted in Folsom and Lubar, *Philosophy of Manufactures*, 411–19. Etzler's writings are reprinted in *The Collected Works of John Adolphus Etzler*, John Nydahl, ed. (Delmar, NY, 1977). Two particularly pertinent writings of Roebling are John A. Roebling, *Diary of My Journey from Muehlhausen in Thuringia via Bremen to the United States of America in the Year 1831* (Trenton, 1931) and John A. Roebling, *Final Report of John A. Roebling, Civil Engineer to the President and Directors of the Niagara Falls Suspension and Niagara Falls International Bridge Companies* (Rochester, 1855).

Several of the antebellum utopian communities have been restored. Among the Shaker villages, Shakertown, Pleasant Hill, Kentucky, is particularly well done and also functions as a living historical farm. Many remnants of Robert Owen's New Harmony are accessible at New Harmony, Indiana. Buildings from John A. Roebling's community survive in Saxonburg, Pennsylvania. The best of his bridges built before 1860 is the Cincinnati Bridge between Cincinnati, Ohio, and Covington, Kentucky.

CHAPTER XV

The London Crystal Palace Exhibition and the Recognition of American Technology

The Crystal Palace, the first great world's fair, was the subject of an enormous amount of literature. There was the official literature of the fair: the five-volume *Official Descriptive and Illustrated Catalogue of the Great Exhibition 1851* (London, 1851) and the *Reports by the Juries* (London, 1851). A semiofficial description was John Tallis's *History and Description of the Crystal Palace and the Exhibition of World's Industry in 1851* (London, 1852). More than matching the catalogs and descriptions in volume were the ephemera: thousands of poems, broadsides, and pamphlets described the fair or its exhibits. Newspapers, too, were thorough in their description: the *Times* of London gave extensive coverage throughout the exhibition, and American papers and journals were not far behind.

Visitors to the fair added to the literature. Among the most interesting for their American perspective are Benjamin P. Johnson, *Great Exhibition of the Industry of all Nations* (Albany, 1852), and William A. Drew, *Glimpses and Gatherings, during a Voyage and Visit to London and the Great Exhibition, in the Summer of 1851* (Augusta, 1852). A good description of the American prize winners at the fair is C. T. Rogers's *American Superiority at the World's Fair* (Philadelphia, 1852).

Because of its cultural significance, historians have written extensively on the Crystal Palace. Briggs, *Iron Bridge to Crystal Palace*, includes many pictures of the exhibition. A good analysis of the American reaction to the fair is Robert F. Dalzell, Jr., *American Participation in the Great Exhibition of 1851* (Amherst, MA, 1960); the fair as a showcase of design is the subject of Nikolaus Pevsner, *High Victorian Design: A Study of the Exhibits of 1851* (London, 1951). There is an extensive art historical literature on Powers's *The Greek Slave:* two good examples are Linda Hyman, "*The Greek Slave* by Hiram Powers: High Art as Popular Culture," *Art Journal*, 35 (1976), 216–23, and Vivien M. Green, "Hiram Powers's *The Greek Slave:* Emblem of Freedom," *The American Art Journal*, 14 (1982), 31–39.

CHAPTER XVI

Epilogue: The Role of Technology, Past and Present

Comparing current views of technological change and industrialization with those of the era of the Industrial Revolution is difficult. All historians are influenced by the present in their studies of the past. Some students of the recent past apply understanding of early history to those inquiries. However, reliable returns are not yet in on recent history and even less on the present. As a result, most writings on these subjects are not completely dependable and sometimes emotional.

The American rebellions of the late 1960s and 1970s were followed by many reconsiderations of technology. Victor C. Ferkiss, *Technological Man: The Myth and the Reality* (New York, 1969), and Alvin Toffler, *Future Shock* (New York, 1970), offered differing views of the human effects of technology. One statistical study presuming to show that change seldom had the anticipated results is presented in Donella H. Meadows, Dennis L. Meadows, Jorgen Randers, and William W. Behrens, III, *The Limits to Growth: A Report on the Club of Rome's Project on the Predicament of Mankind* (New York, 1972). Very influential is E. F. Schumacher, *Small Is Beautiful* (New York, 1973), which points out that high technology is not the best approach in all societies and all situations. These and more blatant critiques led to reactions such as the engineer's view taken in Samuel C. Florman, *The Existential Pleasures of Engineering* (New York, 1975), and *Blaming Technology: The Irrational Search for Scapegoats* (New York, 1981).

Areas of current technological enthusiasm comparable to that of the Industrial Revolution have had mixed study. Computer histories are emerging, such as Kent C. Redmond and Thomas M. Smith, *Project Whirlwind: The History of a Pioneer Computer* (Maynard, MA, 1980). A more current compilation is Tom Forester, ed., *The Information Technology Revolution* (Cambridge, MA, 1985), especially Howard Rosenbrook, et al., "A New Industrial Revolution?," 635–47. An open view is Colin Norman, *The God that Limps: Science and Technology in the Eighties* (New York, 1981). A serious look at the present is "Robotics, Future Factories, Future Workers," special issue of *The Annals of the Academy of Political and Social Science* (November 1983). A larger, less studied reach is Richard A. Kasschau, Roy Lachman, and Kenneth R. Laughery, *Information Technology and Psychology: Prospects for the Future* (New York, 1982).

Japanese production has had too little attention. John B. Rae, *Nissan/Datsun: A History of Nissan Motor Corporation in U.S.A., 1960–1980* (New York, 1982) is straight history. One specific comparison is Leonard H. Lynn, *How Japan Innovates: A Comparison with the U.S. in the Case of Oxygen Steelmaking* (Boulder, CO, 1982). A Japanese examination of recent achievements is Masanori Moritani, *Japanese Technology: Getting the Best for the Least* (Tokyo, 1982). A briefer look is Richard Casement, "Tomorrow's Leaders: A Survey of Japanese Technology," *The Economist* (June 19, 1982).

By far, the worst threat from technology is nuclear war. This key government-technology accomplishment has been well written up in Richard G. Hewlett and Oscar E. Anderson, Jr., *The New World, 1939/1946* (University Park, PA, 1962), and Richard G. Hewlett and Francis Duncan, *Atomic Shield, 1947/1952* (University Park, PA, 1969). The ultimate human effects, as stated in Robert Jay Lifton and Richard Falk, *Indefensible Weapons: The Political and Psychological Case against Nuclearism* (New York, 1982); Carl Sagan, Paul Ehrlich, et al., *The Cold and the Dark: The World after Nuclear War* (New York, 1984); and Freeman Dyson, *Weapons and Hope* (New York, 1984), always project other than technological solutions.

The threat cannot be overemphasized, but the dark side of other aspects of history has been exaggerated by a few writers. Most historians still seek to examine past good and evil with all the integrity they can muster; an example of success in this effort is Elting E. Morison, *From Know-How to Nowhere: The Development of American Technology* (New York, 1974). Even more impressively objective and creative are some of the newest studies of specific twentieth-century technologies such as Thomas P. Hughes, *Networks of Power: Electrification in Western Society, 1880–1930* (Baltimore, 1983), and Hugh J. Aitken, *The Continuous Wave: Technology and American Radio, 1900–1932* (Princeton, 1985).

Illustration Credits

We gratefully acknowledge the following persons and institutions for the photographs, drawings, and maps in this book. Illustrations obtained from the National Museum of American History of the Smithsonian Institution are designated by the abbreviation NMAH.

CHAPTER I

1. NMAH; 2. Agostino Ramelli, *Le diverse et artificiose machine* (Paris, 1588), 317; 3. Ramelli, *Le diverse et artificiose machine*, 20; 4. Ramelli, *Le diverse et artificiose machine*, 93; 5. Ramelli, *Le diverse et artificiose machine*, 135; 6. Joseph Moxon, *Mechanick Exercises or the Doctrine of Handy-Works* (3rd edition, 1703; reprint Scarsdale, NY, 1979), facing 185; 7. Moxon, *Mechanick Exercises*, facing 1; 8. Francis Vivares engraving of G. Perry and Thomas Smith painting, Upper Works, Coalbrookdale, 1758. Elton Collection: Ironbridge Gorge Museum Trust, Telford, UK; 9. Giovanni Branca, *Le Machine* (Rome, 1629), 25; 10. Thomas Savery, *The Miner's Friend* (London, 1698; reprint 1828); 11. J. T. Desaguliers, *A Course of Experimental Philosophy* (London, 1744), facing 430; 12. Carroll W. Pursell, Jr., *Early Stationary Steam Engines in America* (Washington, 1969), 3; 13. NMAH; 14. Pursell, *Early Stationary Steam Engines*, 4; 15. NMAH; 16. Museum of American Textile History, North Andover, MA; 17. Museum of American Textile History; 18. Museum of American Textile History; 19. Library of Congress; 20. Elton Collection: Ironbridge Gorge Museum Trust.

CHAPTER II

1. Library Company of Philadelphia, Philadelphia, PA; 2. NMAH; 3. New York State Historical Association, Cooperstown, NY; 4. NMAH; 5. NMAH; 6. NMAH; 7. Benjamin Franklin, *An Account of the New Invented Pennsylvanian Fire Places* (Philadelphia, 1744; reprint Providence, 1974); 8. Hopewell Village National Historical Site, Elverson, PA.

CHAPTER III

1. NMAH; 2. NMAH; 3. Historic American Building Survey, Library of Congress; 4. NMAH; 5. John Worrell, Old Sturbridge Village, Sturbridge, MA; 6. NMAH; 7. NMAH; 8. NMAH; 9. University of Pennsylvania, Philadelphia, PA; 10. Stephen E. Kramer.

CHAPTER IV

1. George S. White, *Memoir of Samuel Slater* (Philadelphia, 1836), frontispiece; 2. NMAH; 3. NMAH; 4. Patrick Malone, Slater Mill Historic Site, Pawtucket, RI; 5. NMAH; 6. Museum of American Textile History, North Andover, MA; 7. NMAH; 8. Library of Congress; 9. Robert Vogel, NMAH; 10. NMAH; 11. National Archives; 12. National Archives.

CHAPTER V

1. National Portrait Gallery, Smithsonian Institution; 2. National Archives; 3. NMAH; 4. NMAH; 5. NMAH; 6. NMAH; 7. NMAH; 8. NMAH; 9. New-York Historical Society, New York, NY; 10. NMAH; 11. NMAH; 12. NMAH; 13. American Philosophical Society, Philadelphia, PA; 14. NMAH; 15. NMAH.

CHAPTER VI

1. NMAH; 2. New York State Agricultural Society *Transactions*, 1846; 3. Thomas Jefferson Memorial Foundation; 4. NMAH; 5. R. L. Ardrey, *American Agricultural Implements* (Chicago, 1894), 109; 6. NMAH; 7. NMAH; 8. Sleepy Hollow Restorations, Tarrytown, NY; 9. NMAH; 10. Sleepy Hollow Restorations; 11. NMAH; 12. Oliver Evans, *Young Mill-Wright and Miller's Guide* (13th ed., 1850; reprint New York, 1972), plate 22; 13. Colvin Run Mill, Fairfax, VA; 14. Samuel H. Daddow and Benjamin Bannan, *Coal, Iron and Oil: Or the American Practical Miner* (Pottsville, PA, 1866); 15. Eli Bowen, *The Pictorial Sketchbook of Pennsylvania* (Philadelphia, 1852), 177.

CHAPTER VII

1. Joseph Wiedel; 2. M. M. Baggs, *Memorial History of Utica* (Syracuse, NY, 1892) through Robert E. Hager; 3. New-York Historical Society, New York, NY; 4. NMAH; 5. NMAH; 6. Maryland Historical Society, Baltimore, MD; 7. NMAH; 8. NMAH; 9. NMAH; 10. American Philosophical Society, Philadelphia, PA; 11. American Philosophical Society; 12. [James Rumsey], *Explanation of a Steam Engine and . . . Applying It to Propel a Boat* (Philadelphia, 1788), plate 3; 13. NMAH; 14. NMAH; 15. NMAH; 16. NMAH; 17. NMAH; 18. NMAH.

CHAPTER VIII

1. Library of Congress; 2. NMAH; 3. NMAH; 4. NMAH; 5. National Portrait Gallery, Smithsonian Institution; Gift of H. H. Walker Lewis in memory of his parents, Mr. and Mrs. Edwin A. S. Lewis; 6. NMAH; 7. NMAH; 8. J. G. H. Warren, *A Century of Locomotive Building by Robert Stephenson and Company, 1823–1923* (Newcastle, UK, 1923), frontispiece; 9. Science Museum, London; 10. Science Museum, London; 11. NMAH; 12. NMAH; 13. NMAH; 14. NMAH; 15. NMAH; 16. NMAH; 17. NMAH; 18. NMAH; 19. New York Public Library, Astor, Lenox and Tilden Foundations; 20. NMAH; 21. Joseph Wiedel; 22. Joseph Wiedel; 23. NMAH; 24. National Gallery of Art, Washington, DC, gift of Mrs. Huttleston Rogers.

CHAPTER IX

1. NMAH; 2. NMAH; 3. Oliver Evans, *Young Mill-Wright and Miller's Guide* (13th ed., 1850; reprint New York, 1972), plate 4; 4. James Francis, *Lowell Hydraulic Experiments* (Lowell, 1845); 5. NMAH.

CHAPTER X

1. NMAH; 2. NMAH; 3. "A Visit to the Norris Locomotive Works," *United States Magazine* (October 1855), reprinted in *Railroadians of America Book No. 2*, 90; 4. NMAH; 5. "A Visit to the Norris Locomotive Works," 88; 6. "A Visit to the Norris Locomotive Works," 92; 7. "A Visit to the Norris Locomotive Works," 83; 8. "A Visit to the Norris Locomotive Works," 78; 9. "A Visit to the Norris Locomotive Works," 82; 10. NMAH; 11. NMAH; 12. "A Visit to the Norris Locomotive Works," 86; 13. Old Colony Historical Society, Taunton, MA; 14. NMAH; 15. NMAH; 16. NMAH; 17. NMAH; 18. NMAH; 19. Sheldon Museum, Middlebury, VT; 20. NMAH.

CHAPTER XI

1. Steven Lubar; 2. Mr. Fitzroy Newdegate; 3. NMAH; 4. NMAH; 5. NMAH; 6. American Antiquarian Society, Worcester, MA; 7. International Museum of Photography of George Eastman House, Rochester, NY; 8. Historic American Engineering Record Collection, Library of Congress; 9. Museum of American Textile History; 10. Collection of John Colony, in the Historic American Engineering Record Collection, Library of Congress; 11. Library of Congress; 12. Museum of American Textile History; 13. Museum of American Textile History; 14. Baker Library, Harvard Business School; 15. Museum of American Textile History; 16. NMAH.

CHAPTER XII

1. NMAH; 2. New York Public Library; 3. NMAH; 4. NMAH; 5. *Harper's Weekly* (February 19, 1859); 6. NMAH; 7. David N. Johnson, *Sketches of Lynn* (Lynn, MA, 1880); 8. Lynn *Directory*, 1855; 9. *Leslie's Weekly* (March 7, 1860).

CHAPTER XIII

1. NMAH; 2. NMAH; 3. NMAH; 4. NMAH; 5. NMAH; 6. Mattatuck Museum, Waterbury, CT; 7. NMAH; 8. NMAH; 9. Springfield Armory Museum, Springfield, MA; 10. NMAH; 11. NMAH; 12. NMAH; 13. NMAH; 14. *United States Magazine* (September 15, 1854).

CHAPTER XIV

1. Robert and Robert Dale Owen, eds., *The Crisis* (London, 1833); 2. Hancock Shaker Village, Pittsfield, MA; 3. NMAH; 4. J. A. Etzler, *The New World* (Philadelphia, 1841); 5. *The New World*, 5; 6. *Harper's New Monthly Magazine* (May 1887); 7. National Archives; 8. NMAH; 9. NMAH; 10. National Archives; 11. Rensselaer Polytechnic Institute, Troy, NY.

1. Library of Congress; 2. Collection of Business Americana, NMAH; 3. *Art Journal Illustrated Catalogue*; 4. National Museum of American Art, Smithsonian Institution; Museum purchase in memory of Ralph Cross Johnson; 5. *Punch*, Vol. 20 (January–June 1851); 6. Library of Congress; 7. C. T. Rogers, *American Superiority at the World's Fair* (Philadelphia, 1852); 8. Library of Congress; 9. NMAH; 10. NMAH; 11. NMAH; 12. NMAH; 13. NMAH; 14. NMAH; 15. Collection of Business Americana, NMAH; 16. NMAH; 17. Collection of Business Americana, NMAH; 18. NMAH; 19. Collection of Business Americana, NMAH; 20. Collection of Business Americana, NMAH.

Index

eponymic theory of, 75–77; exhilaration of, 277–78; government support for, 86; nature of, 84; and science, 77, 97; stages of, 74, 88; and technology transfer, 71–72. *See also* Patent system

Inventor as hero, 75–76

Investment, 154–55; in railroads, 131

Iron: import of, 106; use of in locomotives, 168

Ironbridge, England, 69

Iron production, 40, *41*, 106–8; and agriculture, 108; in Great Britain, 13, 15, 69–71, 106; and tariffs, 88; in United States, 70–71

Japan, 273–74

Jefferson, Thomas: attitude toward technology, 57, 188; and patent system, 78, 103; plow design of, 97; and James Rumsey, 117

Jennings, Isaiah, *76*

Jigs and fixtures. *See* Gauges

John Bull (locomotive), 124, *130*; and American locomotive design, 138–43, *142, 143*; construction of, 133–35, *135*; as symbol, 150

Johnson, Walter, 253

Jouffroy, Marquis de, 69

Kay, John, 20

Kempton, Jerome, 202

Kennedy, Joseph C. G., 253

Kentucky rifle. *See* Pennsylvania rifle

Labor: at armories, 228–29; at clock factories, 223, *226*; at Lowell textile mills, 196, 199; on railroads, 144–45; at southern New England textile mills,

63–64, 192, 196, 199

Labor conditions, 93

Labor movement, 164

Labor scarcity, 157

Lancaster Turnpike, 114

Land: and politics, 34; and social status, 34; as source of wealth, 32–34

Law: and commercial mills, 103; and entrepreneurship, 154; and incorporation, 156; and labor movement, 164; patent acts, 78, 83, 84

Lee, Mother Ann, 239

Lerow, John A., 261

Liebig, Justus, 99

Lightning rod, 80, *80*

Lime, 99

Litchfield, Connecticut, 223

Liverpool and Manchester Railroad, 127, 132, *132*, 133, 135

Livingston, Robert R., 84, 95, 118

Locomotives, 123; construction of, 168–76; design of, 138–43; in Great Britain, 123; manufacture of, 143. *See also* under names of locomotives

Logan, George, 57

London Society of Arts, 95

Lotteries, 154

Lowell, Francis Cabot, 66

Lowell, Massachusetts, 66, 193–202; hours of work, *200*; regulations at, *201*

Lowell Machine Shop, 183, 199

Lowell Offering, 199

Luddism, 153, 187

Luther, Seth, 163

Lynn, Massachusetts, 214–15, *216*

Machines. *See* Agricultural machinery; Textile machinery

Machine shops, 133, 167–84; Augustus Alfred's, 176–78; at Merrimack Manufacturing Company, 178; at Norris Locomotive Works, 167–76, *172*; use of drawings at, 168–69,

178

Machine tools, 51, 167; drill press, 21; grinding machines, 21, 182; lathe, *12*, 21, 51, *52*, 173, *173*; milling machine, 182, *183*; planer, 21, 173, *173*; slotting engine, 173, *175*

Machining, 15, 21

Machinists, 173–74, 181–82; at textile mills, 178

McCormick, Cyrus, 76, *76*, 77, 98–99, 258

Management, of railroads, 143–45. *See also* Factory management

Manayunk, Pennsylvania, 202

Mann, Thomas, 93

Manufacturing statistics: 1810, 164; 1860, 164–65

Manure, 99

Market forces, 270–71

Marketing, of clocks, 221–22

Markham, Isaac, 181–82

Mass production. *See* American system of manufactures

Material improvement, American desire for, 27, 31

Mechanics, 61–65. *See also* Machinists

Mechanics institutes, 91

Mechanization, 152–53; attitudes toward, 156–57; of gristmills, 102–5; and industrialization, 153; of sailing shops, 245

Merchants, and tariffs, 88

Metalworking: casting, 169, *170*; forging, *13*, 169, *172*. *See also* Machining

Micrometer, 175, *175*

Middle Atlantic states, industry in, 165–66

Middlebury, Vermont, 181

Midwest, 105, 107; industry in, 166

Military role in promoting technology: in nineteenth century, 227; in twentieth century, 275–76

Mills, 157. *See also* Grist mills

Millstones, 100–102, *102*